# Resistance in Paradise:

## Rethinking 100 Years of U.S. Involvement in the Caribbean and the Pacific

Edited by
Deborah Wei and Rachael Kamel

American Friends Service Committee

in cooperation with
Office of Curriculum Support
School District of Philadelphia

Philadelphia

**Cover illustration:** "Hono," lithograph by Samoan artist Michel Tuffery. (Another Tuffery lithograph, "Vaka E'a," appears on the student handout pages after each lesson.) Both are copyright © 1991 by Michel Tuffery. Used by permission.

**Design:** Gerry Henry

**Resistance in Paradise** is published by

American Friends Service Committee
Community Relations Division
1501 Cherry St.
Philadelphia, PA 19102

in cooperation with
Office of Curriculum Support
School District of Philadelphia
21 & Parkway
Philadelphia, PA 19102

ISBN 0-910082-33-2



*The following material is used by permission:*

Field, Michael. "Papuata Girls Boarding School," *America Samoa, Nonviolence and the Mau* (University of Hawaii / Polynesian Press, 1994). Reprinted with permission.

Field, Michael. "Black Saturday" from *Mau: Samoa's Struggle for Freedom* (University of Hawaii / Polynesian Press, 1990). Reprinted with permission.

Figiel, Sia. "We" from *Where We Once Belonged* (Pasifika Press, 1996). Reprinted with permission.

Mariposa (Fernandez, Maria Teresa). *Ode to the Diasporican* © 1995. 720 E. 213th Street, Bronx NY 10457. (718) 515-3475. Reprinted with permission.

McMullin, Dan Taulapapa. "The Shark" from *The Demon Anchors,* published in *Folauga,* a Samoan-Language Journal for Young People. Vol. 2 (Wellington, New Zealand: Learning Media Ltd., 1998). Reprinted with permission.

Sierra Club Legal Defense Fund. "Hawai`i's Natural Heritage" from Natural History of the Hawaiian Islands, 1995. Reprinted with permission.

Smith, Wayne. Comments from "Island Under Siege: The U.S. Blockade of Cuba" by Pedro Prada published by Ocean Press. Reprinted with permission.

Trask, Haunani Kay and Miliani Trask, "The Aloha Industry," *Cultural Survival Quarterly* (Winter 1992). Reprinted with permission.

Verharen, Theodore. "O le Solo o le Va o le Foagoago o le Lalolagi" from *The Samoan Islands,* Vol. I, English translation from a German translation by Dr. Augustin Kramer. (University of Hawaii Press, 1994) pp. 541-542. Reprinted with permission.

Walker, Alice. "A Letter to President Clinton" from *Anything We Love Can Be Saved.* Copyright © 1997 by Alice Walker. Reprinted by permission of Random House, Inc.

Printed in the United States of America. 

# Contents

# Foreword

In the summer of 1996, staff and volunteers of the American Friends Service Committee (AFSC) met to plan how to strengthen the organization's work with Asian and Pacific Islander communities, both in the United States and in their countries of origin. Those present at the meeting were well aware that the year 1998 would mark the hundred-year anniversary of the emergence of the United States as a global power, holding sway over territories in the Caribbean and the Pacific, far beyond the North American continent.

In a few short months in 1898, in what is known as the Spanish-American War, the United States replaced Spain as the ruling power in the Philippines, Cuba, Puerto Rico, and Guam. Hawai`i and American Samoa were annexed by the United States in the same year. Within AFSC, the discussion of the significance of the centennial of these events led to a vision of creating this curriculum guide. From the outset, the aim of the guide was to help students and teachers in the United States understand how this history, and its enduring impact, is perceived from the vantage point of these island nations.

As with other AFSC efforts, a paramount concern was that the story should be told mainly by members of the affected communities. Among the more than two dozen authors of this volume are many people whose lives have been shaped by the history they relate, whether as immigrants, as political exiles, as activists fighting for the sovereignty of their homelands — or as all three. They have joined together for this project, along with a multiracial group of educators and activists, in a collaborative writing team that defined the format and content of the guide and prepared the individual chapters.

Through the collective vision and sustained efforts of this team, this book has become a reality. Many of the writers featured here have never met each other personally. Belief in the common goal of breaking silences, of giving voice to perspectives that are often neglected in mainstream U.S. education, has carried this project forward to completion.

## Acknowledgments

Many people joined the authors and editors of this guide in making this book a reality. First and foremost, Thoai Nguyen, national coordinator of AFSC's Asia Pacific Program during the preparation of the guide, worked tirelessly to provide overall coordination to the project. Invaluable feedback and support were provided by members of the program's advisory committee, including Pat Benson Duldulao, Joanne Dufour, Vera Haile, Ramsay Liem, Elena Mangahas, Mariagnes Medrud, Craig Shimabukuro, Sally Soliai, Roy Takumi, and Deborah Wei.

Additional members of the writing team included Melinh Jenkins, Kathy Kelly, Mariagnes Medrud, and Klancy Miller. Bill Bigelow and Debi Duke helped to conceptualize the book in its early stages. Ramon Bosque Perez helped with important information.

In addition to those named above, many other colleagues and friends reviewed the manuscript and gave helpful suggestions for improving its accuracy and clarity, including Kilali Alailima, Nancy Aleck, Frank Bonilla, Bahiya Cabral, Ruth Cadwallader, Nelson Carasquillo, Pat Clark, Karen Cromley, Harold Jordan, Lisa Nakamura, June Shimokawa, Mike Yarrow, and Isaac Wheeler.

Other AFSC colleagues who helped with resources, contacts, and advice included Ed Nakawatase, Dick Erstad, Saralee Hamilton, and Sultana Alam. The support and guidance of Joyce Miller, director of AFSC's Community Relations Division, was crucial to the success of this project. AFSC Board members Donald Gann, Paula Rhodes, and Mariagnes Medrud also lent vital support to this effort.

The contributions of Linda Love, director of AFSC's Literature Resources Unit, are too numerous to detail. Editorial and research assistance were provided by Sally Chan, Amanda Bergson Shilcock, and Bela August Walker.

Many collegial organizations lent their support and assistance to this effort, including *Rethinking Schools,* the Network of Educators on the Americas, the National Coalition of Education Activists, the American Social History Project of the City University of New York, and the Caribbean Cultural Center. Funding support for this project was provided by the Fund for the Four Directions, the Thomas and Mary Shoemaker Fund, and the AFSC Board of Directors.

Most important, this guide is possible only because of the persistence and faith of the peoples of Cuba, Guam, Hawai`i, the Philippines, Puerto Rico, and Samoa, and the efforts of people of conscience who have sought social justice throughout our history together as people on this planet. It is to their strength and dedication we owe the greatest of debts.

# A Letter to the Teacher

We all want our work to be meaningful, and we want students to value the content that we teach. In history as a discipline, we know that today's students sometimes feel that this material has little to do with their lives. One of the ways that we can counteract that perception is to make history more real for students by using the actual voices of the people we are studying and by showing the very real connections of "history then" to "history now."

This guide connects us with actions taken a century ago that directly shape the world in which we live today. Nineteen ninety-eight marks the hundredth anniversary of the first U.S. foreign interventions beyond the North American continent, affecting Guam, Puerto Rico, Hawai`i, American Samoa, the Philippines, and Cuba. Most of this history is unknown by U.S. students — and their teachers — but it is painfully familiar to the people in each of these countries.

Their stories suggest answers to questions that we often grapple with today. Why is the role of the United States not always welcomed by all peoples? Why do some students, and their families, feel unconnected to the "American Dream?" How can we form common bonds of understanding across differences of experience, language, religion, and culture in its broadest sense?

The information and activities included here should assist you as a teacher to build connections with students, as well as introducing content that may not have been fully explored in traditional textbooks. The use of primary sources, and a willingness to explore topics in a more complete context, enable us to help students discover the "real story," and to hear multiple voices telling it.

Too often, the teaching of U.S. history has been more a matter of "cheerleading" than of critical analysis. Such an approach has used history as a vehicle for building national myths, celebrating wars won, and extolling national values. In today's world, it seems more important to equip students to appreciate the place of the United States in the community of nations and their own place in a diverse, multiracial society.

Because this guide gives voice to perspectives that are not often presented, it can pose challenges in the classroom. Exploring new information, especially information that evokes strong feelings, can be a difficult experience for teachers and students alike. It can also be a door to new understandings about ourselves, both as individuals and as members of a nation. Understanding one another's experiences, however difficult it may be, is, we believe, the first step toward true sharing.

## How to Use This Guide

This guide opens with an introductory chapter, addressed mainly to teachers, that examines the events of 1898 and their aftermath. Student lessons at the end of the chapter explore general themes regarding the role of interpretation in history.

The remainder of the book is dedicated to chapters on each of the countries that came under U.S. rule in this period. Each of the country-specific chapters includes a brief historical overview followed by a series of lessons, including suggested activities and corresponding handouts for students. Both the overviews and the handouts are written to be accessible to students at the secondary level. Terms that may be unfamiliar are signaled in each chapter overview and in each lesson, and are defined in a glossary at the back of the guide.

Student readings include a wealth of primary sources: newspaper articles and political cartoons from the time of the Spanish-American War, historical documents, personal testimonies, and more. Also included are a broad range of contemporary pieces, both fiction and nonfiction. The overall approach is multidisciplinary; many of the materials and activities included here can be used for classes in history, social studies, or English. The suggested activities include role plays, debates, writing exercises, classroom discussions, and the creation of stories, poems, or cartoons, among others.

Many of the lessons included here engage students in developing their own critical readings, whether of historical narratives, media representations, or policy debates. By listening to voices that have mainly been left out of the historical record, students can learn to understand how our vision of history and of the world we live in is reshaped according to who is looking and who is being seen.

You may also opt to use the primary sources reproduced here in other ways that best meet your students' needs. Please consider sharing with us your "best practices" with this material; we all have much to learn from one another as we explore new resources and consider new ideas.

In general, we welcome your reactions, ideas, and suggestions for this guide. We are committed, as you are, to helping students better understand the world, so that they can assume their role as active participants in it. Our hope is that this guide will help you to achieve that goal.

# Reframing the Spanish-American War in the History Curriculum

*Overview*
**Baltazar Pinguel**

*Lessons*
**Deborah Wei**
**Stephen R. Shalom**

PLEADING time constraints, or the need to teach about issues that will resonate for students, teachers have often dropped the Spanish-American War from the history curriculum. The mere mention of this war causes eyes to glaze over, heads to nod. For most people in the United States, all that remains of that time are perhaps a few fragmentary images: the battle cry "Remember the *Maine*!" or Teddy Roosevelt and his "Rough Riders" charging up San Juan Hill. For students, these events seem dry as dust and impossibly remote.

In reality, the Spanish-American War, which spanned a mere ten months during 1898, represents a defining moment in U.S. and world history, one that has affected hundreds of millions of lives in large parts of the globe. The war and its aftermath marked the emergence of the United States as a global power, pursuing interests and prerogatives far beyond its own territory. It would not be an exaggeration to say that the Spanish-American War set the stage for U.S. foreign and military policy during the twentieth century. Likewise, images and attitudes forged in that period continue to shape the stance of the United States toward the rest of the world today.

What are the barriers that cut us off from this period in history? What lies beneath the frozen, stereotypical images of century-old military campaigns? More to the point, what do we lose when we allow this era to sink beneath the weight of historical amnesia?

The curriculum materials presented in this guide explore the legacy of that war from a distinct point of view: that of the island nations in the Caribbean and the Pacific, nations whose destiny has been framed for centuries by the tension between foreign domination and the quest for independence. For these peoples, the war lives on, underlying profound questions of culture, society, and language, as well as political and economic issues. Among the vanquished, history is not forgotten.

This opening chapter summarizes the events of the Spanish-American War and places them in the context of the social, economic, and political forces shaping U.S. policy at the time. The remaining chapters examine the history and present-day realities of the countries that came under U.S. influence as a result of the Spanish-American War: Cuba and Puerto Rico in the Caribbean and Guam and the Philippines in the Pacific. The annexation of Hawai`i and American Samoa by the United States was closely related to the war and also occurred in the same period, and so chapters on these areas are also included.

Using this guide can help students and teachers alike deepen their appreciation for the importance of history — and the terrible costs of forgetting the past. This centennial year of the Spanish-American War offers a signal opportunity to remind ourselves that we cannot know who we are, or where we are going, until we know where we have been.

## The Spanish Empire and the Drive for Independence

As the original sponsor of Columbus's voyages of discovery and conquest, Spain was the first European power to begin the era of overseas colonial domination. At its height, the Spanish empire included most of Latin America, much of the Caribbean, the Philippines, and various Pacific islands. By the 1800s, however, the desire for independence was growing throughout the colonies of the European powers, and the much-weakened Spanish empire was a key target. Most Latin nations achieved their independence from Spain in the earlier years of the nineteenth century. In the Pacific and Caribbean islands, however, independence was postponed.

In 1868, the Puerto Rican people launched the famous "Grito de Lares" (the Cry of Lares, a Puerto Rican mountain town) and declared a

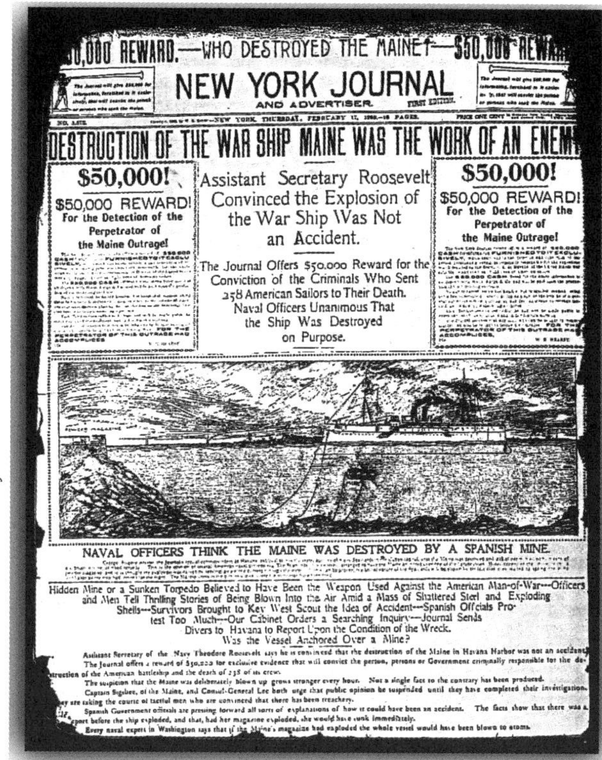

...000 REWARD.—WHO DESTROYED THE MAINE?—$50,000 REWA...

NEW YORK JOURNAL

AND ADVERTISER. FIRST EDITION.

NEW YORK, THURSDAY, FEBRUARY 17, 1898.—16 PAGES. PRICE ONE CENT

DESTRUCTION OF THE WAR SHIP MAINE WAS THE WORK OF AN ENEM...

$50,000!

$50,000 REWARD! For the Detection of the Perpetrator of the Maine Outrage!

Assistant Secretary Roosevelt Convinced the Explosion of the War Ship Was Not an Accident.

The Journal Offers $50,000 Reward for the Conviction of the Criminals Who Sent 258 American Sailors to Their Death. Naval Officers Unanimous That the Ship Was Destroyed on Purpose.

$50,000!

$50,000 REWARD! For the Detection of the Perpetrator of the Maine Outrage!

W. R. HEARST.

NAVAL OFFICERS THINK THE MAINE WAS DESTROYED BY A SPANISH MINE.

Hidden Mine or a Sunken Torpedo Believed to Have Been the Weapon Used Against the American Man-of-War---Officers and Men Tell Thrilling Stories of Being Blown Into the Air Amid a Mass of Shattered Steel and Exploding Shells---Survivors Brought to Key West Scout the Idea of Accident---Spanish Officials Protest Too Much---Our Cabinet Orders a Searching Inquiry---Journal Sends Divers to Havana to Report Upon the Condition of the Wreck. Was the Vessel Anchored Over a Mine?

Assistant Secretary of the Navy Theodore Roosevelt says he is convinced that the destruction of the Maine in Havana Harbor was not an accident.

The Journal offers a reward of $50,000 for exclusive evidence that will convict the person, persons or Government criminally responsible for the destruction of the American battleship and the death of 258 of its crew.

The suspicion that the Maine was deliberately blown up grows stronger every hour. Not a single fact to the contrary has been produced.

Captain Sigsbee, of the Maine, and Consul-General Lee both urge that public opinion be suspended until they have completed their investigation. ...ey are taking the course of tactful men who are convinced that there has been treachery.

Spanish Government officials are pressing forward all sorts of explanations of how it could have been an accident. The facts show that there was a ... port before the ship exploded, and that, had her magazine exploded, she would have sunk immediately.

Every naval expert in Washington says that if the Maine's magazine had exploded the whole vessel would have been blown to atoms.

AMERICAN SOCIAL HISTORY PROJECT

*The explosion of the U.S.S.* **Maine***, as announced in the* **New York Journal** *of 17 February 1898.*

short-lived democratic republic. Twenty years later in the South Pacific, in 1888, the Spanish governor in Pohnpei and 200 of his soldiers were killed by the Micronesians in a surprise attack.[1] On February 24, 1895, the so-called "Grito de Bayre" took place, marking the commencement of the Cuban war of independence against Spain. On August 23, 1896, drawing inspiration from their Cuban counterparts, Filipinos, led by the revolutionary organization Katipunan, staged the "Cry of Pugadlawin," which marked the beginning of the Philippine revolution against Spain.[2]

All of these resistance movements were met with the utmost violence by the Spanish authorities. In the Philippines, members of the Katipunan were executed, tortured, or banished to Guam; in December 1896, eighty of these Filipino exiles were massacred by Spanish soldiers as they were attempting to escape from Guam's Agaña prison.[3] In Cuba, villagers were forced into heavily garrisoned zones, to cut off the rebels from their civilian base of support. The inhuman enforcement of this policy of *reconcentración* earned for the Spanish governor of Cuba, Valeriano Weyler, the nickname "the Butcher of Cuba." Spanish atrocities sparked widespread sympathy for the rebels in the United States, and support for Cuban independence was one of the principal rationales offered to the public for the U.S. war with Spain.[4]

## Ten Months in 1898

On February 15, 1898, the U.S. battleship *Maine* exploded while docked in the harbor of Havana, Cuba, which at that time was a Spanish colony. The yellow press and U.S. policy makers found it convenient to blame the Spanish, and the United States quickly declared war on Spain.[5] Questions were raised from the beginning, however, about whether an act of sabotage had really taken place. Finally, in 1976,

CORBIS-BETTMANN

*This 1898 photograph shows the wreckage of the* **U.S.S. Maine** *in Havana Harbor.*

*When a U.S. warship shelled Fort Santa Cruz in Guam, the Spanish governor of the island mistook the firing for a salute.*

an underwater exploration of the wreck of the *Maine* showed that the explosion was actually caused by a fire in the coal bunker, not by sabotage.

By 1898, Spain had become one of the Europe's weakest powers, politically and militarily. Independence movements in both Cuba and the Philippines were on the verge of success. The Spanish-American War was a notably one-sided exercise. The Battle of Manila Bay on May 1, the first major engagement of the war, resulted in the total destruction of the Spanish fleet, with U.S. casualties placed at eight wounded.[6] The conquest of Puerto Rico met with minimal resistance, while Guam was captured without a fight on June 21. (The Spanish commander of Guam, who did not know about the outbreak of the war, even apologized for not having returned what he assumed to be a salute fired by the U.S. Navy the previous day, explaining that his forces had run out of ammunition.)[7] A July 3 engagement near the coast of Havana ended in another rout of the Spanish fleet, with 323 dead and 151 wounded, while the United States suffered only a single casualty.

On December 10, 1898, the United States and Spain signed the Treaty of Paris, ending the Spanish-American War. Through this treaty, the United States gained control of the Philippines and Guam in the Pacific and Puerto Rico in the Caribbean. Since support for Cuban independence had been so prominently featured in the discussion of the war in the United States, Cuba maintained formal independent status. The Cuban government was obliged, however, to incorporate the highly concessionary terms of the Platt Amendment of 1901 (see Lesson 2.2) into its new constitution. The U.S. military occupation of Cuba officially ended in 1902, when the island became a de facto U.S. protectorate.[8]

## The Philippine-American War

While the United States nominally recognized Cuba's independence, the Filipinos, who had already declared their independence from Spain on June 12, 1898, did not achieve even such token recognition. By the time the Spanish-American war came to the Philippines, the rebels already controlled nearly the entire

*Filipino insurgents, believing that they had achieved their independence, marched through the streets of Manila in 1898 to celebrate Spain's defeat. By early 1899, they were back at war — this time with the United States.*

national territory, with only the capital of Manila remaining under Spanish control.[9] As detailed in the chapter on the Philippines, the Filipino rebels aided U.S. forces against what they understood to be their common enemy, Spain. Nonetheless, the United States and Spain agreed to shut out the representatives sent by the Philippines to the negotiations that resulted in the Treaty of Paris, during which the United States bought the Philippines from Spain for $20 million. By a stroke of the pen, the Philippine struggle for national independence, already at an advanced stage, moved back to square one.

LIBRARY OF CONGRESS

*A sense of the grandeur at the emerging U.S. role as a world power is evident in this photograph of the "Triumphal Bridge" at the 1904 World's Fair.*

Following the signing of the Treaty of Paris, the Filipinos began another war for their independence, this time against the United States. For the United States, this war was militarily far more expensive than the war against Spain. For the Filipinos, the cost was devastating; as many as 250,000 of them died of the direct and indirect effects of the war, the great majority civilians.[10]

The U.S. occupiers in the Philippines soon turned to the very tactics for which they had condemned the Spanish. The first measures they instituted included *reconcentración* and the Brigandage Act, under which independence fighters were reclassified as common bandits. National heroes in the eyes of the Philippine people, such as Macario Sakay, became known as bandits in the U.S. press and passed with that stigma into recorded history. The Philippine-American war was also marked by the systematic use of torture by U.S. soldiers.

Reports of U.S. atrocities sparked enormous controversy in the United States, as discussed below in the section entitled "Against the Grain" (see page 8). At the same time, supporters of the war in government and the press whipped up enormous patriotic fervor, branding opponents of U.S. territorial expansion as traitors. This political climate helped seal congressional support for the U.S. annexation of Hawai`i, which was approved in 1898. The following year, U.S. control of what became known as American Samoa was also institutionalized through an agreement among the United States, Great Britain, and Germany.[11] A little more than a century after fighting its own war of independence, the United States had joined the nations of Western Europe as a colonial power.

## The Hunger for Land, The Drive for Markets

Although in some ways the Spanish-American war marked a new era for the United States, it represented a continuation of previous trends, rather than a change of direction. In the decades following the American Revolution, U.S. territorial expansion proceeded essentially uninterrupted, culminating in the Mexican-American War of 1847. In this war, Mexico, which had won its independence from Spain only thirty-seven years earlier, in 1810, lost approximately a third of its territory — what is now the southwestern United States.

As early as 1823, U.S. President James Monroe had warned the European powers not to seek more colonies in the Western Hemisphere. The "Monroe Doctrine," as this policy was known, held that the United States should become the dominant influence in the hemisphere. Toward mid-century, some southern landowners sought to annex Cuba and Nicaragua, bringing them into the union as additional slave states. Such plans, however, were abandoned after the 1857 defeat of William Walker's invasion of Nicaragua with a mercenary army. Other political figures posed the issue in explicitly racist terms, arguing that U.S. dominance of the hemisphere was part of a divine plan giving "white Americans the right, even the obligation, to 'bring civilization' to people of color," a philosophy that came to be known as Manifest Destiny.[12]

The 1870s and 1880s were a period of sustained growth for the U.S. economy. Burgeoning industries could count on reliable markets, as well as cheap labor supplied by immigrants. By the 1890s, however, two complementary phenomena threatened to derail U.S. economic growth — and with it, the country's economic and political stability.

First, the available land had been largely claimed. As in previous eras, the U.S. government's initial response was to seize more land from the Indians. The Indian Appropriation Act, passed in 1871, nullified all treaties between the United States and Indian nations, opening up vast new areas of land to white settlers. In 1889, 1.9 million acres of Seminole and Creek land were taken over in the great Oklahoma Land Rush. In February 1890, eleven million acres of Sioux territory in South Dakota were also opened for settlement by whites. Resistance by the Sioux culminated at Wounded Knee on December 28, 1890, in which 153 Indians, including men, women, and children, were massacred by the U.S. Seventh Cavalry. Over the next few years, similar losses of land were suffered by the Crow, Cherokee, Potawatomi, and other Indian peoples.[13] By mid-decade, however, the United States had reached the end of its internal "frontier": possibilities for further expansion on the North American continent had been exhausted.

At the same time, technological advancements had greatly accelerated the growth of industrial production, to the point where production outstripped demand. The United States had become the world's leading economic power, producing more than England, France, and Germany combined — but without a big enough market to absorb what it produced. Further, with the opening of farm lands in Argentina, Canada, and Russia, the price of U.S. wheat and corn dropped. The precariousness of the boom economy was underscored by a major stock market crash in 1893, in which 600 banks, 74 railways, and 15,000 other businesses failed. The crash resulted in a panic by investors, resulting in $43 million in gold leaving the country, thereby threatening the collapse of the gold standard.[14] To restore the stability of its economic system, the United States needed to open new markets and new territories.

By the 1880s, the fledgling U.S. labor movement was fighting for such demands as the eight-hour day.* In 1886, the Haymarket Affair marked a historic standoff between capital and labor. A bomb was thrown at a peaceful labor demonstration in Chicago's Haymarket Square, killing seven of a large contingent of police who had ordered the crowd to disperse. Seven labor leaders, only two of whom were present at the march, were sentenced to death after being convicted of conspiracy in the bombing, even though to this day it is not known who was responsible. Around the world, workers' organizations and numerous public figures decried the unfairness of the trial. Although the sentences against two of the defendants were eventually commuted to life in prison, four of them were hanged (another committed suicide just before his execution). William Dean Howells, a leading U.S. literary figure of the time, wrote that "this free Republic has killed four men for their opinions."[15]

Prominent editors and business owners of the day openly argued that regardless of the guilt of the defendants, their hanging was necessary to stop the growth of the labor movement in its tracks. This strategy, however, proved unsuccessful, and throughout the 1890s labor militancy grew rapidly in response to the spreading economic crisis. As strikes grew larger and more numerous, efforts to contain them also grew more violent, with local police, private security guards, and the National Guard seeking to suppress the labor movement by force of arms. In the same era, populist outrage over the behavior of business monopolies, or trusts, led to the passage in 1890 of the Sherman Anti-Trust Act. Ironically, although the act had not been written with labor in mind, it was applied more vigorously against labor unions than against the trusts themselves; the first time it was used successfully was to suppress the historic Pullman Strike of 1894-95.[16]

The displacement of numerous workers by the economic crisis also sparked increasing anti-immigrant sentiment. The openly racist Chinese Exclusion Act of 1882 was the first to single out a particular ethnic group for exclusion from immigration. The act was followed by other statutes targeting all Asians, establishing a racially exclusionary framework for U.S. immigration law that remained in place until 1965. The opening of Ellis Island in 1892 initiated the tightening of immigration from Europe as well. In 1894, a group of Bostonians formed the Immigration Restriction League to campaign for a literacy test to screen out "uneducated undesirables."[17] Expressions of prejudice against all immigrants were highly racialized, including groups (such as Italians or Jews) who are considered to be "white" according to modern understandings.

The 1890s also brought concerted attacks on the gains of African Americans. The post–Civil War Reconstruction Era, spanning the period from 1865 to 1877, witnessed dramatic advances for African Americans, including the passage of the Fourteenth and Fifteenth Amendments and the Civil Rights Act of 1875, which prohibited racial discrimination or separation in public accommodations. The following decades, however, saw many reversals. In 1883, the U.S. Supreme Court overturned the 1875 act. In 1896, in its ruling on *Plessy v. Ferguson*, the court declared the Jim Crow** law of Louisiana to be

*May 1 is celebrated around the world (with the exception of the United States) to honor the labor movement, in commemoration of the Haymarket Martyrs and the struggle for the eight-hour day.

** The term "Jim Crow" refers to the practice of legally enforced racial segregation, as practiced in the southern United States until overturned by the civil rights movement of the 1950s and 1960s. Under such policies, racial discrimination was legal in employment, housing, and other areas. African Americans (and, in some cases, other people of color) were restricted to segregated schools, and public services such as restaurants, public transportation, and even drinking fountains were separated by race.

constitutional.[18] This ruling was not to be reversed until 1954, when the modern civil rights movement was gathering momentum.

On the global scene, the late nineteenth century saw a mad scramble for colonial domination by the European powers. Africa, Asia, Latin America and the Caribbean, and the Pacific were treated as so many melons to be carved up by Britain, Germany, France, Portugal, Spain, Italy, and even smaller European countries such as the Netherlands and Belgium. In the east, Japan flexed its muscles toward China and Korea. The United States, for its part, had not yet entered the fray, having been occupied with acquiring land on its own continent, subduing the North American Indian population, and recovering from the Civil War. By the 1890s, however, the logic of U.S. global expansion was inexorable. Overseas colonies represented new territories, new markets, and new sources of raw materials. A war would prime the pump of economic growth and provide a safety valve for social and political pressures. The Spanish-American War, when it arrived, provided an answer to many dilemmas.

FREE LIBRARY OF PHILADELPHIA

*This cartoon, entitled "Anti-War," was published during the Philippine-American War to mock those opposing U.S. intervention.*

## Against the Grain: Opposition Voices*

U.S. annexation of the Philippines not only sparked the Philippine-American War, it also provoked a heated and sometimes bitter debate in the United States. William McKinley was elected president in 1896 "vow[ing] that annexation of foreign territory would be viewed by his administration as 'criminal aggression'" (Zwick, "Imperialists and Anti-Imperialists: The Roots of American Non-Intervention Movements"). When the Treaty of Paris made it clear that he was about to renege on this vow, a group of prominent citizens in Boston formed the Anti-Imperialist League. For a time the organization spread across the country, with branches forming in New York, Philadelphia, Cincinnati, Chicago, Minneapolis, and other areas.

Among the founders of the League were many people whose names are still known today, including Jane Addams, a leading suffragist and the founder of the Women's International League for Peace and Freedom (WILPF); Samuel Gompers, one of the founders of the American Federation of Labor; steel magnate Andrew Carnegie; former president Grover Cleveland; muckraker and reformer Ida Wells Barnett; and lawyer Moorfield Storey, who later became the first president of the National Association for the Advancement of Colored

*Information in this section draws on the work of historian Jim Zwick in his 1996 electronic publication, Anti-Imperialism in the United States, 1898-1935. This work, which is available on the World Wide Web at http://www.accinet.net/~fjzwick/ail98-35.html, combines contemporary analytical articles with extensive selections of original writings and cartoons from the era under discussion. Direct quotes are cited here to the individual articles in which they occur on the website.

AMERICAN SOCIAL HISTORY PROJECT

*"Civilization Begins At Home" was the title of this anti-war cartoon, published during the Philippine-American War. Depicted in the background are lynchings and shootings of African Americans.*

People (NAACP). The League's first appeal for membership declared that "we are in full sympathy with the heroic struggles for liberty of the people in the Spanish Islands, and therefore we protest against depriving them of their rights by an exchange of masters" (cited in Zwick, "Sitting in Darkness: An Unheeded Message About U.S. Militarism").

The League's first slate of officers included author Samuel Clemens, who is better known by his penname, Mark Twain. Upon studying the text of the Treaty of Paris, Twain wrote that "We do not intend to free but to subjugate the people of the Philippines. And so I am an anti-imperialist. I am opposed to having the eagle put its talons on any other land" (cited in Zwick, "Sitting in Darkness"). The treaty was hotly debated in the Senate and ultimately passed by only one vote — after U.S. troops fired on Philippine independence fighters, their erstwhile allies, in the incident that precipitated the Philippine-American War. (See Chapter 7, "The Philippines," for additional details; Lesson 7.1 also includes excerpts from the Senate debate on ratification of the treaty.) As the war continued, its opponents were frequently branded as traitors; Mark Twain's comment in response was that "the country is divided, half patriots and half traitors, and no man can tell which from which" (cited in Zwick, "Sitting in Darkness").

The debate over the Philippine-American war was heavily colored by the racist strain in

AMERICAN SOCIAL HISTORY PROJECT

*In this cartoon, John Bull, the symbol of Great Britain, is looking up toward Uncle Sam and saying "It's really most extraordinary what training will do. Why, only the other day I thought that man unable to support himself." Note how the figures representing Puerto Rico, Hawai`i, Cuba, the Philippines, and Guam all echo racist images of Africans. (The "Ladrones" is an obsolete name for the Mariana Islands, where Guam is located.)*

CORBIS-BETTMAN

***This 1888 cartoon shows Uncle Sam examining the Haitian Republic. In 1804, following a slave revolt, Haiti became the second independent nation in the Americas. It was later under U.S. military occupation from 1915 to 1934.***

U.S. political culture. Among the white population, support for the war was whipped up with openly racist portrayals of the Filipinos as "savages with feathers in their hair or as black-faced, grass-skirted Sambos" (Zwick, "Sitting in Darkness"). These images had no connection with Filipino culture or history; rather, they were adopted from racist depictions of Native Americans and African Americans. Likewise, many of the U.S. soldiers who fought in the war were veterans of the Indian Wars, and their comments in letters home and similar materials reveal that they viewed this latest war as the logical extension of their conquest of North America (see Lesson 7.2).

Many African Americans worked to oppose U.S. interventionism, drawing the parallels between what was happening in the Philippines and the frequently violent discrimination they faced at home. They also formed their own anti-imperialist organizations, such as the National Negro Anti-Expansion, Anti-Imperialist, Anti-Trust, and Anti-Lynching League, which was founded in 1899. In the 1920s and 1930s, the NAACP continued to speak out against the racist character and consequences of U.S. intervention in Haiti, Santo Domingo (known today as the Dominican Republic), and other countries in the Caribbean and Central America.

Other progressive social movements of the day were also deeply engaged in opposing the U.S. role abroad. WILPF denounced the war as an exercise in male-initiated militarism. Many suffragists joined the Anti-Imperialist League, and in May 1902, the New England Women's Suffrage Association hosted Clemencia Lopez, a Filipina independence activist, who spoke of the "horrors and cruelties" of U.S. occupation of her country (see Lesson 7.1).

It must be noted, however, that the opposition to the war included several contradictory strains. Labor leaders like Samuel Gompers were mainly concerned to protect their membership, which at that period in history was exclusively white, from potential competition by Filipino laborers. Similarly, some of the most prominent opponents of imperialism abroad were advocates of Jim Crow laws at home — such as Sen. Benjamin Tillman, a vice-president of the Anti-Imperialist League who also helped gain passage of literacy requirements for voters that were specifically designed to exclude African Americans. A 1900 anti-imperialist conference passed a resolution supporting African American civil rights — but also threw the movement's support behind presidential candidate William Jennings Bryan, who had close political connections with racist Southern Democrats. These political divisions, as well as disagreements over strategy, weakened the anti-imperialist movement.

## A Century Later

Despite massive domestic opposition to the U.S. role in the Philippines, those who questioned U.S. expansionism lost the political battle, and since then they have largely been written out of history. Many of the questions they raised, however, are as valid today as they were a century ago.

The decades following the Spanish-American War were marked by an uninterrupted process of global expansion by the United States. The country's new territories were quickly put to use; in June 1900, at the height of the Boxer Rebellion in China, the United States sent troops to Beijing from its naval base at Subic Bay in the Philippines. A few years later, the Roosevelt Administration entered into an arrangement with the budding Japanese empire, sanctioning Japanese domination of Korea in return for Japan's support of the U.S. role in the Philippines. This arrangement, formalized through the Taft-Katsura Agreement of 1905, tied U.S. policy in Asia into Korea's lengthy subjugation to Japan, which endured until the end of World War II.[19]

The need for a quick passage from the Atlantic to the Pacific was taken to be another strategic lesson of the war. In 1903, when negotiations with Colombia to build a canal at the narrowest point of the Central American isthmus proved unsuccessful, the United States sponsored the secession of Panama, then part of Colombia. The Canal Zone was acquired a scant two weeks after Panama declared its independence.

In succeeding years, as mentioned above, more U.S. interventions followed. In the Caribbean and Central America, five nations were under U.S. military occupation for lengthy periods, including Cuba, Nicaragua, Panama, the Dominican Republic, and Haiti.[20] Many of these interventions were openly undertaken to defend the interests of U.S.-based corporations, and by the 1920s those who questioned the U.S. role were talking about "economic imperialism" as much as the political variety.

The Philippine-American War was the crucible in which many aspects of the contemporary role of the U.S. military were forged. The "strategic hamlets" of Vietnam, which have endured as a central strategy of modern counterinsurgency warfare, were little more than an updated version of the *reconcentración* invented by the Spanish and adopted by the United States in the Philippines. The maintenance of a large U.S. army, including in peacetime, also dates from that era; between 1898 and 1901 the standing army grew from 26,800 to 104,000 soldiers. Even the recitation of the Pledge of Allegiance was first mandated in 1898 as a compulsory expression of patriotism.

The militias named in the Second Amendment to the U.S. Constitution also began to alter their character in this era. In 1903, "the previously autonomous state militias were expanded and centralized under a national leadership," establishing the National Guard "as a force not only for domestic control and defense but — as seen from their training in Honduras in the 1980s and their later roles in the Gulf War, Somalia, and Haiti — for intervention throughout the world" (Zwick, "Imperialists and Anti-Imperialists"). More recently, the National Guard has also come to play an increasing role in the militarization of the U.S.-Mexico border, in what some analysts have seen as the first

*Tahiti, 1997: Pacific Islanders from Hawai`i, Samoa, Guam, and other nations demonstrate for a nuclear-free and independent Pacific.*

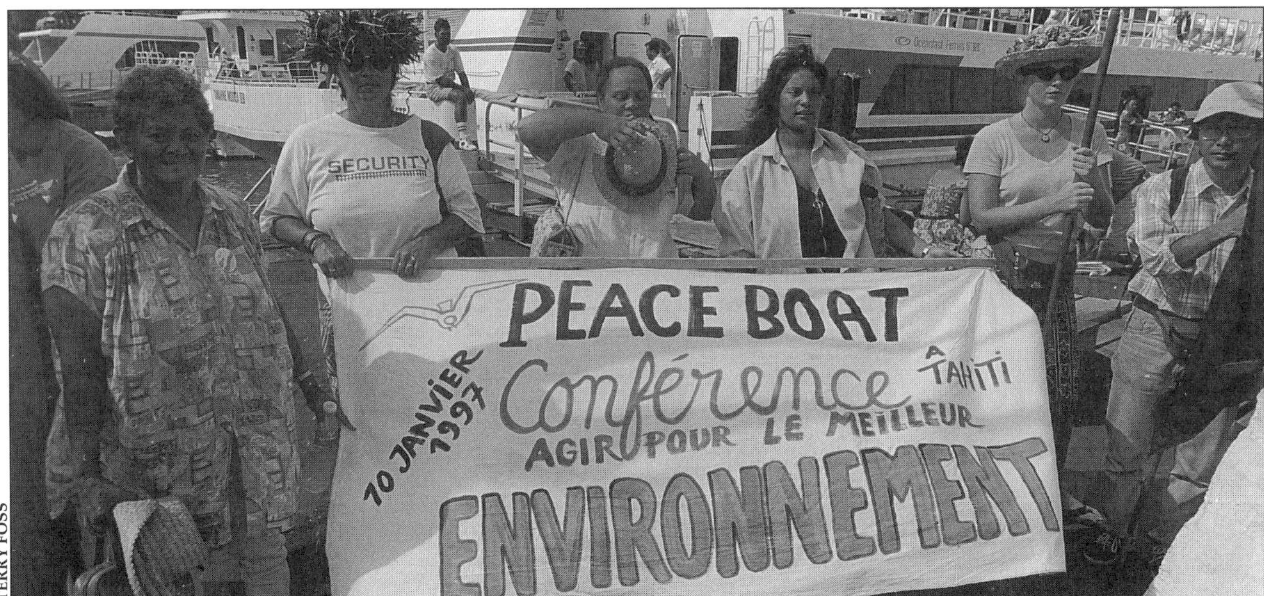


*Pacific Islanders at a 1997 anti-nuclear conference. The sign for the Peace Boat reads, "Act for a Better Environment."*

application of counterinsurgency strategy inside U.S. territory.[21]

Nuclear testing in the Pacific by Western powers has emerged as another enduring legacy of the region's militarization (and a key issue for regional sovereignty movements). Hundreds of nuclear explosions have taken place in the Pacific, starting with the U.S. Navy's tests in 1946 on Bikini Atoll in the Marshall Islands. In 1954 the United States launched one of the biggest and most deadly tests in the Pacific, the "Bravo Test" on the Bikini Atoll. This test involved the atmospheric detonation of a hydrogen bomb at a time when those responsible for the tests knew that winds were blowing in the direction of inhabited atolls. Tests of various sizes continued, irreversibly contaminating many islands and uprooting their populations. Residents became known as "nuclear nomads," forcibly moved from their homes and shuttled from one island to the next due to contamination. Once-healthy people became sick; babies were miscarried or born with deformities. At this writing, the last nuclear test in the Pacific was carried out by France in Mururoa, Tahiti, in 1996; it is not clear whether more such tests may take place in the future. Meanwhile, the many health and environmental problems caused by nuclear fallout and nuclear wastes remain unresolved.

A central purpose of studying history is to understand the present in the light shed by the past. This centennial of the Spanish-American War might best be described as an era of urgent questions without clear answers. The end of the Cold War has not led to a new era of peace, but to a proliferation of regional conflicts, many of which are fanned by racism and ethnic hatred—including in the United States, where the demonization of "enemy" nations continues to rest on thinly veiled racial stereotypes. In many areas of the world, including the Philippines as well as Central and South America, the elimination of the brutal military dictatorships of the 1970s and 1980s has led neither to democratization nor to true independence but rather to deepening impoverishment, coupled with growing dependence on the global market economy. Even in the United States, sustained economic growth has not brought shared prosperity, but rather a widening gap between rich and poor and an overall loss of economic security for a large majority of the population.

This guide, as noted at the outset, offers voices from the island nations whose destiny has been shaped by the entry of the United States onto the global scene a hundred years ago. The experiences and viewpoints presented here differ among themselves; all, however, are deeply engaged with the meanings and possibilities of the elusive concept of sovereignty. What, for a people (or a social group) is independence? What is dependence? What is self-determination? What are their dimensions, and what are their limits? These are questions, not just for a few, but for all of us.

## Notes

[1] Deryk Scarr, *The History of the Pacific Islands: Kingdoms of the Reef* (South Melbourne, Australia: Macmillan, 1990), p. 223.

[2] Teodoro Agoncillo, *The Revolt of the Masses: The Story of Bonifacio and the Katipunan,* (Quezon City: University of the Philippines, 1956), pp. 147-148.

[3] Scarr, *op. cit.,* p. 222.

[4] Thomas A. Bailey, *The American Pageant: A History of the Republic* (Boston: D. C. Heath, 1956), p. 615.

[5] Hugh Thomas, "Remember the Maine?", *New York Review of Books,* April 23, 1998, p. 12.

[6] Gorton C. Carruth, *What Happened When: A Chronology of Life and Events in America* (abridged edition of *The Encyclopedia of American Facts and Dates;* New York: Harper & Row, 1989), p. 571.

[7] Douglas L. Oliver, *The Pacific Islands* (Cambridge, MA: Harvard University Press, 1951), p. 239.

[8] Bailey, *op. cit.,* p. 627.

[9] Stanley Karnow, *In Our Image: America's Empire in the Philippines* (New York: Random House, 1989), p. 111.

[10] Amado Guerrero, *Philippine Society and Revolution* (Oakland, CA: International Assoc. of Filipino Patriots, 1979), p. 17. Estimates of the numbers of casualties range up to 600,000.

[11] Michael J. Field, *Mau: Samoa's Struggle for Freedom* (Honolulu: University of Hawai`i Press, 1990).

[12] Catherine A. Sunshine and Deborah Menkart, Eds., *Caribbean Connections: Overview of Regional History* (Washington: Ecumenical Program on Central America & Network of Educators on Central America, 1991), p. 115

[13] Carruth, *op. cit.*

[14] Philip S. Foner, *History of the Labor Movement in the United States, Vol. 2, From the Founding of the AFL to the Emergence of American Imperialism* (New York: International Publishers, 1975), p. 241.

[15] Richard. O. Boyer and Herbert M. Morais, *Labor's Untold Story* (New York: United Electrical Workers, 1979).

[16] Foner, *op. cit.,* p. 266.

[17] Carruth, *op. cit.*

[18] Carruth, *op. cit.,* p. 561.

[19] B. Cumings, *Korea's Place in the Sun: A Modern History* (New York: W. W. Norton, 1997).

[20] Sunshine and Menkart, *op. cit.,* p. 117.

[21] Timothy Dunn, *The Militarization of the Mexico-U.S. Border, 1878–1992: Low-Intensity Conflict Doctrine Comes Home* (Austin: University of Texas, 1996).

# LESSON 1.1 History and Point of View

**Objective:** To enable students to understand that all study of history is interpretative, and that the "truth" may shift depending on one's perspective.

**Themes:** historical truth, historical perspective

**Vocabulary:** circumnavigation, repelled, aggression

## Suggested Activities

1. You may wish to begin this exercise with a discussion of how students understand the concept of historical truth. Questions for discussion might include: if something is true for one person or group, is it true for everybody? Do facts depend on who is looking at them, or are they independent of the observer? Ask students to share incidents in their personal lives where different people had different understandings of what was going on. Do they believe that just one person's version of these incidents was the "true" one?

2. Have students review the reading included at the end of this lesson. Ask them how this reading fits in with their understanding of such concepts as "truth" or "facts."

3. Ask students to choose another incident in U.S. or world history. Have them draw two commemorative plaques on separate pieces of paper, describing the incident from different points of view. Tell them to be sure that the descriptions on both plaques are factually accurate. Ask them to present their plaques to the class and explain what group of people with what point of view might want to use each.

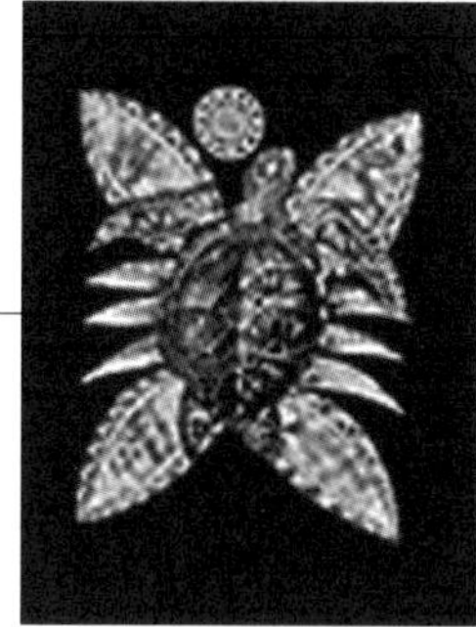

# Reading: Lapulapu and Magellan

On the small island of Mactan in the central Philippines, there are two plaques commemorating the same historical event. One plaque was erected in 1941 and is entitled "Ferdinand Magellan's Death." It reads:

> On this spot Ferdinand Magellan died on April 27, 1521, wounded in an encounter with the soldiers of Lapulapu, chief of Mactan Island. One of Magellan's ships, the *Victoria*, under the command of Juan Sebastian Elcano, sailed from Cebu on May 1, 1521, and anchored at San Lucar de Barrameda on September 6, 1522, thus completing the first circumnavigation of the earth.

The second plaque was erected in 1951 and is entitled "Lapulapu." It reads:

> Here, on 27 April 1521, Lapulapu and his men repulsed the Spanish invaders, killing their leader, Ferdinand Magellan. Thus, Lapulapu became the first Filipino to have repelled European aggression.

Sometimes people say things that are simply untrue. But the information on both of these plaques is accurate: each one is describing a different aspect of the historical truth. Anyone who wants to study history has to learn to sort out truth from falsehood. Beyond that, however, it is also important to recognize that depending on their point of view, people might emphasize different aspects of an event.

In the case of the two plaques on Mactan, the first one was erected in 1941, when the Philippines was still a U.S. colony. The second plaque was put up in 1951, after the Philippines became a formally independent country. Think about the difference between these two plaques in how the facts are presented. How might the change in the political status of the Philippines affected the wording of the plaques?

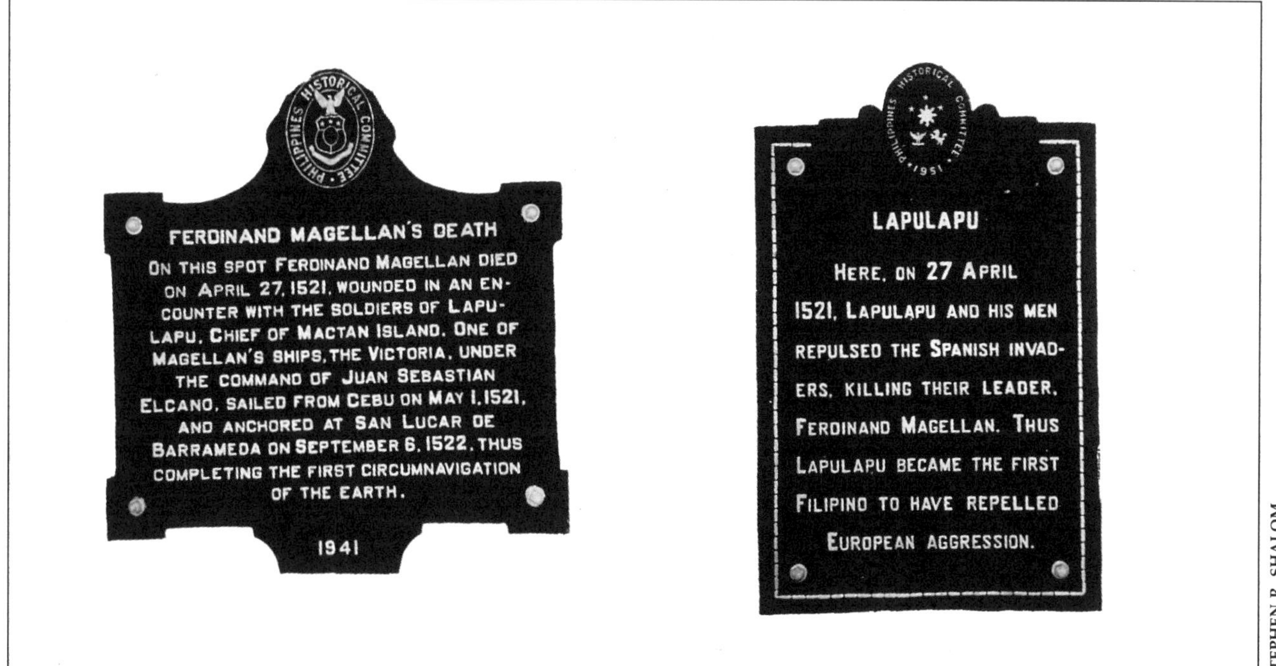


STEPHEN R. SHALOM

# Lesson 1.2 Words, Words, Words

**Objective:** To help students understand key terms and concepts regarding political status and other aspects of the relations between peoples and nations.

**Themes:** political status, terminology

## Suggested Activities

1. Have students read over the worksheet provided at the end of this lesson.
2. Divide students into small groups and ask them to discuss what they have read.
3. Ask students what they know about the early history of the United States. Ask them how terms like "the thirteen colonies," "taxation without representation," "independence," "liberty," and "revolution" were used in the context of history lessons they have received.
4. Now turn the class's attention to the countries listed on the worksheet (which are the same as the countries explored in this guide). In what ways does their situation seem similar to early U.S. history? In what ways does it seem different?

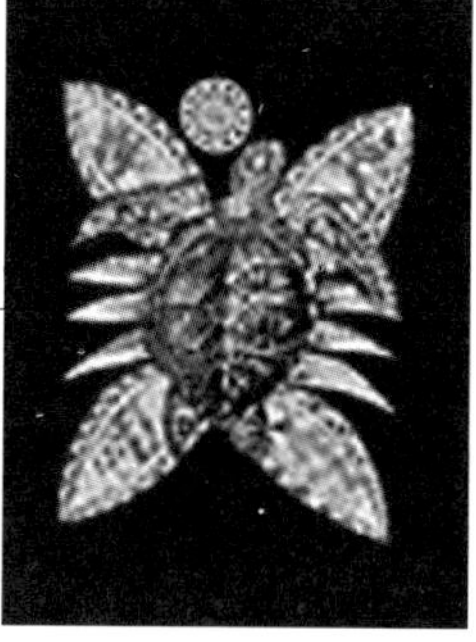

# Worksheet: Terms and Concepts

*Part I of this worksheet summarizes the current status of the various countries annexed by the United States in 1898. Part II presents definitions of key terms used in this guide.*

## PART I:
### *Political Status*

**American Samoa** — American Samoa is controlled by the U.S. Department of the Interior. The people of American Samoa are considered U.S. nationals, but not U.S. citizens. Samoa is classified as an "unorganized and unincorporated U.S. territory."

**Cuba** — Following the Spanish-American War, Cuba was ruled by a U.S. military government until 1902. Cuba then became officially independent, but was obliged to adopt a constitution which said the United States could maintain military bases and control in Cuba in order to protect U.S. interests there. In 1959, Cuba had a revolution and became independent of the United States. To this day, however, the U.S. military continues to maintain the Guantanamo Bay Naval Station on Cuban soil.

**Guam** — After 1898, Guam was placed under U.S. naval control. The United States lost control of Guam briefly in World War II, when Japan took over the island. Since August 1, 1950, Guam has held the title "unincorporated U.S. territory." Residents of Guam elect a nonvoting representative to the U.S. Congress.

**Hawai`i** — In 1893, John L. Stevens, the U.S. ambassador to the Hawaiian Kingdom, conspired with a small group of U.S. and European businessmen to overthrow the Hawaiian government. Hawai`i was proclaimed to be a protectorate of the United States without the consent of the U.S. Congress and in violation of international law. In 1898, Hawai`i was annexed by the United States, and in 1959 it became the fiftieth state. In 1993, U.S. President Clinton signed the "Apology Bill" (PL 103-150), acknowledging the illegality of Hawai`i's overthrow and annexation.

**The Philippines** — In 1898, the United States purchased the Philippines from Spain for $20 million. Outright U.S. rule continued until the Philippines became a commonwealth in 1935. During World War II, Japan occupied the Philippines, with the United States regaining control in 1945. Philippine independence was recognized by the United States in July 1946.

**Puerto Rico** — After 1898, Puerto Rico became a territory of the United States. In 1952, Puerto Rico became a commonwealth of the United States, with a nonvoting representative in the U.S. Congress. The Commonwealth of Puerto Rico has its own constitution. Its residents are citizens of the United States, but those who live on the island cannot vote in national elections.

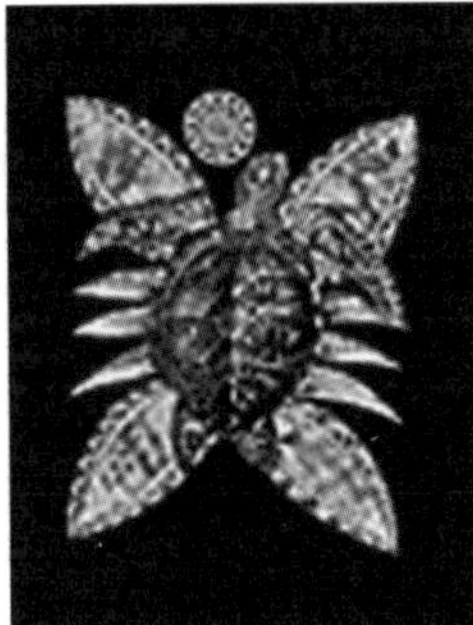

## PART 2:

### *Definitions of Terms*

**Censorship** — Forcible suppression by state authorities of controversial ideas, images, or statements.

**Colonialism** — A system in which one nation exercises military, political, and economic control over another. The nation which is under foreign control is then known as a colony.

**Commonwealth** — A U.S. territory with limited rights of autonomy and self-government.

**Freedom** — Political independence. Possession of civil rights; immunity from the arbitrary exercise of authority.

**Imperialism** — A system in which a nation's authority is extended by territorial acquisition or by establishing economic or political power over other nations.

**Independent** — Not governed by a foreign power; self-governing. Free from the influence, guidance, or control of another or others; self-reliant.

**Liberty** — The condition of being free from restriction or control.

**Nation** — A relatively large group of people organized under a single, usually independent, government; a country.

**Oppression** — Severe and unjust use of force or authority to deprive individuals or groups of their rights.

**Protectorate** — A relationship of protection and partial control assumed by a more powerful nation over a dependent country or region.

**Sovereignty** — Complete independence and self-government. Supremacy of authority or rule as exercised by a sovereign or sovereign state.

**Self-determination** — Freedom of the people of a given area to determine their own political status; independence.

**Territory** — A region that belongs to or is controlled by a country or other political unit. Three different types of territories are held by the United States:

a. *Unincorporated* territories may not become states. Only fundamental rights apply there, as distinguished from formal or procedural rights, such as the right to trial by jury.

b. *Incorporated* territories may become states. All rights guaranteed by the U.S. constitution apply in incorporated territories.

c. *Wholly unorganized and unincorporated* territories are controlled by executive branch officials, not Congress. They have the most limited rights.

---

**Source:** *Definitions adapted from* The American Heritage Dictionary of the English Language, *3d* ed. *(Boston: Houghton Mifflin, 1992).*

# LESSON 1.3 Political Cartoons and Historical Context

**Objective:** To introduce students to the varied public reactions within the United States that were prompted by the Spanish-American war, using political cartoons from 1898.

**Themes:** satire, media images, public opinion

## Suggested Activities

1. Ask students what they know about political cartoons. Where do they usually appear? What purposes do they serve?
2. Break students into groups of four or five and distribute copies of one of the worksheets at the end of this lesson to each group. Ask each group to answer the questions on the worksheet.
3. After the students answer the questions in small groups, have them present their answers to the whole class.
4. After the groups have finished presenting their analyses of the cartoons, ask them to consider how U.S. media portrayed the process of U.S. global expansion 100 years ago. Did anything surprise the students? Were they aware that some people in the United States questioned whether or not the United States should have pursued the course of expansion?
5. Ask students to find political cartoons in current newspapers that portray the United States and its international role. How is the content of these cartoons the same or different from the cartoons of 100 years ago?
6. Have the class select two or three current news stories related to the themes of this guide. Each student can develop her or his own political cartoon based on one of these stories. As an alternative, some students may wish to select a historical event for their cartoon.

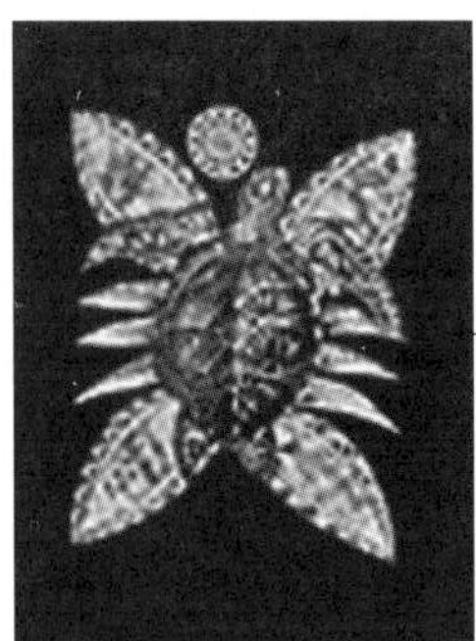



# Worksheet: "Opening Up of the Fishing Season"

*Opening of the Fishing Season*

1. How is the United States portrayed in this cartoon? What assumptions are expressed about the United States by the use of this particular image?
2. How does the cartoon portray the other countries that the United States took possession of in 1898?
3. What is the artist who drew this cartoon trying to say about the United States? Do you think the artist communicated his or her opinion effectively?

---

**Source:** Cartoons of the War of 1898 with Spain; From Leading Foreign and American papers *(Chicago: Bellford, Middlebrook & Co., 1898). Collection of the Library of Congress.*

# Worksheet: "10,000 Miles from Tip to Tip"

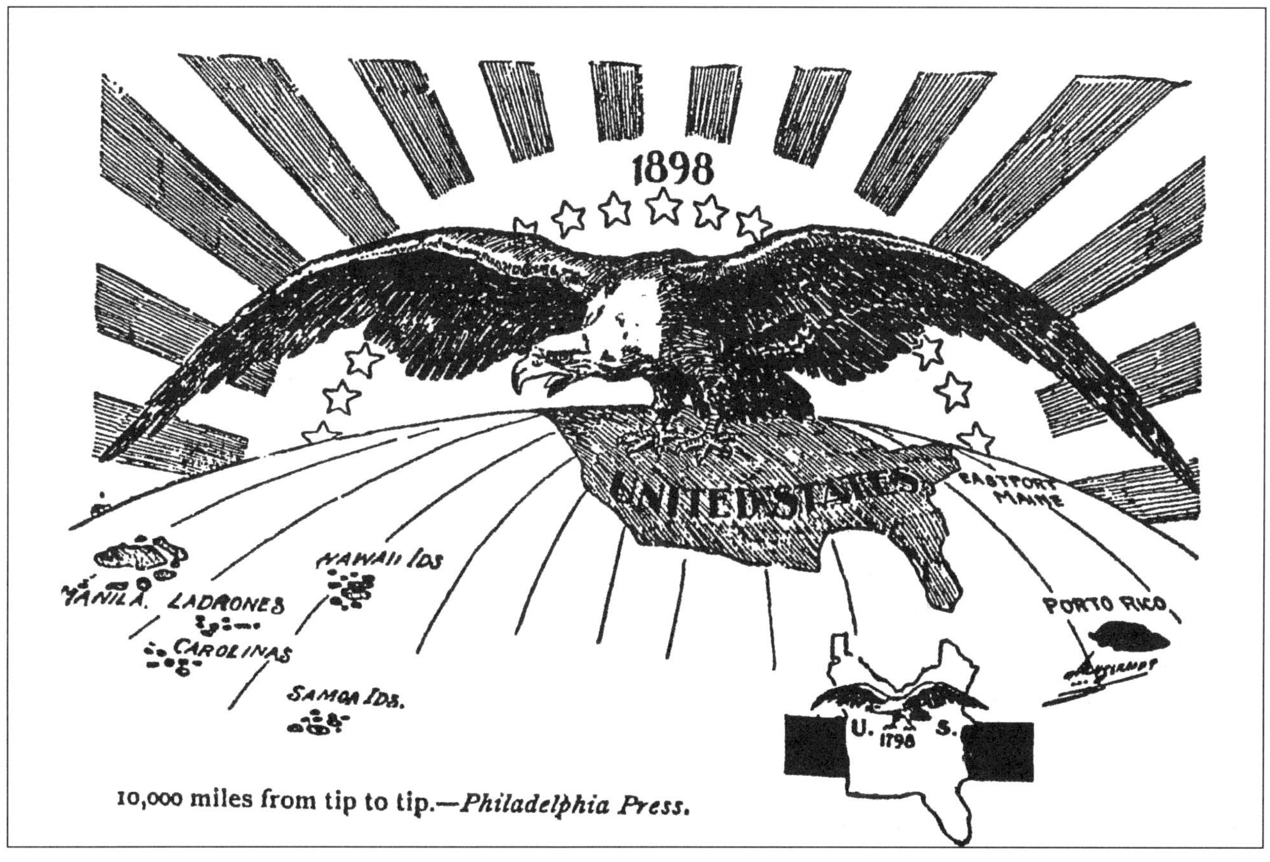


*10,000 miles from tip to tip.*

1. How is the United States portrayed in this cartoon?
2. What is the significance of the two maps and the two dates portrayed in this cartoon?
3. What do you think is the artist's opinion about U.S. expansion? Do you think the artist supports it or opposes it? Why?

---

**Source:** Cartoons of the War of 1898 with Spain; From Leading Foreign and American papers *(Chicago: Bellford, Middlebrook & Co., 1898). Collection of the Library of Congress.*

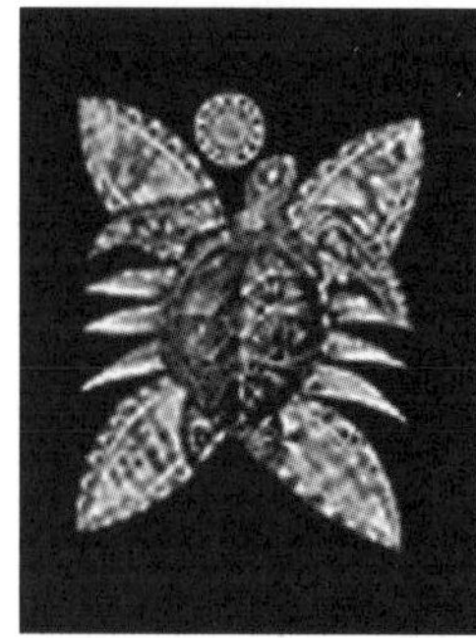

# Worksheet: "No Division Here"

*No division here.*

1. How is the United States portrayed in this cartoon? How are other countries portrayed in the cartoon? What assumptions do these images express about the United States, Spain, England, France, Germany, Austria, and Russia? About Puerto Rico, Cuba, and the Philippines?
2. Based on this cartoon, what could you say about the state of the world in 1898?
3. What do you think is the artist's opinion about U.S. expansion? Do you think the artist supports it or opposes it? What do you think is the artist's opinion of the countries which the U.S. has acquired?

---

**Source:** Cartoons of the War of 1898 with Spain; From Leading Foreign and American papers *(Chicago: Bellford, Middlebrook & Co., 1898). Collection of the Library of Congress.*

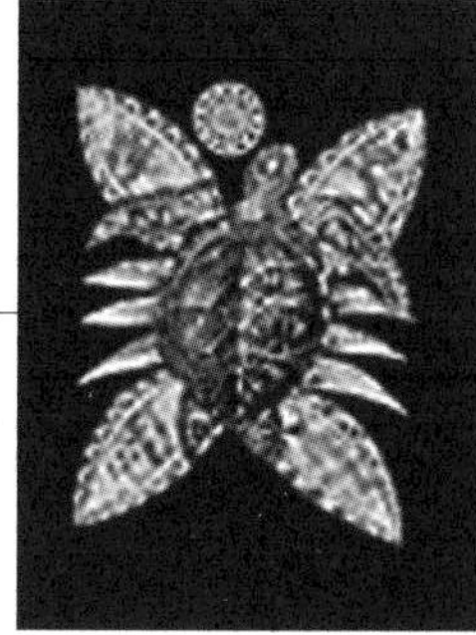

# Worksheet: "Now Will He Let Go?"

*Now, will he let go? If you think he will let go you don't know him.*

1. How is the United States portrayed in this cartoon? What assumptions are expressed about the United States by the use of this particular image?
2. What do you think the caption means?
3. What do you think is the artist's opinion about U.S. expansion? Do you think the artist supports it or opposes it? Do you think the artist communicated his or her opinion effectively?

---

**Source:** *Jim Zwick, Ed.,* Anti-Imperialism in the United States, 1898–1935 *(http://accinet.net/~fjzwick/ail98-35.html), 1996.*

# LESSON 1.4 The Treaty of Paris

**Objective:** To assist students to develop their own critical reading of primary source materials from the Spanish-American War.

**Themes:** colonial powers, international relations, historical analysis

**Vocabulary:** sovereignty, evacuation, cede, archipelago, ratification

## Suggested Activities

1. Distribute the handout at the end of this lesson with excerpts from the Treaty of Paris. Ask students to read Article I and summarize what it says. Supposedly, the Spanish-American War was fought to support Cuban independence. Does Article I of the treaty support this interpretation of the role of the United States?
2. Have students read Articles II and III. Ask them what territories the United States acquired as a result of the treaty. Do they think the people of the countries listed had a say in the writing of the treaty?
3. Ask students whether and how the treaty refers to the inhabitants of the affected countries. Inform them that at the time this treaty was signed, Cuba, Puerto Rico, and the Philippines had nearly succeeded in winning their independence from Spain. What do they think about whether Spain had the right to "give" these territories to the United States?
4. Ask students to imagine that they are a member of the independence movement in one of these former Spanish colonies at the time of the Treaty of Paris. Have them write a letter or journal entry expressing their feelings about the treaty and its impact on their lives.

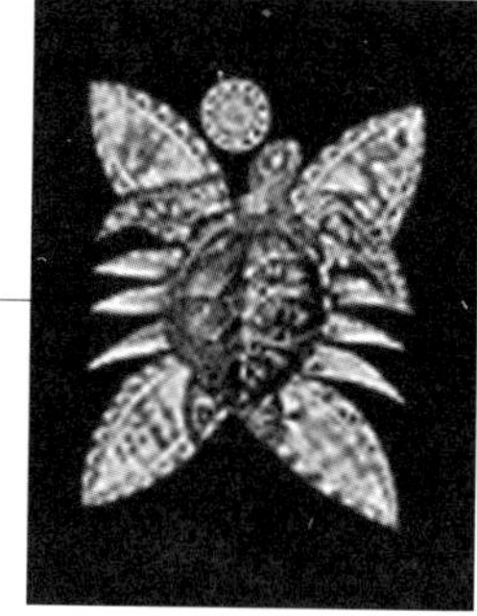

# Reading: Excerpts from the Treaty of Paris

## Article I

Spain relinquishes all claim of sovereignty over and title to Cuba.

And as the island is, upon its evacuation by Spain, to be occupied by the United States, the United States will so long as such occupation shall last, assume and discharge the obligations that may under international law result from the fact of its occupation, for the protection of life and property.

## Article II

Spain cedes to the United States the islands of Porto Rico and other islands now under Spanish sovereignty in the West Indies, and the island of Guam in the Marianas or Ladrones.

## Article III

Spain cedes to the United States the archipelago know as the Philippine Islands, and comprehending the islands lying within the following line: [*specification of location follows*]

The United States will pay to Spain the sum of twenty million dollars ($20,000,000) within three months after the exchange of the ratifications of the present treaty . . .

---

**Source:** *N. Kanellos, Ed.,* Reference Library of Hispanic America, *Vol. I (Detroit: Educational Guidance Service, 1993).*

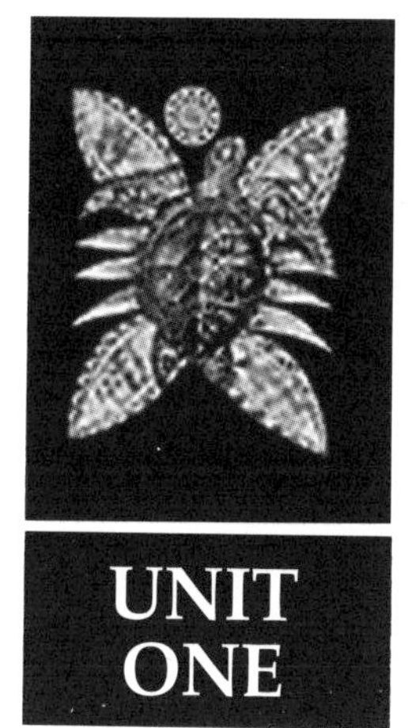

UNIT ONE

# THE CARIBBEAN

# 2.

# Cuba

*Overview*

Juan Antonio Blanco
Rachael Kamel

*Lessons*

Deborah Wei
Liz Hottel
Deborah Menkart
Eric Joselyn

CUBA is the largest island in the Caribbean Sea. It is also the Caribbean island that lies closest to the U.S. mainland, with the northwestern end of Cuba lying only ninety miles to the south of Key West, Florida.

Beginning in about 500 BC, a people known as the Arawaks began to populate the Caribbean. They came from the Orinoco River basin in South America (an area that is part of modern Venezuela, Brazil, and Guyana). Cuba was mainly populated by the Tainos, a branch of the Arawaks. The Tainos were also the principal ethnic group in the areas known today as Puerto Rico, Jamaica, Haiti, and the Dominican Republic. Modern anthropologists are unsure how many people populated the Caribbean islands before the coming of the Europeans; estimates range from 60,000 to as high as seven million. The Taino-Arawaks were mainly farmers and fishers, trading extensively among their islands in wooden canoes.

Christopher Columbus visited Cuba briefly on his first voyage but did not establish a settlement there. In 1508, a Spanish explorer began to circulate tales of the gold to be found in Cuba, and in 1510, a Spanish conquistador, Diego Velazquez, brought an army of 300 men to conquer the island. Hundreds of men, women, and children were indiscriminately slaughtered by this invading army. The Taino-Arawak chieftain Hatuey led the islanders in fighting back against the Spanish invaders. Eventually, however, the Arawaks were defeated and Hatuey was captured and burned alive. To this day, Hatuey is remembered as a symbol of Cuba's resistance to foreign domination.

The Spanish found little gold in Cuba and the other Caribbean islands, and so they turned to mining, cattle farming, and plantation agriculture. They carried out these economic enterprises by enslaving the Arawaks through a system known as *repartimiento,* or the "parceling out" of Indian slaves. This was later replaced by the *encomienda* system, under which tracts of land, together with their Arawak inhabitants, were granted as property to individual Spanish settlers by the Spanish crown. Countless Indians were either worked to death in the mines or killed in epidemics of diseases introduced from Europe. Herds of the newly introduced cattle also trampled the crops on which the Arawaks depended, destroying their food supply.

As the first Spanish foothold in the Western Hemisphere, the Caribbean served as the springboard for the Spanish conquest of Mexico and South America. When the Spanish discovered the Aztec and Mayan civilizations of Mexico and the Incan empire of Peru, many Spanish settlers abandoned Cuba to join in looting Indian gold and silver there. Eventually, howev-

FREE LIBRARY OF PHILADELPHIA

***Havana Harbor is shown in this 1871 engraving.***

er, the colonial economy of Cuba revived because of the island's strategic location as a gateway to the "New World," as well as the highly useful harbor at Havana. Cuba became a major shipping center for plundered Indian gold making its way to Europe and European goods destined for colonial markets. By the eighteenth century, Havana was the most important port in the Americas.

## African Roots

As in other Caribbean islands, most of Cuba's indigenous Taino-Arawak population was destroyed in the encounter with the Spanish colonizers. Spanish settlers searching for alternative sources of labor turned to the enslavement of Africans.* As with the *encomienda* system, slavery caused untold suffering to non-European peoples.

Although the European slave trade began early in the sixteenth century, it did not become widespread as a social institution until the rise of large-scale plantation agriculture. In Cuba (and in Puerto Rico), sugar plantations became economically important toward the end of the eighteenth century. As sugar cane production expanded, the slave population grew dramatically. By 1827, enslaved Africans accounted for some 40 percent of the Cuban population, which was then more than 700,000. By mid-century, Africans and people of African descent in Cuba outnumbered whites.

Cuba's population also included a higher proportion of free Africans than other European colonies in the Western Hemisphere. Free Africans and their descendants engaged in many different trades, attaining a social status that was barred to them in British colonies. Conditions were nonetheless harsh for slaves, however. Some slaves managed to run away, establishing their own fortified communities, known as *palenques*, in Orient province in the eastern part of the island. Slave rebellions were also common.

## Reaching for Independence

Inspired by the ideals of the French Revolution of 1789, most of Spain's Latin American colonies fought for their independence in the early years of the nineteenth century. Beginning in 1810, revolts began to break out in one country after another; by 1825, virtually the entire continent was free from European rule.** The leaders of these rebellions were the *criollos*, or Latin American–born descendants of Spanish settlers. As in the United States, Indians and people of African descent were not included as equal participants in these newly formed nations. (An exception to this pattern was the Republic of Haiti, where a former slave, Toussaint L'Ouverture, led a rebellion in 1801 that ended French colonial rule and freed all the slaves.)

In the Caribbean, and especially in Cuba, slave-owning planters opposed independence because they feared rebellions among their slaves. Major slave rebellions occurred in Cuba in 1810 and 1812. The fears of the slave owners were also fueled by the experience of neighboring Haiti. Following the establishment of the Haitian Republic, some 30,000 French colonists left Haiti for Cuba, bringing as many of their slaves with them as they could.

Although the plantation owners feared independence, other Cubans desired it. Cubans of African descent, whether free or enslaved, wanted to put an end to slavery. In addition, other *criollos*, including merchants and small farmers, believed Cuba could compete better in international trade if it modernized the sugar industry and replaced slavery with wage labor. The capital for this modernization came chiefly

*Chapter 3, Puerto Rico, offers additional detail on African slavery and the influence of African culture in the Caribbean.

**Portugal's only colony in the Americas, Brazil, won its independence in 1822, the same period as most Spanish colonies.

from the United States, and U.S. investors came to have a growing interest in Cuba's economy.

In 1868, a group of Cuban *insurrectos* (rebels) declared the island's independence. The headquarters of their rebellion was Yara, in Orient province, a center of anti-slavery activity. When a Puerto Rican uprising the same year was quickly put down, many of the Puerto Rican independence fighters came to fight alongside the Cubans, as a way of continuing their struggle against Spain. There was also widespread sympathy for the Cubans in the United States, where many people sent arms or supplies to the *insurrectos,* and some even came to join them in their fight.

FREE LIBRARY OF PHILADELPHIA

*In this nineteenth century painting, Cuban* **insurrectos** *battle Spanish regulars.*

The Ten Years War, as this rebellion is known, ended in 1878. Neither the *insurrectos* nor the Spanish were able to win a decisive victory. Concessions that were made by Spain to end the war included home rule for Cuba, amnesty for the *insurrectos,* and freedom for the slaves who fought with the rebels. Slavery was completely abolished by 1886, but many of the other reforms promised by Spain were never carried out, and talk of independence began once again.

Jose Marti (1853–1895) was a central figure in Cuba's final war of independence from Spain. Exiled in his teens for pro-independence activities, he returned to Cuba following the amnesty of 1878. He was soon forced to leave once again. In 1881, he settled in New York, where he spent the next fourteen years speaking and rallying support for the cause of Cuban independence. Marti spoke of a new vision of independence, which would include freedom not only from Spanish rule but also from all forms of injustice, especially racial discrimination (see Lesson 2.1). Although he admired the democratic ideals of the United States, he also warned of the danger of the growing U.S. influence in Latin America.

During and after the Ten Years War, many Cubans had moved to the United States, becoming a major influence in such cities as Key West and Tampa, Florida. These Cuban immigrants also became a crucial base of support for the Cuban independence movement, forming committees to raise funds for the cause and helping exiled *insurrectos.* By 1895, the conditions were ripe for another rebellion. Marti founded the Cuban Revolutionary Party in Tampa and returned to Cuba to join the battle for independence. He was killed by Spanish forces only four months later.

## A Double-Edged Sword

Appealing to memories of the U.S. War of Independence from Britain, supporters of Cuban independence rallied support for their cause among the U.S. public. In 1896, with the Cuban rebels gaining ground, the Spanish general Valeriano Weyler was sent to put down the insurrection. The U.S. press reported the many atrocities committed by his forces, and public opinion turned against the Spanish worldwide.

Early in 1898, U.S. President William McKinley warned the Spanish that if they did not grant Cuban independence, the United States would step in. To underline his warning, he sent the battleship *U.S.S. Maine* to Havana harbor. When the ship blew up on February 15, 1898, more than 260 U.S. sailors lost their lives. The U.S. press was quick to blame Spanish sabotage and clamored for war with Spain.* On April 18, the U.S. Congress recognized Cuban independence and demanded Spain's withdrawal. On April 24, war was declared. As detailed in chapter 1, the war quickly widened to include all of Spain's remaining colonies in the Caribbean and the Pacific.

SPAIN
CUBAN INSURRECTIO
CUBA
POSSESSION IS NINE POINTS OF THE LAW
BURNING AT BOTH ENDS.
PRESIDENTIAL SMOKER—"You can't get it to draw that way—better give it to me, gents; I'll smoke it."

CORBIS-BETTMAN

*U.S. President William McKinley stands at the back in this 1898 cartoon, offering to "smoke" the cigar representing Cuba.*

U.S. motives for intervention in Cuba were complex. By the end of the nineteenth century, trade with Cuba and investments there had considerable importance to the U.S. economy. Some U.S. investors feared that the continuing war would damage their Cuban holdings. Others wanted to continue the expansion of the United States by adding new territories, such as Cuba. In 1869, near the start of the Ten Years War, the United States had made an offer to Spain to buy the island for $100 million. This offer was rejected.

At the close of the Spanish-American War, Spain gave up all claims to Cuba. Cubans continued to press for their independence, however, since U.S. troops remained in Cuba as an occupying force until 1902. Part of the price for U.S. withdrawal was Cuban acceptance of the Platt Amendment (see Lesson 2.2). When the United States finally recognized Cuban independence in 1902, the new nation's constitution included an amendment written by a U.S. senator, Orville H. Platt, which said that U.S. forces could intervene in Cuba under certain conditions. The U.S. naval station at Guantanamo Bay was also established under this agreement. Although the Platt Amendment was finally abrogated in 1934, the U.S. maintains its naval base at Guantanamo to this day.

## The Road to Revolution

Over the following decades, the Cuban desire for independence and sovereignty was frustrated time and again. U.S. troops returned in 1906 to intervene in a conflict between rival political parties, staying until 1909. In 1912,

*As noted in chapter 1, a 1976 investigation showed that the cause of the explosion was a fire in the ship's coal bunker, not sabotage.

when discrimination against Afro-Cubans sparked an uprising by sugar workers, the U.S. marines returned to occupy U.S.-owned sugar mills until the revolt was suppressed by Cuban government troops. Armed uprisings occurred in the 1920s and again in the 1930s.

Corruption was widespread in the Cuban government, and several leaders who came to power promising reforms proved to be as corrupt as their predecessors. Foreign control of the Cuban economy continued to grow. U.S. firms controlled many businesses, especially the sugar industry, the backbone of Cuba's economy. Their holdings included more than 70 percent of the country's farmland. U.S. organized crime figures also controlled the underground (illegal) economy, and Cuba became known as a haven for prostitution and pornography. These underground industries catered mainly to tourists from the United States.

From the 1930s onward, a sergeant in the Cuban army, Fulgencio Batista, became increasingly powerful in Cuban politics. Until the 1950s, Batista mainly worked behind the scenes to manipulate the results of Cuban elections. Then, in 1952, he seized power as a dictator. Batista's dictatorship was supported by the United States. While he was in power, he protected U.S. business interests, building a huge fortune for himself in the process. Most Cubans, however, lived in grinding poverty. The middle class, as well as the poor, hated and feared the Batista dictatorship.

In 1956, a new generation of *insurrectos* took up arms — this time, against the Batista dictatorship. The leader of this movement was a young lawyer named Fidel Castro. He led a guerrilla army based in the southeastern Sierra Maestra mountains. This revolutionary movement enjoyed broad popular support from throughout Cuban society. Not only poor people but also many Cuban landowners, church officials, and business owners supported the effort to oust the dictatorship, and they persuaded the U.S. government to stop supplying arms to Batista. At the end of 1958, Batista fled the country, taking as much of the national treasury with him as he could. The revolutionary army entered Havana in January 1959. In February, a new Cuban government was declared, with Fidel Castro as its leader.

## Collision Course

In April 1959, Castro traveled to Washington to appeal for economic aid from the U.S. government. The Eisenhower Administration, however, refused to support the new government, because of its strong commitment to Cuban sovereignty.

On May 17, 1959, the new Cuban government signed an agrarian reform law, which was designed to break up large plantations, or *latifundios*, and distribute the land to landless peasants. The law also nationalized (that is, returned to Cuban control) the land holdings of the U.S. agribusiness giant United Fruit (now United Brands). Although the Cuban government offered compensation to United Fruit and other landowners for their property, the policy of nationalization was unacceptable to the U.S. government. Two days after agrarian reform was instituted in Cuba, then-President Dwight D. Eisenhower approved the Pluto Plan, a secret plan to destabilize the Cuban government by the U.S. Central Intelligence Agency (CIA).

Agrarian reform also turned many wealthy Cubans against the new government. Those whose lands or businesses had been seized felt they had been treated unfairly. Some of them started a new underground movement to oppose the Castro government. Thousands of Cubans, mainly wealthy people and professionals, left the island, mostly for Miami, Florida. Many of them hoped to bring down the Cuban government in order to regain their lost property.

Because the U.S. government was also opposed to Castro, it opened its borders to these Cuban exiles. It also provided funds and other support for their plans to retake the island. In 1960, the CIA began to train an exile army in the jungles of Guatemala. When John F. Kennedy assumed the U.S. presidency in 1961, he agreed to let the exiles' invasion of Cuba go forward. In April 1961, the exiles' force landed at the Bay of Pigs. The Cuban government had learned of their plans, however, and the invasion was easily repulsed.

U.S. hostility toward the Cuban government continued to mount. An economic embargo was imposed on the island in 1961 (see Lesson 2.3). As confirmed many years later (in congressional hearings in 1976), the CIA also continued its destabilization efforts throughout the 1960s. Such CIA activities included plots to assassinate Fidel Castro as well as support for sabotage and terrorism by anti-government groups both in Miami and inside Cuba.

From its beginnings, the Cuban revolution included people with many different political beliefs. Some were mainly committed to nationalism — the idea that Cuba should pursue its own independent destiny. Others were mainly committed to socialism — the idea that public control of the economy helps to end poverty and injustice. All were agreed, however, that Cuba should be free from U.S. political and economic domination. Faced with unbending U.S. opposition, Cuba turned toward the Soviet Union as a protector and ally. The United States was also actively involved in persuading other countries to boycott Cuba, limiting the available options for the island's government.

In 1961, the Cuban government declared itself to be socialist. In 1962, it accepted a Soviet offer of installing short- and medium-range nuclear missiles on the island, to ward off the threat of a U.S. invasion. This led directly to a political confrontation, known in Cuba as the October Crisis and in the United States as the Cuban Missile Crisis. U.S. President Kennedy ordered a naval blockade of Cuba and demanded the withdrawal of the Soviet missiles. After six days, the Soviets agreed to dismantle their missile sites. Recently declassified documents reveal that to win this Soviet concession, Kennedy had promised not to invade Cuba.

## The Knife Edge of Independence

In the United States, Cuba after the revolution is usually portrayed as a pawn of the Soviet Union. Cubans living on the island, however, tell the story in more complex terms. After the missile crisis, the Cuban government was unhappy at being drawn into what it saw as a political game between the United States and the Soviet Union. It was also angry at having been excluded from the negotiations, despite the fact that it was at the very center of the crisis.

Throughout the 1960s, Cuba became increasingly

MILAGROS CISNEROS

*Leadership of the Cuban Baptist Student-Worker Association, 1995.*

alienated from other Communist nations, such as the Soviet Union and its allies in Eastern Europe (known as the Eastern bloc). Although economic and military ties were not severed, they were significantly diminished. Cuba directed its own foreign policy toward supporting national liberation movements in Africa and Asia, as well as the radical guerrilla movements of Latin America. Political and military training were provided to these movements by Cuba's military and intelligence agencies.

MILAGROS CISNEROS

*Cuban musicians, 1995.*

Domestically, Fidel Castro gave many speeches that were critical of the Eastern bloc. He criticized the Soviet Union for relying on "material incentives" (that is, money) to build up socialist economies, rather than inspiring new generations with revolutionary ideals and commitments. Volunteer work and mass mobilization became features of Cuban society in those years. He also felt the Soviets were not supportive enough of national liberation struggles in the Third World (the colonized or formerly colonized nations of Africa, Asia, and Latin America).

By the end of the 1960s, however, the Cuban model was in crisis. Guerrilla movements throughout Latin America were being defeated. The attempt to build up Cuba's economy through state ownership combined with "moral incentives" (that is, motivations based on values rather than monetary rewards) resulted in a generalized economic and financial crisis. Meanwhile, the Soviet invasion of Czechoslovakia in 1968 spelled defeat for reformers seeking greater political openness within the Eastern bloc.

Faced with continuing hostility from the U.S. government, Cuba decided to rebuild a closer alliance with the Soviet Union. The price of this strategy was the "sovietization" of Cuban society, as Cuba began to copy the political and economic systems of the USSR. From this era onward, the Cuban government began to place greater limits on personal and political freedoms for its citizens. Although this approach was adopted for reasons of national security and survival, it undermined the democratic and humanistic ideals of the Cuban revolution.

Throughout the 1970s and 1980s, Cuba made a major effort to ensure the economic, social, and cultural rights of its population. At the same time, political and civil rights, such as freedom of speech, freedom of association, freedom of the press, and freedom of religion, were severely limited. The resulting paradox is that Cuba emerged as the only Third World country with a "First World"* health and educational system. Indicators of the quality of life in Cuba, such as life expectancy, literacy, or infant mortality, are similar or even superior to those of many industrialized nations. The relationship of the Cuban people to their government cannot be understood without taking into account both sides of this equation.

## Searching for Survival and Identity

Beginning with the fall of the Berlin Wall in 1989, the communist governments of the former

*The term "First World" refers to the advanced industrial countries, including the United States, Europe, and Japan.

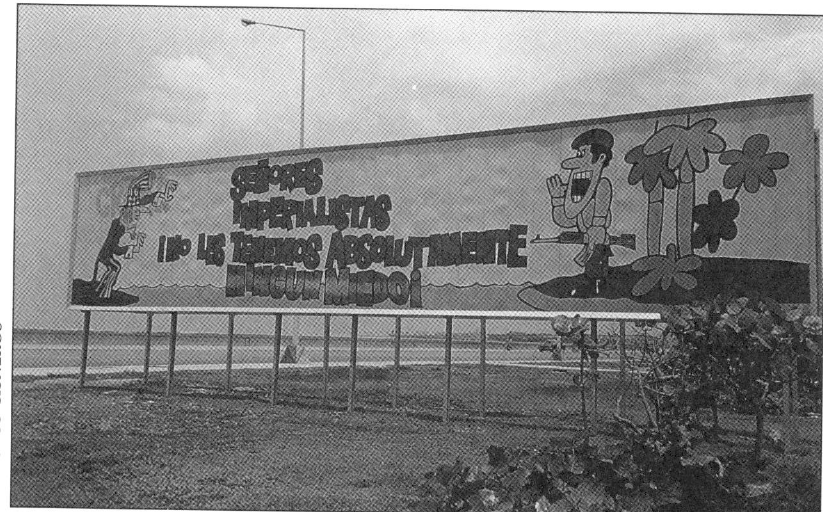


MILAGROS CISNEROS

*This 1995 photograph shows a Cuban billboard. The Cuban soldier at right is shouting to Uncle Sam, "Mr. Imperialist — We're not afraid of you at all!"*

Eastern bloc were dissolved one after another. This process came to a climax with the breakup of the Soviet Union in 1991. This in turn brought an end to Soviet economic support for Cuba, which had been considerable.

Also in 1989, U.S. President George Bush ordered the invasion of Panama, signaling a disposition to use military force once again to pursue U.S. interests in the Western Hemisphere. The 1990s thus began with Cuba standing alone in a world increasingly dominated by conservative forces, including aggressive opposition from the United States.

The end of the Cold War could have been a time for the United States to pursue the normalization of relations with Cuba. Instead, the U.S. government decided to deepen the embargo by passing the Cuban Democracy Act of 1992 (see chronology in Lesson 2.3). Their hope was to bring down the Cuban government once and for all. The stiffening of the embargo, coupled with the loss of Soviet economic support, has caused tremendous human suffering in Cuba, with widespread shortages of basic necessities such as food and medicines.

For Cubans, the 1990s have been a time of soul-searching. Responding to the current crisis has required Cubans to think about where they came from, how they reached their present situation, and what could be done about their future.

In the 1950s, two major goals pushed the Cubans into revolution: the demand for full sovereignty and independence, and the quest for a fairer, more just society. Can Cuba's achievements in these areas be preserved? Can the Cuban economy be restructured to make it competitive in international markets without the Soviet safety net? Can Cuba move away from political intolerance and restrictions on civil rights, most of which were copied from the now-disappeared Soviet Union?

Many younger Cubans believe that all of these new goals can and must be achieved. Numerous proposals have been introduced in recent years to reform and improve both the Cuban economy and the country's political and legal system. Others, however, argue that

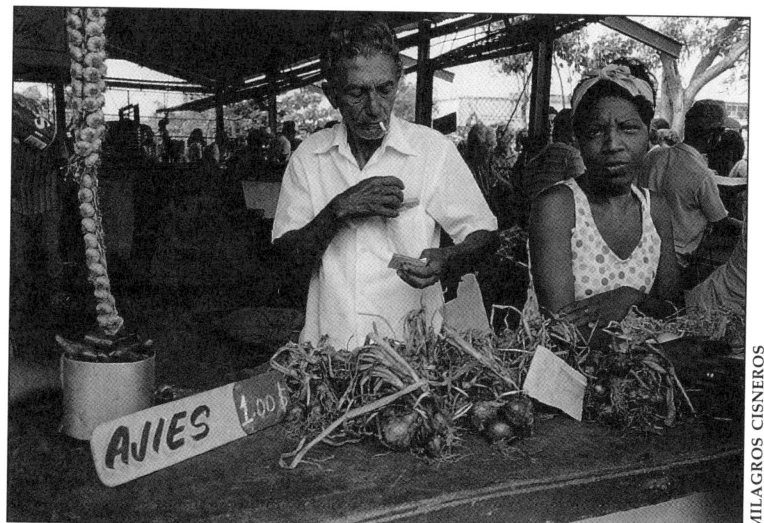


MILAGROS CISNEROS

***Cuban market, 1995.***

MILAGROS CISNEROS

*Havana, 1995.*

stepped-up U.S. attempts to destabilize Cuba mean that any change is dangerous.

## Reconciliation or Revenge?

Defenders of the U.S. embargo against Cuba argue that it creates pressure for political reform inside Cuba. In many ways, however, deepening the embargo has had exactly the opposite effect. Between 1992 and 1995, for example, the Cuban government relaxed some of its restrictions on civil, political, and economic freedoms. When the U.S. government adopted the Helms-Burton Act in 1996, however, the Cuban government restored many of these controls. The more Washington stiffens its confrontational posture, the more Cuban authorities resist change and reform.

Officially known as the Cuban Liberty and Democratic Solidarity Act, the Helms-Burton Act extends the U.S. embargo by imposing sanctions on third countries that trade with Cuba (see chronology in Lesson 2.3 for additional details). This move by the U.S. government prompted an enormous international outcry. Major U.S. allies and trading partners, including Canada, Mexico, and the European Union, have criticized the Helms-Burton Act as a violation of their national sovereignty. They have objected to the idea that domestic U.S. laws could be imposed on activities that did not take place in the United States or involve U.S. citizens.

In response to Helms-Burton, several countries enacted "biteback" laws forbidding their own companies from complying with the U.S. restrictions. Most of these governments are developing closer economic ties with Cuba. Inside Cuba, the Helms-Burton Act helped to solidify broad support from Cuban citizens and outrage against the United States as the principal author of the island's economic troubles.

In the United States, many voices have been raised calling for a change in U.S. policy toward Cuba. By early 1998, 112 representatives in the U.S. Congress had signed on as cosponsors of the Cuban Humanitarian Relief Act (H.R. 1951), which would lift the embargo on food and medicine. In 1997, the American Association of World Health published a report detailing the extensive human suffering caused by the embargo. Many religious leaders and human rights groups have called for an end to the embargo on humanitarian grounds. Even the former head of the U.S. Southern Command, Gen. John J. Sheehan, has stated publicly that Cuba poses no threat to U.S. security.

The principal supporters of the embargo are found within the Cuban exile community in the United States and their allies in Congress. They believe that the United States should not normalize relations with Cuba until the current Cuban government has fallen and they have regained the property they owned before the revolution. They argue that violations of human rights by the Cuban government justify continuing U.S. sanctions.

At this writing, in the spring of 1998, many signs of change are in the air. In January, Pope John Paul II visited Cuba, celebrating mass in Havana's Plaza of the Revolution. He called on the Cuban government to restore political freedoms and respect the rights of dissidents — while denouncing the U.S. embargo as "ethically unacceptable." In March, the Clinton Administration eased some restrictions, while leaving the overall embargo in place.

In April 1998, the prime minister of Canada, Jean Chretien, paid a high-profile visit to Cuba to mark the opening of a new international airport terminal, half of which was financed by Canada. Following his visit, several reports were published of unofficial negotiations between U.S. businesses and Cuban officials. Business interests have begun lobbying to lift the embargo so that they can gain access to Cuban markets and investment opportunities. Also in April, the United Nations voted down a U.S.-sponsored motion condemning Cuba for violations of human rights.

Inside Cuba, most people today are caught within a political dilemma. They would like to radically change their present situation, but they don't want to play into the hands of U.S. policy while doing so. Any chaotic situation in Cuba, they fear, might offer a pretext for a U.S. invasion, perhaps allowing the exile community in Miami to seize power. If such a scenario ever came to pass, it could mean not only the end of Cuba's sovereignty, but also the loss of social and economic fairness in Cuban society, which has been achieved through more than four decades of risks and sacrifices.

If U.S. policy were to change, however, a different scenario could be imagined. If U.S. citizens could travel freely to Cuba, and Cuban visitors could enter the United States, people in both countries could enter into dialogue. If the U.S. economic blockade were lifted, Cuba would receive a flood of offers of trade and investment — from businesses that would press for economic reforms and greater efficiency. If the United States were to make a formal commitment to respect Cuba's independence and sovereignty, then Cuban citizens could not be accused of "helping the enemy" every time they advocated for political reforms inside Cuba. Similarly, if the United States returned the obsolete naval base at Guantanamo to Cuba, it would be sending a signal to the Cuban people that a century of "gunboat diplomacy" and superpower politics was at an end.

In this scenario, the twenty-first century could witness a new era of mutual respect and cooperation between Cuba and its powerful neighbor to the north, the United States.

## References

Medea Benjamin, *Cuba: Talking About Revolution* (Hoboken, NJ: Ocean Press, 1994). 2d ed. 1997. Published in association with Global Exchange.

N. Kanellos, Ed., *Reference Library of Hispanic America*, Vol. I (Detroit: Educational Guidance Service, 1993).

*The Latino Experience in U.S. History* (Paramus, NJ: Globe Fearon, 1994).

Marifeli Perez-Stable, *The Cuban Revolution: Origins, Course, and Legacy* (New York: Oxford University Press, 1993).

Catherine A. Sunshine and Deborah Menkart, Eds., *Caribbean Connections: Overview of Regional History* (Washington: EPICA/NECA, 1991)

**Vocabulary:** wage labor, atrocities, sabotage, abrogate, guerrilla, sovereignty, agrarian reform, agribusiness, repulsed, embargo, destabilization, bloc, normalization

# Lesson 2.1 Our America

**Objectives:**

- To give students a basic introduction to Jose Marti, a leader of the Cuban independence movement in the late nineteenth century whose writings inspired peoples throughout Spain's colonial holdings.
- To help students think critically about the importance of racial and cultural awareness in political decision making.

**Themes:** national identity, racial identity, independence movements

**Vocabulary:** plantain, foregone, viable, pillory, emanates, animosity, foments, imperative, antagonism, eminence, provocation, pompous, formidable

## Suggested Activities

1. Distribute the handout at the end of this lesson with excerpts from "Our America," a famous essay by Jose Marti. Read over the introductory section with students.
2. Have students read the excerpts aloud in class. Because of its poetic style, this essay's sentences are extremely long and may be difficult for students to comprehend. Use the questions that follow each portion of the text to help walk students through the piece.

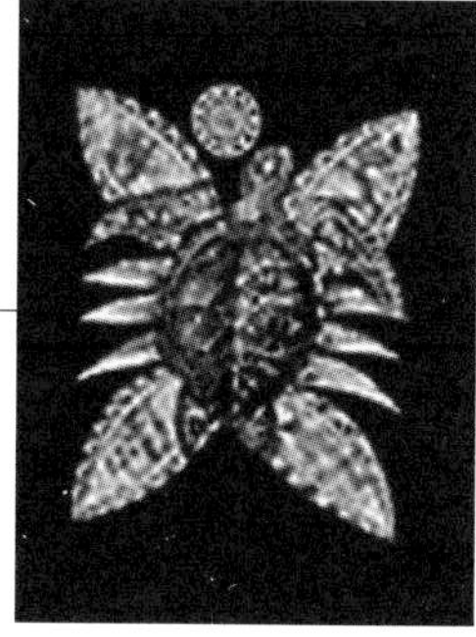

# Reading: "Our America" by Jose Marti

*Jose Marti was a Cuban patriot of the late nineteenth century who fought against Spanish colonial rule. His writings inspired people in Spanish colonies throughout the Caribbean and the Pacific to resist Spanish domination. Marti spent many years in exile in the United States planning his insurrection against Spain. He returned to Cuba when his Cuban Revolutionary Party (PRC) began its final battle for independence from Spain in 1895. The Spanish colonial government countered with a brutal campaign to suppress the revolution, and Marti was killed within four months of the start of the insurrection. Still, his legacy has lived on in the form of his writings.*

*The passages below are excerpted from "Our America," a famous essay that Marti published in* La Revista Ilustrada *(The Illustrated Review) on January 10, 1891. In this essay he distinguishes between two extremely different Americas. One, which he refers to as North America (that is, the United States), clung to a European world view and permitted full citizenship and participation only to people of European descent. The other, which he terms "Our America" (what is now known as Latin America), offered the possibility of creating a new, original synthesis blending the European experience with the culture and perspective of the indigenous and African peoples who also make up the population of the hemisphere.*

*It is interesting to note that enduring differences in language between the United States and Latin America reveal some of the very differences in outlook that Marti is discussing. In the United States, people commonly refer to "the Americas," reflecting the idea that North and South America are different continents. In Latin American usage, during Marti's time and continuing up to the present, people think of America as a single continent. Part of Marti's argument is that the North American half of the continent was following a path that was not true to the unique blend of peoples and cultures that exists throughout the hemisphere. This approach, he believed, would not provide a workable path to freedom or development for the emergent nations of Our America.*

---

## Our America: Excerpt 1

" What are we?" is the mutual question, and little by little they furnish answers. . . . The youth of America are rolling up their sleeves, digging their hands in the dough, and making it rise with the sweat of their brows. They realize that there is too much imitation, and that creation holds the key to salvation. "Create" is the password of this generation. The wine is made from plantain, but even if it turns sour, it is our own wine! That a country's form of government must be in keeping with its natural elements is a foregone conclusion. . . . Freedom, to be viable, has to be sincere and complete. If a republic refuses to open its arms to all, and move ahead with all, it dies. The tiger within sneaks in through the crack; so does the tiger from without. . . . Nations should live in a atmosphere of self-criticism because criticism is healthy, but always with one heart and one mind. Stoop to the unhappy, and lift them up in your arms! Thaw out frozen America with the fire of your hearts! Make the natural blood of the nations course vigorously through their veins. The new Americans are on their feet, saluting each other from nation to nation, the eyes of the laborers shining with joy. The natural statesman arises . . . *He reads to apply his knowledge, not to imitate. Economists study the problems at their*

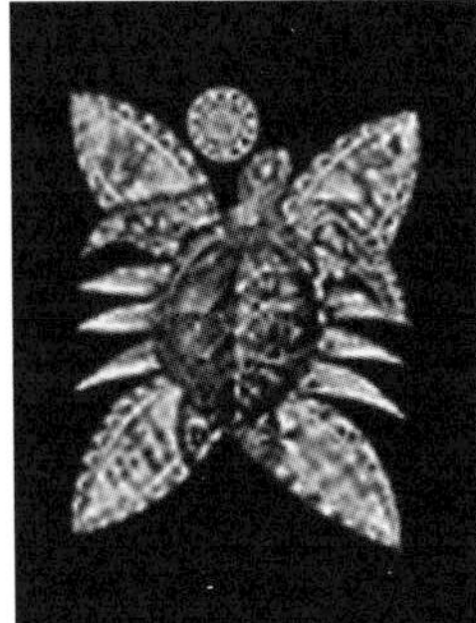

*point of origin. . . . Playwrights bring native characters to the stage. Academies discuss practical subjects. . . . In the Indian republics, the governors are learning Indian.* [Italics added.]

### Questions for Discussion

1. The first paragraph of this excerpt begins with the question: "What are we?" What is Marti saying about "the youth of America?" What are they trying to create? What does he mean when he says, "The wine is made from plantain, but even if it turns sour, it is our own wine?"
2. Look specifically at the lines that are italicized at the end of this passage. What does Marti see happening in Our America (Latin America)? How does he believe intellectuals — people with education — should attempt to include all the people in their countries as they move toward creating government, education, and culture? How might this approach be different from the way the United States was formed?

---

## Our America: Excerpt 2

But perhaps Our America is running another risk that does not come from itself but from the difference in origins, methods, and interests between the two halves of the continent, and the time is near at hand when an enterprising and vigorous people who scorn or ignore Our America will even so approach it and demand a close relationship. And since strong nations, self-made by law and shotgun, love strong nations, and them alone; . . . since its good name as a republic in the eyes of the world's perceptive nations puts upon North America a restraint that cannot be taken away by childish provocations or pompous arrogance . . . among Our American nations, the pressing need of Our America is to show itself as it is, one in spirit and intent, swift conqueror of a suffocating past, stained only by the enriching blood drawn from hands that struggle to clear away the ruins, and from the scars left upon us by our masters. The scorn of our formidable neighbor who does not know us is Our America's greatest danger. And since the day of the visit is near, it is imperative that our neighbor know us, and soon, so that it will not scorn us. Through ignorance it might even come to lay hands on us. Once it does know us, it will remove its hands out of respect. One must have faith in the best in men and distrust the worst. One must allow the best to be shown so that it reveals and prevails over the worst. Nations should have a pillory for whoever stirs up useless hates, and another for whoever fails to tell them the truth in time.

### Questions for Discussion

1. In this section, Marti begins to talk directly about North America (the United States). What is the risk that he refers to in the opening sentence of this passage?
2. What does Marti mean when he says "The scorn of our formidable neighbor who does not know us is Our America's greatest danger?" What does he believe should be done to guard against that danger?

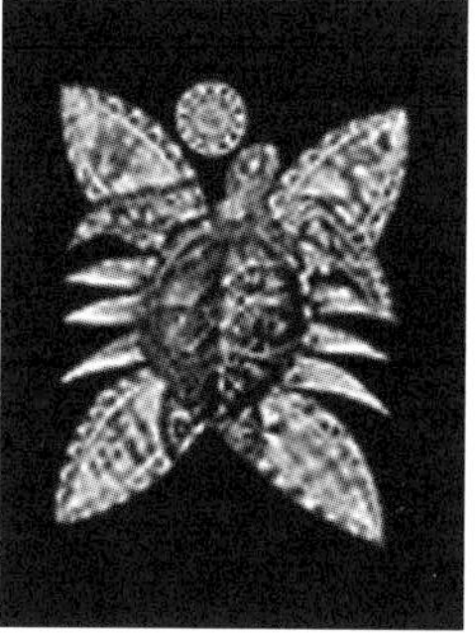

## Our America: Excerpt 3

There can be no racial animosity, because there are no races. . . . The soul, equal and eternal, emanates from bodies of various shapes and colors. Whoever foments and spreads antagonism and hate between the races, sins against humanity. . . [I]n a period of internal disorder, . . . the rapidity with which the country's character has been accumulating [can] be turned into a serious threat for the weak and isolated neighboring countries, declared by the strong country to be inferior and perishable. The thought is father to the deed. And one must not attribute . . . a fatal and inborn wickedness to the continent's fairskinned nation simply because it does not speak our language, or see the world as we see it, . . . or look charitably from its still uncertain eminence upon those less favored by history, who climb the road of republicanism by heroic stages. . . . [T]he problem can be resolved, for the peace of centuries to come, by appropriate study, and by tacit and immediate unity in the continental spirit. With a single voice the hymn is already being sung. The present generation is . . . sowing the seed of the new America throughout the Latin nations of the continent and the sorrowful islands of the sea!

### Questions for Discussion

1. Marti states, "There can be no racial animosity, because there are no races." What does he mean by this statement? What does this passage say about how Marti understands racial differences? Does his understanding agree with yours? Why or why not?
2. In this passage Marti speaks about racism as a tool which allows some countries or peoples to oppress others. He makes an eloquent statement countering racism and outlines why racism is dangerous. Which sentences in the passage make this point most directly? How would you restate them in your own words?
3. Look specifically at the sentence: "The thought is father to the deed." Give some examples from U.S. and world history in which racism was "the thought" which led to certain "deeds." (Examples might include the colonization of the Americas, the enslavement of Africans, the British takeover of Ireland, the Nazi Holocaust). Could these various historical events have occurred if their perpetrators had not believed in their own racial superiority?

---

**Source:** *Translation excerpted from N. Kanellos, Ed.,* Reference Library of Hispanic America, *Vol. I (Detroit: Educational Guidance Service, 1993).*

# Lesson 2.2 The Platt Amendment

**Objectives:**

- To introduce students to the use of primary source documents in historical analysis.
- To permit students to develop their own critical reading of the political status of Cuba negotiated following the Spanish-American War.

**Themes:** sovereignty, unequal relations between nations

**Vocabulary:** compact, defraying, revenues, plenipotentiaries

## Suggested Activities

1. Have students review the text of the Platt Amendment in the reading at the end of this lesson. Explain that the Platt Amendment was written to define the relationship between the United States and Cuba. It provided the basis for ending the U.S. military occupation of Cuba that followed the Spanish-American War.
2. Inform students they are going to do an exercise to help them understand the implications of the Platt Amendment. Tell them to imagine that while the United States was fighting for its independence from Great Britain, a fictitious country known as the Republic of Zargosta entered the war with Britain and drove the British out of North America. Tell them to take their copy of the Platt Amendment, crossing out the words "the United States" wherever they appear and replacing them with "the Republic of Zargosta." Then tell them that wherever they see the word "Cuba" they should cross it out and insert the words "the United States."
3. Ask students to break into small groups and read the treaties as they now stand. What rights does the Republic of Zargosta now have in the United States? How do they feel about this? Would they consider the United States to be an independent country under these conditions? Why or why not?
4. Have the class reconvene. Remind students that one of the stated reasons that the United States went to war with Spain was to help Cuba gain independence. How do they think the Cuban people might have felt when they learned about the Platt Amendment?

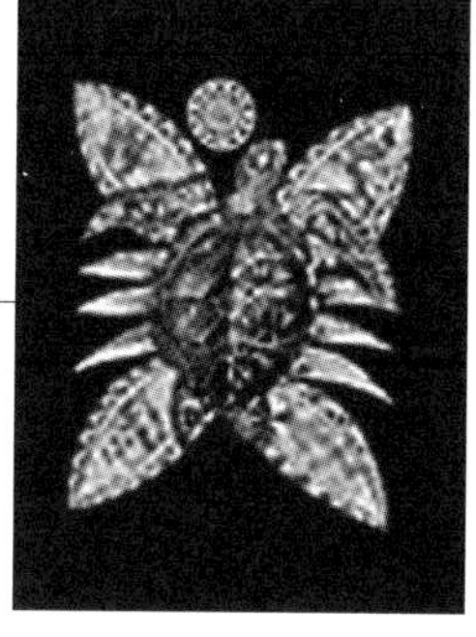

# Reading: The Platt Amendment

*The paragraphs below are excerpted from the Platt Amendment of 1902. Following the Spanish-American War, U.S. troops remained in Cuba for four more years. The United States agreed to withdraw its occupying army from Cuba only when Cuba agreed to include this document in its constitution. The amendment was written in the United States by Sen. Orville H. Platt.*

## Article I

The Government of Cuba shall never enter into any treaty or other compact with any foreign power or powers which will impair or tend to impair the independence of Cuba, nor in any manner authorize or permit any foreign power or powers to obtain by colonization or for military or naval purposes, or otherwise, lodgement in or control over any portion of said island.

## Article II

The Government of Cuba shall not assume or contract any public debt to pay the interest upon which, and to make reasonable sinking-fund provision for the ultimate discharge of which, the ordinary revenues of the Island of Cuba, after defraying the current expenses of the Government, shall be inadequate.

## Article III

The Government of Cuba consents that the United States may exercise the right to intervene for the preservation of Cuban independence, the maintenance of a government adequate for the protection of life, property, and individual liberty, and for discharging the obligations with respect to Cuba imposed by the Treaty of Paris on the United States, now to be assumed and undertaken by the Government of Cuba.

## Article IV

All acts of the United States in Cuba during its military occupancy thereof are ratified and validated, and all lawful rights acquired thereunder shall be maintained and protected.

## Article V

The Government of Cuba will execute, and as far as necessary, extend the plans already devised, or other plans to be mutually agreed upon, for the sanitation of the cities of the island, to the end that a recurrence of epidemic and infectious diseases may be prevented, thereby assuring protection to the people and commerce of Cuba, as well to the commerce of the Southern ports of the United States and the people residing therein.

## Article VI

The Island of Pines shall be omitted from the boundaries of Cuba specified in the Constitution, the title thereof being left to future adjustment by treaty.

## Article VII

To enable the Unites States to maintain the independence of Cuba, and to protect the people thereof, as well as for its own defense, the Government of Cuba will sell or lease to the United States lands necessary for coaling or naval stations, at certain specified points, to be agreed upon with the President of the United States.

## Article VIII

The present Convention shall be ratified by each party in conformity with the respective Constitutions of the two countries, and the ratifications shall be exchanged in the countries, and the ratifications shall be exchanged in the city of Washington within eight months from this date. In witness whereof, we the respective Plenipotentiaries, have signed the same in duplicate, in English and Spanish, and have affixed our respective seals at Havana, Cuba, this twenty-second day of May, in the year nineteen hundred and three.

---

**Source:** *Excerpted from N. Kanellos, Ed.,* Reference Library of Hispanic America, *Vol. I (Detroit: Educational Guidance Service, 1993), p.106.*

# LESSON 2.3 Role Play on the U.S. Embargo of Cuba

**Objective:** To familiarize students with current debates concerning the U.S. embargo of Cuba.

**Themes:** international relations, policy advocacy, power politics

**Vocabulary:** guerrilla, covert action, sabotage, consortium, expropriation, assets, humanitarian, subsidiary, remittances, codifies, apocalyptic

## Suggested Activities

1. Prior to carrying out this role play, have students read the overview portion of this chapter as background. This reading may be given as homework the night before the role play is to be performed. The chronology of the embargo included at the end of this lesson presents some additional details and can be used as a supplementary reading.
2. To begin the role play, explain to the students that the class is going to hold a hearing to determine whether or not to continue the U.S. embargo of Cuba. You might wish to point out that although the "pro" and "anti" roles are roughly balanced in the role play, this is not reflective of opinion in the international community, which is overwhelmingly opposed to the continuation of the embargo.
3. The class will need to select a Hearing Board, composed of three students who will not be part of any group, but will direct the entire process. Divide the remainder of the class into nine groups and give each group copies of one of the role sheets included at the end of this lesson. The role sheets present actual statements made by supporters and opponents of the embargo. The source of each statement is identified on the sheet.
4. Each group should choose one member to serve as its delegate. The other members will counsel and support the delegate.
5. Each group should discuss and agree on their group's answer to the following questions:
   - How does the embargo affect you?
   - What do you stand to gain or lose from a change in the embargo?
   - Which of the other groups do you think might share your views? Why?
6. Place three desks for the Hearing Board in the front of the room, facing the rest of the class. Each group should arrange its desks in clusters. Only the delegates will be permitted to speak before the Hearing Board. The other students should be in constant contact with their delegates, passing them notes and

whispering to suggest questions or arguments.

7. As the exercise begins, each delegate should present a brief summary of their group's stance. When each presenter finishes, the Hearing Board will ask pointed questions (included in their role sheet). The other presenters may join in the questioning, but they must first be recognized by the board.
8. When the hearing is concluded, the board should vote on whether or not to continue the U.S. embargo against Cuba.
9. Reconvene the class to "debrief" by discussing the exercise after it is over. Ask students to abandon their roles and then share their reactions to the outcome of the hearing. What do they think the policy implications will be of the board's decision? How might the decision affect the day-to-day lives of people in Cuba? What about governmental relations between Cuba and the United States? What impact do they think the decision might have on such issues as immigration to the United States? International trade? Local politics in Florida (where the Cuban exile community has considerable political clout)?

# Reading: Chronology of the U.S. Embargo Against Cuba

**January 1959:** After seven years of guerrilla war, the July 26 Movement under the leadership of Fidel Castro establishes a new government in Cuba, ousting former dictator Fulgencio Batista.

**March 1960:** U.S. President Dwight D. Eisenhower approves a plan of covert action and economic sabotage against Cuba. In the first months of 1960, the U.S. government wages a campaign to prevent Cuba from receiving loans and credits from Western European and Canadian institutions. A consortium of European banks, under pressure from the United States, cancels plans to loan $100 million to Cuba.

**July 1960:** President Eisenhower cancels the unfilled balance of Cuba's sugar quota for the U.S. market for 1960. (Like other sugar producers in the Caribbean, Cuba was previously guaranteed the right to export a certain amount of its sugar to the U.S. market.)

**August 1960:** Cuba orders the expropriation (seizure) of twenty-six of the largest U.S. companies operating in Cuba.

**October 1960:** In what the U.S. media describe as a "quarantine" of Cuba, the Eisenhower Administration bans U.S. exports to that country, except for food, medicines, and medical and hospital supplies. Companies wishing to sell these goods to Cuba can do so under a "general" license (no specific license application is required). Imports from Cuba continue to be allowed.

**January 1961:** The United States cuts off diplomatic relations with Cuba.

**April 1961:** The Bay of Pigs invasion is launched. With the support and guidance of the U.S. Central Intelligence Agency, Cuban exiles stage an attack on the island, hoping to overthrow the government. Their attempt fails miserably.

**September 1961:** The Foreign Assistance Act of 1961 authorizes the U.S. president to establish and maintain "a total embargo upon all trade between Cuba and the United States."

**February 1962:** U.S. President John F. Kennedy extends the embargo to prohibit Cuban imports into the United States.

**March 1962:** The embargo is further tightened to prohibit imports into the United States of goods made from or containing Cuban materials, even though they may come from other countries.

**August 1962:** In order to pressure other countries not to support Cuba, the U.S. Congress amends the Foreign Assistance Act of 1961 to prohibit U.S. aid "to any country which furnishes assistance to the present government of Cuba."

**February 1963:** The Kennedy Administration prohibits cargoes purchased by the U.S. government from being transported on foreign vessels that call at a Cuban port.

**July 1963:** The U.S. Treasury Department issues the Cuban Assets Control Regulations. These regulations include the essential features of the U.S. economic embargo against Cuba that has been in effect ever since. All Cuban assets in the United States are frozen, meaning that neither Cuban citizens nor the Cuban govern-

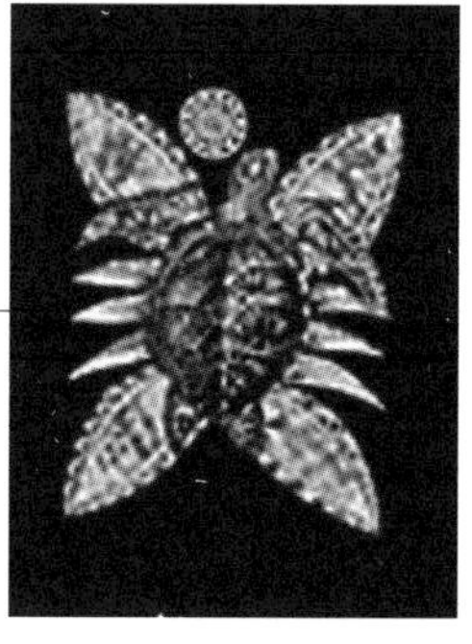

ment may have access to them. A special license from the Treasury Department is required for all financial and commercial transactions between Cuba and the United States, as well as between private citizens of both countries. As part of this restriction, U.S. citizens are prohibited from spending their own money during travel to Cuba.

**May 1964:** The U.S. Commerce Department revokes its prior general license policy for export to Cuba of foods, medicines, and medical supplies. The Commerce Department adopts a broad policy of denying requests for commercial sales of food and medicine to Cuba and permits only limited humanitarian donations.

**July 1964:** The Organization of American States (OAS) passes a resolution obliging its members to enforce a collective trade embargo on Cuba. The resolution excludes sales of food, medicines, and medical equipment. The United States, however, persists in its policy of denying licenses for such sales.

**July 1974:** The U.S. Treasury Department relaxes some of its Cuban regulations, allowing, among other things, the importation of Cuban books and records. Restrictions are also relaxed on travel to Cuba by scholars and journalists.

**July 1975:** The OAS repeals its regional trade embargo against Cuba, prompting U.S. President Gerald Ford to end the ban on trade with Cuba by foreign subsidiaries of U.S.-based firms. Instead, the U.S. government now requires only that U.S. companies obtain individual licenses for transactions involving their overseas subsidiaries.

**March 1977:** U.S. President Jimmy Carter removes restrictions on travel to Cuba by U.S. citizens.

**April 1982:** U.S. President Ronald Reagan restores severe restrictions on travel to Cuba by U.S. citizens.

**October 1992:** U.S. President George Bush signs the Cuban Democracy Act (CDA), which outlaws trade with Cuba by foreign subsidiaries of U.S. corporations and imposes severe restrictions on foreign ships that visit Cuba before attempting to enter U.S. ports. The CDA also gives the Treasury Department for the first time the authority to impose fines of up to $50,000 for violations of the embargo.

**March 1996:** The Cuba Liberty and Democratic Solidarity Act (the Helms-Burton Act) becomes law. This law seeks to impede the present Cuban government from achieving economic recovery by deterring foreign investment. Among other measures, the Helms-Burton Act allows foreign companies to be taken to court in the United States if they are "trafficking" in properties in Cuba formerly owned by U.S. citizens that have been nationalized by the Cuban government. ("Trafficking" is expansively defined to include not only direct investment in such properties but also any activities involving such properties that benefit the so-called "trafficker.") In addition, the act "codifies" the existing Cuban Asset Control Regulations, which means that any future modification of those regulations would require an act of Congress.

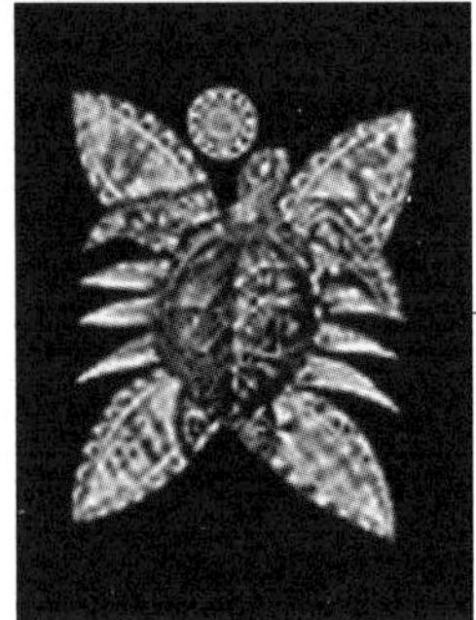

## Current Embargo Restrictions

The bulk of U.S. prohibitions against trade with Cuba are set forth in regulations enforced by the Treasury Department's Office of Foreign Assets Control and the Commerce Department's Bureau of Export Affairs. These include a ban on U.S. exports to Cuba, Cuban imports into the United States, and even transactions with Cuba by foreign subsidiaries of U.S.-based corporations. Also banned are credits and the transfer of money or property by U.S. nationals to Cuban nationals.

On March 20, 1998, following a visit to Cuba by Pope John Paul II, the Clinton Administration relaxed some of the existing embargo restrictions. Direct humanitarian flights to Cuba from the United States are now permitted. Cuban-Americans are now allowed to send up to $1200 a year to their relatives on the island (although other transfers of funds are still banned). Some of the bureaucratic barriers to sales of medicine to Cuba have also been removed.

Other provisions of the embargo that remain in force include:

- Entry is denied to U.S. ports by any ship which has docked in Cuba during the prior 180 days. U.S. ports are also closed to third-country vessels carrying "goods in which Cuba or Cuban nationals have an 'interest,' whatever the cargo's origin or destination. This prohibition applies to a third-country vessel carrying third-country goods which incorporate even trace amounts of Cuban-origin products or produce."
- Re-exports to Cuba of U.S.-origin goods and technical data are banned.
- Exports are banned to Cuba by third-country companies of goods containing 20 percent or more U.S.-origin components; individual licenses are required for those goods containing over 10 percent U.S-origin components.
- Licenses are required for humanitarian donations, which may only be directed to nongovernmental organizations, of which there are very few in Cuba. Under no circumstance is the sale of food authorized.

---

**Source:** *Adapted from "Denial of Food and Medicine: The Impact of the U.S. Embargo on Health and Nutrition in Cuba," American Association for World Health, March 1997.*

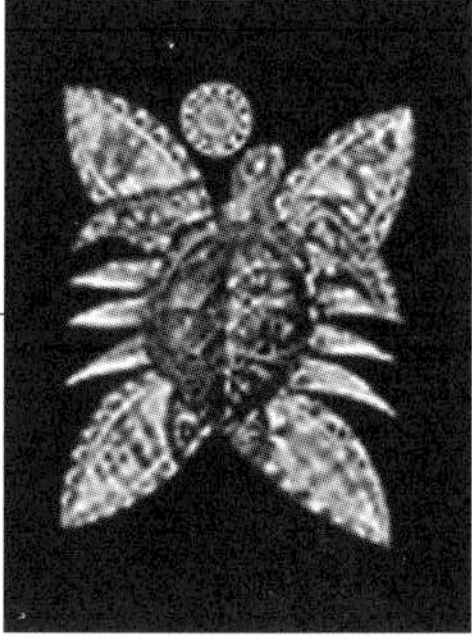

# Cuba Embargo Role Play

## Role: Hearing Board

*Below are examples of questions that may be used by the Hearing Board to question the delegates:*

- What right do you have to speak on Cuban affairs?
- What could happen that would make you change your position?
- If you don't get your way, what do you plan to do about it?
- (To the pro-embargo side) How can you justify the fact that we trade with other governments that you have criticized, including China?
- (To the pro-embargo side) Do you think other countries have the right to embargo the United States if they are critical of our domestic policies?
- (To the anti-embargo side) You say it isn't fair. Isn't a country free to choose who it trades with?
- (To the anti-embargo side) Cuba has a lot of internal problems. Wouldn't we just be condoning their violations of human rights by trading with them?
- (To the anti-embargo side) During the revolution, Cuba took property away from its rightful owners. Was that fair? Wouldn't trading with Cuba now show approval of this behavior?

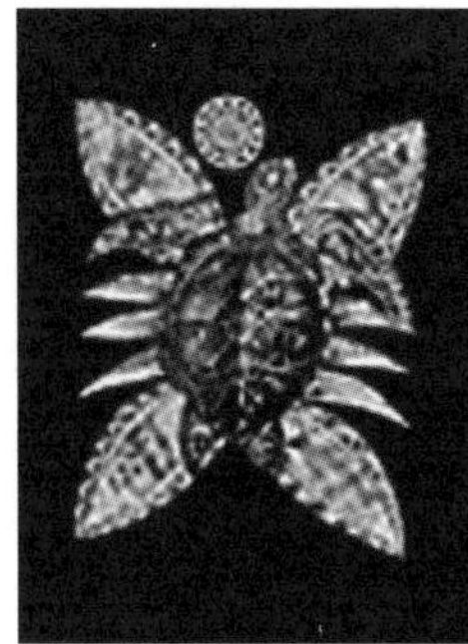

# Cuba Embargo Role Play

## Role: Human Rights Advocate

*Congressional testimony by the Interreligious Foundation for Community Organization.*

The Interreligious Foundation for Community Organization [IFCO; also known as Pastors for Peace] is a 30-year-old national ecumenical agency which has been working for reconciliation in the area of U.S./Cuba relations since 1991. In these last seven years, we have taken dozens of delegations and humanitarian aid missions to Cuba. We have visited Cuba with diverse groups of concerned U.S. citizens — including clergy and diocesan delegations, Rotarians, health care professionals, and congressional staff. We have seen with our own eyes the many ways in which the archaic U.S. trade sanctions have had a brutal impact on the people of Cuba — particularly on Cuban children and families, on the infirm and the elderly, on the most vulnerable Cuban citizens.

Let us share with you these pictures of the things we have seen in Cuba:

- Parents who don't have syringes to give insulin to their diabetic child.
- No spare parts for ambulances, for automobiles, for elevators, for medical equipment.
- A communal playroom for elementary school kids who have no other access to toys.
- A beloved Baptist pastor who died after a kidney transplant (and in how many developing nations would the pastor of a poor urban church have access to an organ transplant free of charge?) without the cyclosporin needed to sustain her new kidney. . .
- Children on a pediatric cancer ward vomiting twenty times a day because the anti-nausea drugs which suppress the side effects of their chemotherapy are not available.
- A woman who walked three miles to the church where we were staying, to thank us for the donation of a wheelchair: she explained that, until they received that chair, her adult son with full-blown cerebral palsy had not been able to leave their house since he'd gotten too big to carry.
- A father of two young girls who explained, "I used to wear size 32 jeans, and now I wear size 27; it's because what food there is, we give first to our daughters."

Cuba's critics here in the United States would like to blame all these shortages on the Cuban government. But we have found that the Cuban people hold a very different view. They weren't suffering all these dire shortages before 1991. When goods were available in Cuba, they were distributed equitably by the very same Cuban government now in power. The basic needs of eleven million people were met for many years. And the U.S. embargo had only a marginal impact, because 85% of Cuba's economy was tied to the Soviet bloc. With the Soviet collapse and the end of the "cold war," Cuba would have been an easy new market for the United States. As the Cuban people understand it, our government passed up a golden opportunity to open a new era in U.S./Cuba trade relations, and chose instead to implement the so-called Cuban Democracy Act (CDA) and tighten the stranglehold of its archaic economic sanctions.

---

**Source:** *Excerpted from testimony to House Ways and Means Committee, Subcommittee on Trade, Hearing on U.S. Economic and Trade Policy Toward Cuba, May 7, 1998.*

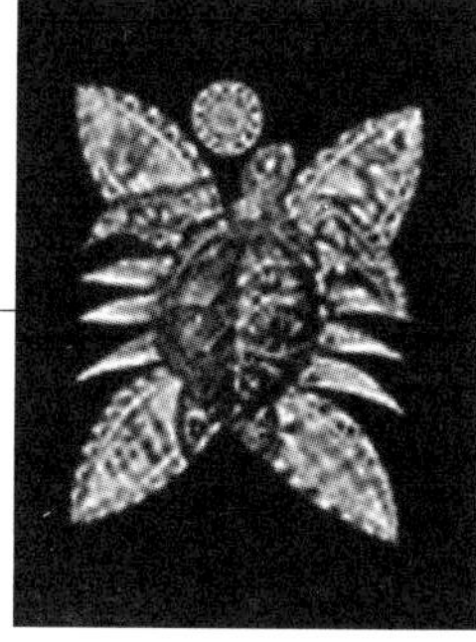

# Cuba Embargo Role Play

## Role: Jorge Mas Canosa

The trade prohibition imposed on Castro's regime advances four important U.S. policy objectives, which also serve the interests of the Cuban people.

- First, it is an enduring symbol of this country's firm stance against totalitarianism and a clear message to those who would rule by the force of violence and repression rather than the will of reason and public consent.
- Second, it forced the Soviet Union to pay a tremendous, and ultimately unsustainable, price (approximately $100 billion since 1960) in order to maintain a far reaching military outpost and subsidize an aggressively hostile Marxist dictatorship in the Western hemisphere.
- Third, it limited Castro's ability to self-generate the resources necessary to project military power and support Communist insurgencies abroad.
- Fourth, it limits Castro's ability to provide his inner circle and the privileged "nomenklatura" [party officials] of the Communist party with the perks and prerogatives essential to maintaining their loyalty to the "maximum leader."

As a result, the embargo today serves as the major obstacle to the finding of substitute markets, credit, and assistance at the crucial time when the Eastern bloc, Castro's former political and economic base of support, has collapsed. With nowhere to turn for aid, Castro must reform or leave. Since he is incapable of reform, he will be forced from power, perhaps by the same ones who until the day before were part of his entourage. . . .

Opposition groups in Cuba have declared that it is Castro who gains and the Cuban people who suffer when countries trade and provide credits to Castro's regime. Most Cuban opposition groups have called for the support of efforts to strengthen Castro's economic isolation. The Cuban Democratic Coalition, for example, which is the largest opposition organization inside Cuba, has declared its support for a new U.S. legislative initiative to strengthen the U.S. embargo against Cuba.

The opinion of those who are leading the opposition inside Cuba, those on the front lines of the struggle, is that we must deprive Castro of the resources he needs to maintain his repressive apparatus. We must deplete the "reserve of the Comandante."

To do that, it is essential that we not only strengthen the embargo, but also that we invite our friends and allies around the world to join us in increasing the economic pressure on Castro.

*(Jorge Mas Canosa, who died in 1997, was the longtime head of the Cuban-American National Foundation, a Cuban exile group dedicated to overthrowing Cuba's present government.)*

---

**Source:** *Cuban-American National Foundation (http://www.canfnet.org).*

# Cuba Embargo Role Play

## Role: International Trade Analyst

If the blockade were lifted ...

- The United States could export up to $400 million in grain sales to Cuba.
- The United States could supply all Cuba's fertilizer and pesticide requirements (totaling around $150 million).
- U.S. agricultural sales to Cuba could be an estimated $300 million.
- Cuba would purchase about $90 million in U.S. medical supplies.
- The United States could sell Cuba 20,000 tons of cotton, 5,000 of polyester and rayon fibers, and about $1 million in thread.
- U.S. port authorities anticipate that there would be a dramatic expansion in shipping.
- By purchasing Cuban citrus, the United States could save $34 million dollars a year.
- The United States could capture 60 percent of Cuba's nickel exports.
- $6.5 million per year could be saved by purchasing Cuban sugar.
- Cheaper U.S. imports of Cuban seafood, coffee, tobacco, rum, honey, and marble would be possible.
- The U.S. tourist industry and cruise lines could benefit by around $1 billion a year.

The question before us is simple: Is it in the interests of the United States to begin to lift the trade embargo against Cuba and at long last to take other measures to move towards a more constructive relationship with that island?

My answer is an unequivocal "yes." It is indeed in the interests of the United States to take those steps. Why? Because that is the best way to achieve our remaining objectives in Cuba. I say "remaining" because all our foreign policy goals have long since been achieved. We used to say to the Cubans that once they had removed their troops from Africa, once they had stopped intervening in revolutionary situations in Central America and other parts of the world, and once they had significantly reduced their military relationship with our principal global rival, the Soviet Union, that then we could begin to improve relations with them.

Clearly, all those conditions have been fulfilled. That and more. The Soviet Union has collapsed. The Cold War is over. Cuba is no longer a concern to us or anyone else. It is prepared to live in peace with its neighbors and play a constructive role within the international community. But none of that has made any difference. Rather than improving relations as we'd promised, we've actually increased the pressure against Cuba . . .

Other nations note this profound inconsistency in our policy toward Cuba and conclude that it is driven not by concern for human rights, not by legitimate foreign policy concerns, but by domestic politics. They thus see no reason to support us. "Pander to [a] tiny percentage of voters in Miami or Union City if you wish," one Canadian diplomat noted some years back, "but don't expect us to share your obsession or follow your lead" . . .

— *Wayne Smith, former chief of the U.S. Interests Section in Havana*

---

**Source:** *Pedro Prada,* Island Under Siege: The U.S. Blockade of Cuba *(Hoboken, NJ: Ocean Press, 1995).*

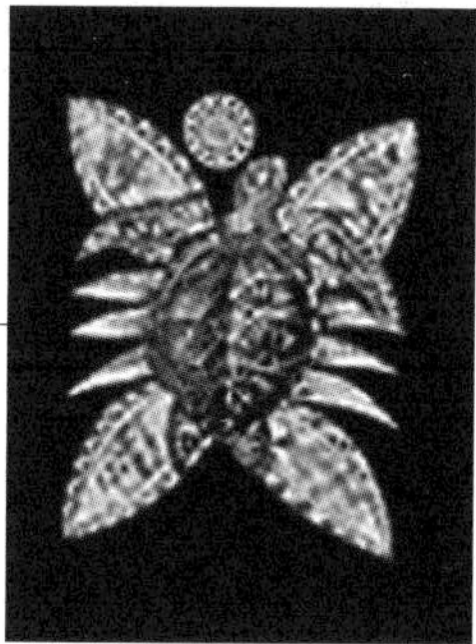

# Cuba Embargo Role Play

## Role: Rep. Diaz-Balart

*Rep. Lincoln Diaz-Balart (R-FL), a Cuban-American, is a leading congressional spokesman for the Cuban exile community.*

There is a pathologically unstable tyrant in the final years of his dictatorship just 90 miles from our shores. His four-decade record of brutality, rabid hostility toward the Cuban exile community, anti-Americanism, support for international terrorism, and proximity to the United States, is an ominous combination.

When considering the potential threat from Castro, the following must be noted.

Despite the end of the Cold War, Castro continues to espouse a hard line, using apocalyptic rhetoric, proclaiming socialism or death, ranting about a final reckoning with the United States, and punishing any Cuban who advocates genuine political or economic reform.

Castro maintains one of Latin America's largest militaries with capabilities completely inconsistent with Cuba's economic reality and security needs.

Despite Cuba's economic failure, Castro has the capability to finance special projects through his network of criminal enterprises and billions of dollars of hard currency reserves that he maintains in hidden foreign accounts. Castro has a proven capability to penetrate U.S. airspace with military aircraft and to conduct aggressive shoot-down operations in international airspace just outside the U.S. . . .

It is important, Mr. Speaker, that we explain at this time what our embargo against Castro is and what it is not. We must counter the massive disinformation campaign by those who wish to lift the embargo against Castro. The way to do that is with the facts. Our embargo is an embargo against U.S. credits, financing and mass tourism to Castro. It is not an embargo on medicine or humanitarian assistance.

---

**Source:** *Congressional Record, March 18, 1998, p. H1280.*

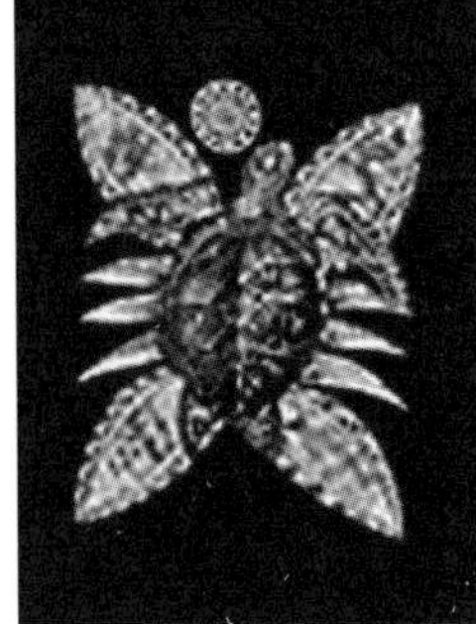

# Cuba Embargo Role Play

## Role: Author Alice Walker

March 13, 1996

President Bill Clinton
The White House
Washington, DC

Dear President Clinton:

Thank you very much for the invitation to the White House while I was in Washington in January. I am sorry circumstances made it impossible for us to meet. . . .

I love Cuba and its people, including Fidel. The bill you have signed to further tighten the blockade hurts me deeply. I travel to Cuba whenever I can to take medicine and the small, perhaps insignificant comfort of my presence, to those whose courage and tenderness have inspired me practically my entire life.

I have seen how the embargo hurts everyone in Cuba, but especially Cuban children, infants in particular. I spent some nights in utter sleeplessness worrying about them. . . .

The bill you have signed is wrong. Even if you despise Fidel and even if the Cubans should not have shot down the planes violating their air space. . . . The bill is wrong, the embargo is wrong, because it punishes people, some of them unborn, for being who they are. Cubans cannot help being who they are. Given their long struggle for freedom, particularly from Spain and the United States, they cannot help taking understandable pride in who they are. They have chosen a way of life different from ours, and I must say that from my limited exposure to that different way of life, it has brought them, fundamentally, a deep inner certainty about the meaning of existence (to develop one's self and to help others) and an equally deep psychic peace. One endearing quality I've found in the Cubans I have met is that they can listen with as much heart as they speak. . . .

[T]he dream of the revengeful and the greedy is to retake Cuba, never mind the cries of children who can no longer have milk to drink, or of adults whose ration card permits them one egg a week. Would you want Chelsea to have no milk, to have one egg a week? You are a large man, how would you yourself survive? . . .

One cannot justify starving them to death because their leader is a person of whom some people, themselves imperfect, human, disapprove. . . .

I often disagree with you . . . Still, I care about you, Hillary, and Chelsea, and wish you only good. I certainly would not deprive you of food in protest of anything you have done! . . .

Sincerely,

*Alice Walker*

---

**Source:** *Alice Walker,* Anything We Love Can Be Saved *(New York: Random House, 1997), pp. 212–216*

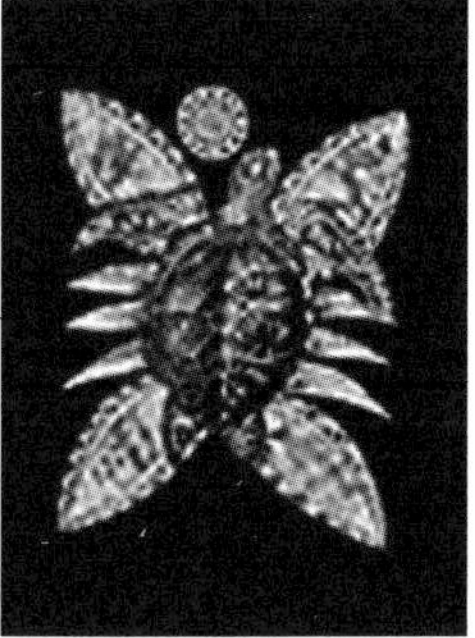

# Cuba Embargo Role Play

## Role: U.S. State Department

*Excerpt from a speech by Jeffrey Davidow, Assistant Secretary of State for Inter-American Affairs, to the American Enterprise Institute, July 28, 1997.*

I always find it fascinating that often those who would be the first to support the U.S. government when it speaks out strongly against anti-democratic elements or efforts in Venezuela, or Paraguay, or Guatemala, seem relatively complacent about the continuation of an anti-democratic regime in Cuba. I find it interesting that some who urge the U.S. government to develop strategies that extol the free market and emphasize the need for clear rules of the commercial game are sometimes willing to let that all take a back seat, if there is a prospect of some financial advantage to come from maneuvering in the non-free and murky waters of the Cuban economic system. And, call me naive, but I just do not understand how organizations that rightfully urge international cooperation for the protection of human rights or for freedom for political prisoners or for other problems which are of legitimate transnational concern occasionally become mute when discussing Cuba.

It is Cuba that is out of touch with reality, not U.S. policy towards Cuba. Our policy is consistent with the thrust of our basic approach in this hemispheric democracy, free markets, international cooperation on transnational issues. It is Cuba's implacable hostility to the concepts of democracy and freedom that makes our relationship with the Cuban government so different from our relationship with the other nations of the hemisphere. The Cuban government actively opposes the aspiration of its people to democracy. It does not permit free elections, it imprisons those who advocate basic liberty, and it works to thwart the development of independent institutions that it cannot dominate and control. On the economic side, some have made much of Cuba's so-called reforms that have allowed a small self-employment sector to develop. But Cuba still does not recognize the fundamental right of private property, and is hostile to the very idea of "profit." It does not allow an individual to employ anyone outside of his family, and does not permit a person to seek to better his or her life by working for another. There are no independent labor unions, and no rule of law to enforce contracts and rights. The rest of the hemisphere generally supports the free flow of investment, the right to organize and join a union, and a legal system that will enforce the rights of all. Cuba is outside of this consensus.

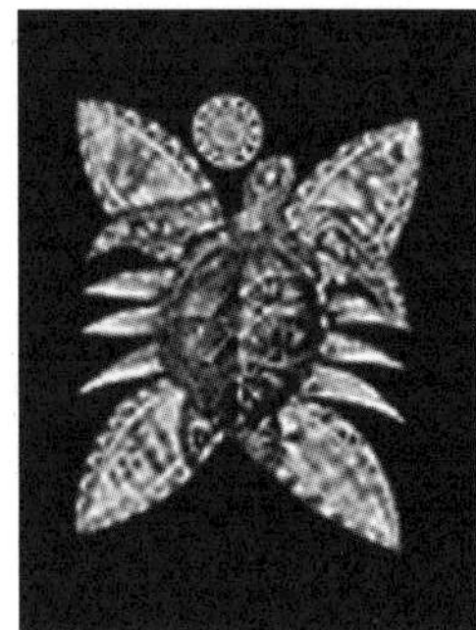

# Cuba Embargo Role Play

## Role: Public Health Specialist

### Report from the American Association for World Health

After a year-long investigation, the American Association for World Health has determined that the U.S. embargo of Cuba has dramatically harmed the health and nutrition of large numbers of ordinary Cuban citizens. As documented by the attached report, it is our expert medical opinion that the U.S. embargo has caused a significant rise in suffering — and even deaths — in Cuba. For several decades the U.S. embargo has imposed significant financial burdens on the Cuban health care system. But since 1992 the number of unmet medical needs — patients going without essential drugs or doctors performing medical procedures without adequate equipment — has sharply accelerated. This trend is directly linked to the fact that in 1992 the U.S. trade embargo — one of the most stringent embargoes of its kind, prohibiting the sale of food and sharply restricting the sale of medicines and medical equipment — was further tightened by the 1992 Cuban Democracy Act.

A humanitarian catastrophe has been averted only because the Cuban government has maintained a high level of budgetary support for a health care system designed to deliver primary and preventive health care to all of its citizens. Cuba still has an infant mortality rate half that of the city of Washington, DC. Even so, the U.S. embargo of food and the de facto embargo on medical supplies have wreaked havoc with the island's model primary health care system. The crisis has been compounded by the country's generally weak economic resources and by the loss of trade with the Soviet bloc. . . .

Specifically, the AAWH's team of nine medical experts identified the following health problems affected by the embargo:

1. *Malnutrition* The outright ban on the sale of American foodstuffs has contributed to serious nutritional deficits, particularly among pregnant women, leading to an increase in low-birthweight babies. . . . By one estimate, daily caloric intake dropped 33 percent between 1989 and 1993.
2. *Water Quality* The embargo is severely restricting Cuba's access to water treatment chemicals and spare parts for the island's water supply system. This has led to serious cutbacks in supplies of safe drinking water, which in turn has become a factor in the rising incidence of . . . water-borne diseases.
3. *Medicines & Equipment* Of the 1,297 medications available in Cuba in 1991, physicians now have access to only 889 of these same medicines — and many of these are available only intermittently. Because most major new drugs are developed by U.S. pharmaceuticals, Cuban physicians have access to less than 50 percent of the new medicines available on the world market. . . .
4. *Medical Information* Though information materials have been exempt from the U.S. trade embargo since 1988, the AAWH study concludes that in practice very little such information goes into Cuba or comes out of the island due to travel restrictions, currency regulations, and shipping difficulties. Scientists and citizens of both countries suffer as a

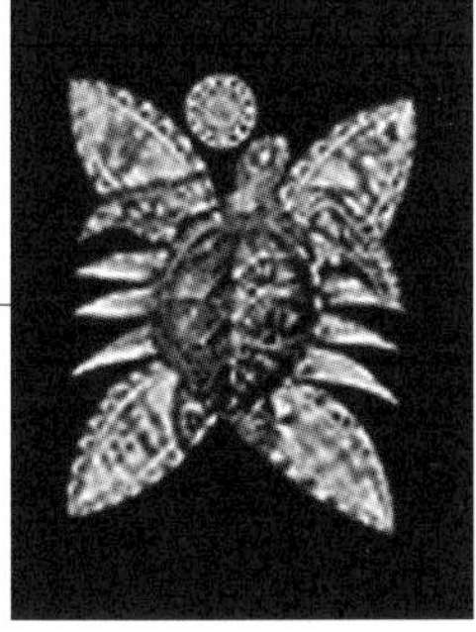

result. Paradoxically, the embargo harms some U.S. citizens by denying them access to the latest advances in Cuban medical research, including such products as Meningitis B vaccine, cheaply produced interferon and streptokinase, and an AIDS vaccine currently undergoing clinical trials with human volunteers.

Finally, the AAWH wishes to emphasize the stringent nature of the U.S. trade embargo against Cuba. Few other embargoes in recent history — including those targeting Iran, Libya, South Africa, Southern Rhodesia,* Chile, or Iraq — have included an outright ban on the sale of food. Few other embargoes have so restricted medical commerce as to deny the availability of life-saving medicines to ordinary citizens. Such an embargo appears to violate the most basic international charters and conventions governing human rights, including the United Nations charter, the charter of the Organization of American States, and the articles of the Geneva Convention governing the treatment of civilians during wartime.

Such a stringent embargo, if applied to most other countries in the developing world, would have had catastrophic effects on the public health system. Cuba's health-care system, however, is uniformly considered the preeminent model in the Third World.

The Cuban constitution makes health care a right of every citizen and the responsibility of the government. The system is based on universal coverage and comprehensive care, essentially free of charge to the population. Over the years, the central government has placed a top priority on public health expenditures in the national budget and allocated considerable human resources to public health strategies that have earned praise from the World Health Organization, the Pan American Health Organization, UNICEF, and other international bodies and individual health care authorities.

Consequently, in the 1990s Cuba's health statistics more closely approximated those of the nations of Europe and North America than of developing countries . . .

*The former name of Zimbabwe.

**Source:** *"Denial of Food and Medicine: The Impact of the U.S. Embargo on Health and Nutrition in Cuba," American Association for World Health, March 1997.*

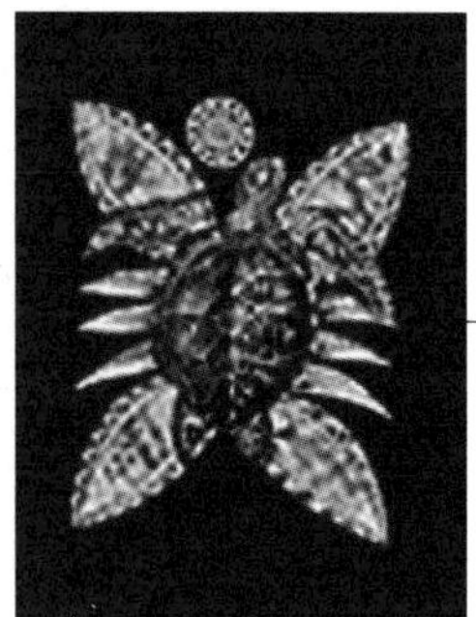

# Cuba Embargo Role Play

## Role: Heritage Foundation

*Kim Holmes is Vice-President and Director of Foreign and Defense Policy Studies for the Heritage Foundation, a conservative think-tank in Washington, DC.*

Since the U.S. imposed a trade embargo on Cuba thirty-two years ago, much has changed in the world of communism. Fidel Castro's patron, the Soviet Union, has collapsed. Communist China is embracing capitalism. And Marxist-Leninism is a creed that survives only in a few dreary outposts like North Korea and Cuba.

Because communism is on the run, some people believe that the embargo on Cuba should be lifted. Since the world has changed so much, they ask, why bother worrying about this last redoubt of communism in the Caribbean? Critics of the embargo argue that Fidel Castro no longer threatens the security and vital national interests of the United States. They also insist that the trade embargo is a Cold War anachronism that serves only to perpetuate Castro's stranglehold on the Cuban people. They maintain that the embargo has never worked because Castro remains in power, and that the best way to encourage economic and democratic reforms in Cuba is to end the embargo and trade with Castro.

These arguments are dangerously misguided. To be sure, the world has changed — but this should not mean that Cuba should be treated any differently. In fact, it should not be treated differently at all. The point is that while the world has changed, Cuba has not — at least not enough to justify lifting the embargo.

The U.S. imposed the embargo on Cuba because Castro was a communist dictator who repressed his people, stole the property of foreigners, and threatened U.S. security and interests. The embargo should be lifted when Cuba becomes a free-market democracy committed to the rule of law and peaceful relations with the U.S. and its neighbors. So far these conditions have not been met. Fidel Castro remains a repressive dictator who still threatens U.S. security and interests. Moreover, ending the trade embargo now would not promote economic and democratic reforms in Cuba.

— *Kim Holmes*

---

**Source:** *Excerpted from Kim Holmes, "Keep the Arms Embargo on Cuba," Committee Brief No. 14, A Special Report to the Senate Foreign Relations Committee, Heritage Foundation, Washington, DC, June 1995.*

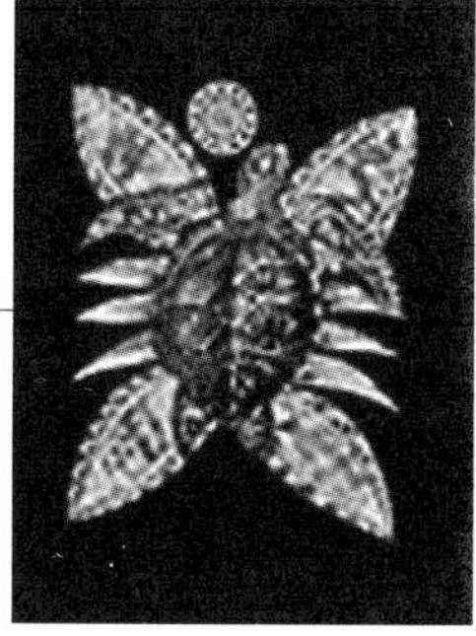

# Cuba Embargo Role Play

## Role: Cuban Government

In 1994 alone, Cuba lost a billion dollars as a result of the U.S. embargo. This figure includes both income that was not received and additional expenditures occasioned by U.S. policy. The amount of this loss was equivalent to 50 percent of all of Cuba's imports for the year.

For three consecutive years, the United Nations has condemned the U.S. blockade of Cuba. Last year, the only countries to vote negatively on this UN resolution were the United States and Israel. Yet the United States, rather than listening to the voice of the world community, is preparing to internationalize its blockade through the Helms-Burton Law.

Apparently, the end of the Cold War does not apply to all countries equally. The text of Helms-Burton expressly states that the goal of this legislation is to bring about the overthrow of the Cuban government. . . .

The United States has used its control of the international banking system to freeze funds used by Cuban enterprises for international commerce. For example, on May 13, 1994, the Cuban fishing fleet in Canada transferred $45,000 to the firm Servinaves Panama, to pay for services rendered to a Cuban ship that was crossing the Panama Canal. This funds transfer was sent out by the Bank of Toronto, but never reached its destination, because the Foreign Assets Control Office of the U.S. Department of the Treasury retained the funds.

All of Cuba's international commerce is subject to sizable additional fees because of the additional costs to foreign firms of doing business with Cuba that are created by the U.S. blockade. For example, imports of grain, which are essential to the Cuban economy, cost $80 per metric ton, whereas before the deepening of the U.S. embargo in 1992, they cost $40 per metric ton. In 1994 alone, the total cost of such additional charges is at least $60 million.

The blockade specifically targets Cuban production for export markets, one of Cuba's few means of obtaining foreign exchange. In the case of the sugar industry, our principal export industry, the embargo caused additional costs for fuel, fertilizer, herbicides, and pesticides amounting to $8 million in 1994.

U.S. pressure has been especially intense in the case of the energy industry. For example, U.S. officials visited a Mexican firm that was involved in helping to bring on line one of Cuba's principal oil refineries. The U.S. officials told the executives of the Mexican firm that their business with Cuba violated agreements between Mexico and the United States and could damage relations between those two countries. . . .

The U.S. blockade has had devastating effects on Cuba. The daily per capita nutritional intake of the Cuban population has fallen by 40 percent in proteins, 64 percent in carbohydrates, 67 and 62 percent in vitamins A and C, 22 percent in iron, and 19 percent in calcium. Since 1989, we have observed a progressive and accelerated deterioration in nutrition of our citizens, without mentioning the many other effects of blockade on daily life. . . .

The lack of food and industrial products imposed by the blockade has resulted in the physical and mental destruction of our population. . . . Shortages of products necessary for maintaining cleanliness and hygiene has brought about the spread of diseases throughout the island. . . .

---

**Source:** *Report by Cuban Chancellor Roberto Robaina to UN Secretary General Butros Butros Ghali, June 9, 1994, quoted in Orlando Perez, "Cuba: the Costs of the Blockade," ALAI/Latin American Information Agency, Aug. 18, 1995, pp. 15–17. Translation by Rachael Kamel.*

# 3.

# Puerto Rico

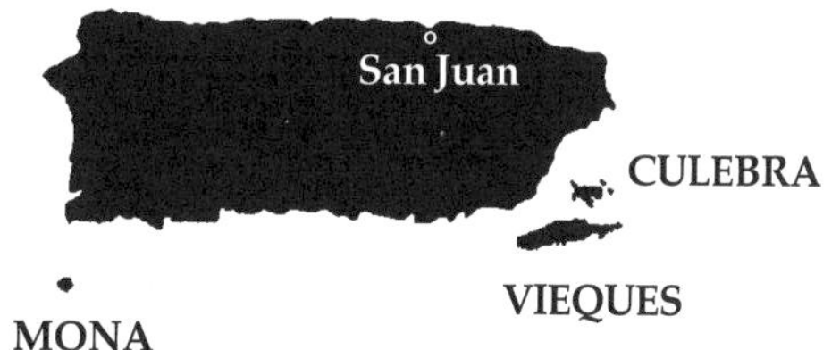


Johnny Irizarry
María E. Mills-Torres
Marta Moreno Vega
Anita Rivera

PUERTO RICO is a mountainous tropical archipelago in the Caribbean that measures 3,423 square miles. Its neighbors include the Dominican Republic and Haiti (two countries that share a single island), Cuba, and Jamaica to the west and the U.S. Virgin Islands and the lower Antilles to the east. South America lies to the south and the U.S. mainland to the north.

Puerto Rico has large modern cities and small country towns. Population centers include the main island of Puerto Rico and two smaller islands, Culebra and Vieques. Puerto Rico's current population is more than 3.5 million people. There are also 2.7 million Puerto Ricans living on the U.S. mainland. Puerto Ricans are the second largest Latino group in the United States. Spanish is the language spoken on the island, with English taught as a second language in the schools.

The Puerto Rican people reflect the varied physical and cultural heritage of the different groups that have mixed together to create the island's population: the original indigenous inhabitants, European settlers (mainly from Spain), and Africans. As a result, Puerto Ricans range across the full spectrum of skin colors. The Puerto Rican experience presents some differences from the traditional ways people in the United States are accustomed to understanding race (see Lesson 3.1, Race and Identity).

## Native Inhabitants and Spanish Colonization

The original name of the island, given by the indigenous Taino-Arawak people, was "Boriken,"* which means "land of the brave people." The Tainos were an agricultural people with highly developed political, social, religious, and cultural beliefs and practices, whose ancestors go back to 4,000 BC.

*Spelled "Borinquen" in modern usage

In 1493, on his second voyage to the Americas, Christopher Columbus claimed Borinquen for Queen Isabella and King Ferdinand of Spain. He originally named the land of the Tainos San Juan Bautista. The island's name was later changed to Puerto Rico, which means "rich port." Within sixty years, most of the Taino population was destroyed through war against the Spanish invaders, through the devastation of slavery in gold mines and plantations, and through diseases that the Europeans brought to the island.

Almost immediately after the arrival of the Spanish, the Tainos began to rebel against colonization. *Caciques* or chiefs led revolts against the invading Spaniards. Famous legends and historical documents from the Spanish themselves tell stories of this resistance, led by famous *caciques* such as Urayoán and Agüeybaná II. Even before the arrival of the Spanish conquistadors, Cacique Urayoán had warned his people of the coming devastation. Legend tells that he had a vision of the coming of white-skinned men riding animals (horses) that would bring great destruction to his people. He was one of the first *caciques* to call his people to rebellion and to spread the word to other *caciques* to resist Spanish colonization.

Many Tainos escaped from the oppression of the Spanish by fleeing to other Caribbean islands, where they joined the Caribs (the native inhabitants of the lower Antillean Islands) in resisting Spanish colonization. Despite the decimation of the Taino people, their influence lives on as a permanent physical and cultural element of Puerto Rican life. For example , many Arawak-Taino words passed into Spanish (and, in some cases, from there into English), such as *huracán* (hurricane) and *hamaca* (hammock). Taino musical instruments, such as maracas and the *guiro* (an instrument made from gourds), continue to play a key role in Puerto Rican musical forms.

Once the Taino population was largely destroyed, the Spanish began enslaving Africans to fill their need for labor. African slavery was a major engine of the Puerto Rican economy from 1508 to March 22, 1873, when it was finally abolished.

## Puerto Rico's African Heritage

Some scholars believe that there is evidence of an African presence in the Americas prior to the Spanish arrival in the late fifteenth century. Archeological studies have discovered what may be African artifacts and human skeletons in parts of Mexico, Central America, and the Caribbean that predate the Europeans by at least 2,000 years. For example, evidence of exchanges between the great Olmec culture of Mexico and the Nubian-Kemetic cultures of Africa during the period 1450–800 BC has been found in La Venta and Palenque in Mexico. Between 1310 and 1491 AD Mandingo merchant explorers from Africa made more than fifty trips to various Caribbean and Central and South American points.*

In addition, the Spanish themselves were deeply influenced by African culture. The Moors of North Africa had a permanent impact on the development of Spanish history, art, and culture through their occupation of Spanish territory, which lasted approximately 800 years. Free Africans, known as *libertos,* originally traveled with the Spanish conquistadors to the Americas. A *liberto* was a man or woman of African origin who came to settle in Puerto Rico from Spain. Two examples are:

- Juan Garrido, who accompanied Juan Ponce de Leon (the first governor of Puerto Rico assigned by the Spanish crown) in exploring the coast of Florida in 1506. Garrido is also known for bringing the first wheat and other new vegetable seeds to the Americas.
- Francisco Gallego, the first Spanish entrepreneur of African origin in Puerto Rico.*

Enslaved Africans were sold to the Spanish by Portuguese slavers working from ports in central-west Africa. African slaves were brought first to the Caribbean islands and from there to other parts of the Americas. The entire Western Hemisphere, including the Caribbean as well as North, Central, and South America, has a common African ancestry, originating from central-west Africa. Historians estimate that anywhere from fifteen to fifty million Africans were taken from Africa between 1482 and 1888. The lack of food and extreme physical abuses experienced in the Middle Passage across the Atlantic often killed up to a third of the enslaved Africans.

As early as 1514, enslaved Tainos and Africans in Puerto Rico joined forces in revolt against slavery. By 1848 more than twenty revolts had occurred. *Cimarrones* (fugitive slaves) planned individual escapes and collective revolts. Many *cimarrones* would escape to the remote mountains of the island or even other Caribbean or Central or South American lands, where they formed free communities. Some of their descendants survive to this day, especially along the Atlantic Coast of Central and South America. Many others were killed in heroic attempts to obtain their freedom.

Throughout the 365 years of slavery in Puerto Rico, there was also a large population of free Puerto Ricans of African descent. In addition to revolting or escaping, slaves could also negotiate to buy their freedom and that of their families. Most free Puerto Ricans of African descent, as well as *mulatos or mestizos,*** worked in a variety of occupations such as agriculture or

*See Asante Molefi K. and Mark Mattson, *Historical and Cultural Atlas of African-Americans* (New York: Macmillan, 1991), p. 17.

*See *The People's Voice: Puerto Rican Culture and History* (Rochester, NY: People's Publishing Group and Rochester City School district, 1993), pp. 30-33.

**Spanish words denoting people of mixed racial origin.

domestic labor, or as artisans, merchants, or ship hands. Many continued the struggle against slavery and racism, becoming abolitionists and freedom fighters. People of African descent have made pronounced contributions to Puerto Rico's historical, social, intellectual, artistic, and cultural development.

African influence may also be traced in many words from African languages that have become a permanent part of Puerto Rican Spanish (and, in some cases, English): *mangó* (mango), *candungo* (storage pot), *mofongo* (a plantain dish), *mondongo* (a stew), *guineo* (banana), or *chévere* (good!). Puerto Rican musical instruments such as *la clave* (also known as *par de palos* or "two sticks"), drums with stretched animal skin such as bongos or congas, and Puerto Rican music-dance forms such as *la bomba* or *la plena* are likewise rooted in Africa. Puerto Rican cuisine also has a strong African influence.

***In this 1898 cartoon, the United States offers shelter to a vulnerable Puerto Rico.***

## Puerto Rico After 1898

By the nineteenth century, Puerto Ricans were a distinct people, aspiring to achieve independence from Spanish rule and establish their own nation. On September 23, 1868, independence fighters struck out in the "Grito de Lares" (Cry of Lares) and declared a democratic republic. Although this uprising was not successful for long, it did win a series of concessions, including a process for achieving full independence from Spain. On July 17, 1898, an independent government was officially installed in Puerto Rico. A week later, however, the island was invaded by U.S. forces. After 400 years of Spanish domination, the island was now under the control of the United States.

By the time of the Spanish-American War, Puerto Rico's indigenous, Spanish, and African roots had blended together into the island's unique political, social, religious, and cultural life. Much of what we know today as Puerto Rican culture had been forged by the end of the nineteenth century. Puerto Rico's artistic and cultural traditions, literature, music, and visual arts are recognized internationally and have made pronounced contributions to the development of artistic expression — in Latin America, among Latinos in the United States, and internationally.

Religion, especially the Catholic Church, has also played a major role in Puerto Rican history, especially in political, social, and cultural traditions. As throughout the hemisphere, the impact of the church has been extremely complex. For the conquistadors, forcible conversion to Christianity served as a justification for the enslavement of the Tainos and Africans. As the centuries passed, however, the Puerto Rican people shaped religion into one of their central modes of cultural expression.

CORBIS-BETTMAN

*This 1939 photograph shows U.S. soldiers camped outside Baymon, Puerto Rico, as they begin an annual march through the island.*

After 1898, a new colonial era entered the lives of the Puerto Rican people. Puerto Rico was now ruled as a possession of the United States. Conflict between the people and their new rulers emerged first over language. Illiteracy was widespread at that time, affecting 85 percent of the population, and the United States expected no resistance from the Puerto Ricans when it imposed English-only laws on the island. Puerto Rican intellectuals and *independentistas* (people who fought for Puerto Rican independence) resisted the replacement of the Spanish language with English. From 1898 until the establishment of the Commonwealth of Puerto Rico in 1952, U.S. governors maintained some type of English-only law over Puerto Rico. In 1952, Spanish once again became the official language of Puerto Rico, although the use of English continues to be required in some educational, governmental, and judicial functions.

In 1917 President Woodrow Wilson signed the Jones Act, which made Puerto Ricans citizens of the United States. Those who chose to reject U.S. citizenship would become exiles in their own homeland. Others left the island as a rejection of U.S. domination. U.S. citizenship, extended in the midst of World War I, brought with it the imposition of military service on Puerto Ricans. Since that time, hundreds of thousands of Puerto Ricans from both the island and the United States have served in the U.S. military, first through the draft and now as volunteers. In many cases Puerto Ricans have been overrepresented in the military and have borne a disproportionate share of casualties — as well as facing racial, ethnic, and language discrimination.

On July 25, 1952, in commemoration of the date of the U.S. invasion of Puerto Rico in 1898, a Puerto Rican constitution was adopted establishing the Commonwealth of Puerto Rico. The U.S. Congress had conferred commonwealth status on Puerto Rico in July 1950; now it was also enshrined in Puerto Rican law. The Popular Democratic Party continued to govern until 1968, when a growing movement favoring statehood for Puerto Rico won the governor's post.

To this day, Puerto Rico remains a territorial possession of the United States. Puerto Rico is subject to the judicial and legal system of the United States, and U.S. federal agencies implement federal laws and programs in Puerto Rico.

Despite their U.S. citizenship, Puerto Ricans still have an anomalous legal status — neither fully independent nor fully a part of the United States. For example, Puerto Ricans on the island cannot vote for the president of the United States, but Puerto Ricans residing in the U.S. mainland can. Puerto Ricans on the island are exempt from federal taxes, but have a system of local taxes very similar to that of the U.S. mainland. A nonvoting "resident commissioner" represents Puerto Rico in the U.S. House of Representatives. (In addition, there are currently three elected U.S. congresspeople of Puerto

Rican descent representing districts in New York and Chicago.)

## Twentieth Century Nationalist Movements

From 1898 until 1947 the U.S. government ran military and civil political administrations on the island of Puerto Rico. In 1948, for the first time, the United States allowed Puerto Ricans to elect their own governor. They voted in Luis Muñoz Marin (1898–1980), a Puerto Rican. Muñoz Marin, who served as governor until 1965, originally believed in independence for Puerto Rico. He later led his party (the Popular Democratic Party, founded in 1938), in establishing Puerto Rico as a Free Associated State. They chose as their party emblem the profile of a Puerto Rican *jíbaro* (peasant) wearing a *pava* (straw hat). Under the emblem they placed the slogan *"Pan, Tierra y Libertad"* (Bread, Land, and Liberty).

Muñoz Marin met with opposition from the nationalist movement, led by Pedro Albizu Campos (1891–1965). The Nationalist Party was founded in 1922, demanding independence for Puerto Rico from the United States. Through the 1950s, the Nationalists continued their fight for Puerto Rican independence. In 1937 the Puerto Rican police opened fire on a peaceful protest march by the Nationalist Party in the city of Ponce. Eighteen people were killed that day and 200 wounded, in what became known as the Ponce Massacre. New groups advocating for independence continued to develop. In 1946 the Puerto Rican Independence Party was founded. Later the Movement for Independence (MPI) was formed; in 1971, this group changed its name to the Puerto Rican Socialist Party.

In 1950 there was another Nationalist uprising. Thousands of independence sympathizers were jailed and more than thirty were killed. Five Nationalists were killed in an attempt to assassinate Governor Luis Muñoz Marin. Shortly thereafter, two Nationalists brought the issue of Puerto Rican independence to world attention when they assaulted Blair House, the residence of President Harry Truman in Washington, DC, while the White House was being renovated. On March 1, 1954, Lolita Lebron and three other Nationalists opened fire on the U.S. House of Representatives, demanding independence for Puerto Rico. Five U.S. congressmen were wounded in that attack and the Nationalists were sentenced to 56 years in prison. Lolita Lebron and the other Nationalists were pardoned in 1979 by President Jimmy Carter. They toured cities in the United States with large Puerto Rican populations and then returned to Puerto Rico, where they were met by hundreds of thousands of cheering Boricuas (people from Borinquen — that is, Puerto Ricans).

A major scandal regarding police surveillance broke in Puerto Rico in the late 1980s, when it was revealed that Puerto Rican and U.S. law-enforcement agencies had worked together from the 1930s onward to maintain files on as many as 75,000 Puerto Rican activists, on both the island and the U.S. mainland. Not only *independentistas* but also unions, religious and cultural groups, women's groups, and others were targeted in this operation. Many activists were subjected to blacklisting and other forms of harassment.*

Armed actions in support of Puerto Rican independence continued through the 1980s; to this day, fourteen independence activists remain in jail in the United States, convicted of acts of "sedition," including bombings and the possession of firearms. These members of a group known as the Fuerzas Armadas de Liberación Nacional (National Liberation Armed Forces) consider themselves to be political prisoners, and their sympathizers have organized a national

*Details are provided in R. Bosque Pérez and José Javier Colón Morera, *Las carpetas: Persecución política y derechos civiles en Puerto Rico* (The dossiers: Political persecution and civil rights in Puerto Rico; San Juan: CIPDC, 1997).

FREE LIBRARY OF PHILADELPHIA

*This 1940 news service photograph, captioned "roaring modernity," played on the contrast between the latest U.S. fighter plane and a Puerto Rican farmer using a horse for transportation. Unintentionally captured was an image of the militarization of Puerto Rico under U.S. dominance.*

and international campaign to press for their release.

## The U.S. in Puerto Rico

Under U.S. rule Puerto Rico has become one of the most militarized territories in the world. Citing Puerto Rico's strategic location in the Caribbean and the need for "national security," the United States has built military bases throughout the island. Militarization has greatly affected the lives of Puerto Ricans. For example, since the 1940s the Puerto Rican island of Vieques has been at the center of a political controversy between the people of Puerto Rico and the U.S. armed forces. In the early 1940s the U.S. Navy seized two-thirds of the land in Vieques to be used for U.S. military purposes. The island's population dropped from 10,000 to 7,000. Today Viequenses (residents of Vieques) live in the central section of their island, while the navy owns and operates the western and eastern sections.

Many people from Vieques and the main island of Puerto Rico have resisted this take-over of their lands by the U.S. Navy through political action. In 1978, for example, a group of fishing communities organized a protest by taking forty small fishing boats into the middle of the navy's weapons-testing exercises. The navy exercises were killing the fish, which local people depended on to survive. Protest actions such as this one continued into the 1980s. Many Puerto Ricans have been arrested for such acts of resistance.

Beginning in the 1950s, the governments of both Puerto Rico and the United States promoted a development strategy for the island known as "Operation Bootstrap." Briefly described, Operation Bootstrap consisted of a plan to transform the island of Puerto Rico from an agricultural society to an industrial one. Tax exemptions prompted more than 100 of the 500

DICK ERSTAD

*A portrait of a local committee of Vieques fishermen in 1964. The Vieques Defense Committee organized to fight the displacement of fishing communities by the U.S. military.*

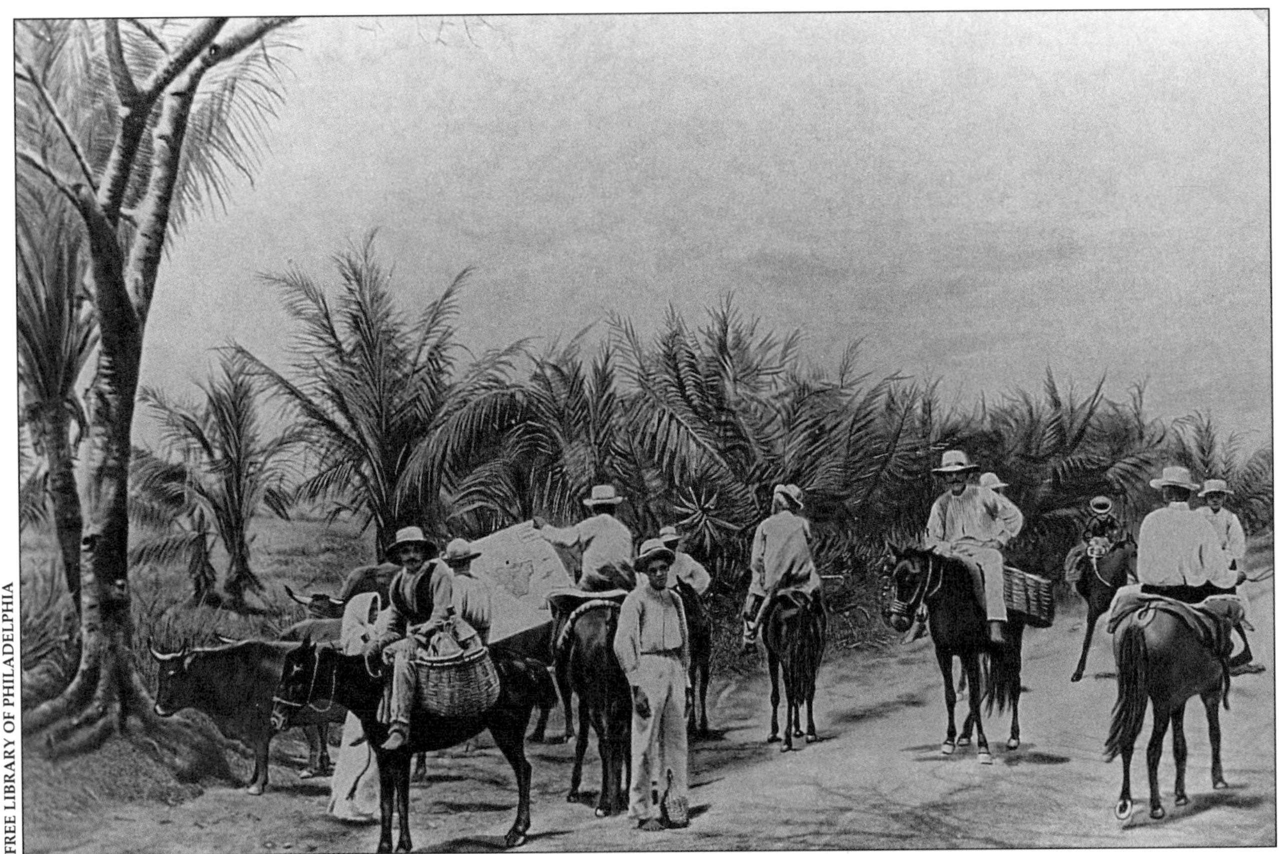

FREE LIBRARY OF PHILADELPHIA

*An early color photograph shows Puerto Rican farmers returning from market near Arecibo.*

largest U.S. corporations to set up operations in Puerto Rico. As a result of this rapid industrialization, Puerto Rican agriculture has been greatly weakened and the island has stopped growing its own food. Today, 85 percent of what Puerto Ricans eat is imported, mostly from the United States.

Industrialization has brought benefits but also costs: the dramatic growth of industry in Puerto Rico and the influx of petrochemical plants in the 1970s have greatly increased environmental pollution in the island. Operation Bootstrap provoked the movement of huge numbers of Puerto Ricans from rural to urban areas as they searched for work. It also created an enormous migration of Puerto Ricans to the United States: more than 40 percent of the Puerto Rican population now lives on the U.S. mainland.

Puerto Rican women have also been the object of population control policies. Beginning in the 1950s, large numbers of Puerto Rican women working in factories were sterilized. Women factory workers were given time off to attend appointments in clinics that were located within the factory itself. Social workers would visit their homes to follow up on women who had missed an appointment at one of these clinics. By 1974, 35 percent of Puerto Rican women of child-bearing age — some 200,000 women — were permanently sterilized. By 1980, Puerto Rico had the highest per-capita rate of sterilization among women in the world. From the 1950s through 1980, Puerto Rico was also used as a testing ground for birth control pills while they were under development. Pills twenty times stronger than the ones used today were tested on Puerto Rican women living in housing projects.

## Migration: Puerto Ricans in the United States

Puerto Ricans started coming to the United States more than a century and a half ago. Their numbers increased after Puerto Rico was ceded to the United States by Spain. A massive wave of migration to the mainland United States began after World War II, as farmworkers came to work in the produce farms of the East Coast while other migrants traveled to the urban areas of the East and Midwest to work in factories. Many U.S. farms and companies recruited workers directly out of Puerto Rico to work as far away as Hawai`i.

In legal terms, Puerto Ricans are not considered immigrants, because they are U.S. citizens. Nonetheless, their motives for coming to the U.S. mainland resemble those of every other immigrant group: pursuit of the "American Dream" and a better social and economic situation for themselves and their families. From the 1940s to the 1960s the labor force participation rate of Puerto Ricans was among the highest of any group in the United States. In those days there was a great demand for factory workers and semi-skilled labor in the United States. In addition, Puerto Ricans were known for their expertise in making cigars, and many of them came to the United States to work in the tobacco industry.

Puerto Rican migrants faced social, educational, housing, and employment discrimination. They also confronted difficulties rooted in language differences. Thousands of Puerto Rican workers, especially women factory workers, were paid lower wages than those paid to white workers. Discrimination came from all directions, including, initially, unequal treatment from labor unions and even exclusion from them.

In recent decades, as U.S. industry has been restructured through automation and the flight of jobs to lower-wage areas of the world, the demand for semi-skilled labor has collapsed in U.S. urban areas, where most of the Puerto Rican population resides. As a result, Puerto Rican communities are facing a situation of extreme unemployment and underemployment, leading to ever-deepening poverty. Puerto Ricans have the lowest median income and highest poverty rate of all Latino groups in the United States. The consequences of such difficult conditions are manifested in high drop-out rates among students, high numbers of single-parent households, drug addiction, lack of access to health care, and other social ills, which have reached alarming proportions within Puerto Rican communities throughout the United States.

These communities have historically responded to their problems by community organizing to build community-based support institutions, including religious, advocacy, and political organizations. Numerous Puerto Rican support institutions have been established to further the search for democratic rights, to improve the delivery of social services, and to promote cultural, spiritual, educational, and economic development for the Puerto Rican community.

In the 1960s and 1970s, one of the best-known Puerto Rican political organizations to emerge from struggles for social justice in the United States was known as the Young Lords. Young Puerto Ricans living in Chicago and in "El Barrio" (East Harlem in New York City) emerged as community political leaders. Their models were the Black Panther Party and the independence movement in Puerto Rico. The Young Lords organized community protest actions and took over institutions such as churches, hospitals, and public service vehicles, to dramatize their demand for human and civil rights, better health and social services, and child care. The Young Lords organized in other cities with high concentrations of Puerto Ricans, including Chicago, Philadelphia, and Hartford, Connecticut. They organized their communities around political and social issues affecting their lives in the United States and over the political status of Puerto Rico. Their attention to this latter issue continued a tradition dating back to the efforts of Puerto Rican exiles in the late 1800s.

## The Future

The future political status of Puerto Rico continues to be a burning issue for all Puerto Ricans (see Lesson 3.3). The three political options are:

1. Commonwealth: the current status, established in 1952.
2. Statehood: Puerto Rico would become a state of the United States.
3. Independence: Puerto Rico would become an independent sovereign nation, in control of its own affairs.

The issues regarding the status of Puerto Rico are complex. Beginning in 1946, the Decolonization Committee of the United Nations required the United States to report to it on a regular basis on the political, social, and economic status of Puerto Rico. After the establishment of the Commonwealth of Puerto Rico in 1952, the United Nations declared that Puerto Rico had reached a new constitutional status and decided that it would no longer require such reports. In 1960, as a result of continued pressure from the Puerto Rican independence movement, the United Nations decided to reopen discussions on the political status of Puerto Rico.

In 1967 a plebiscite (referendum) was held in Puerto Rico on the issue of political status. The majority of the people voted for the continuation of commonwealth status. In 1993 another plebiscite was held; this time 46.3 percent of the people voted in favor of statehood, 48.6 percent voted to continue commonwealth status, and 4.4 percent voted for independence. In 1994, the Puerto Rican legislature requested that the U.S. Congress define the necessary steps to resolve the future political status of Puerto Rico. In response, Rep. Don Young (R-Alaska) introduced a bill in the U.S. House of Representatives (H.R. 856), bringing the United States closer to a national discussion of the future status of Puerto Rico.

Despite the many challenges Puerto Ricans face today, they continue to play a significant role in the politics and government of the United States and to bring a wealth of contributions to all aspects of the economic, political, social, professional, intellectual, artistic, and cultural life of the United States.

---

**Vocabulary:** archipelago, indigenous, conquistadors, colonization, decimation, commonwealth, militarization, sedition, plebiscite

# References

Joy L. DeJesus, *Growing Up Puerto Rican: 20 Puerto Rican Authors Write in Fiction and Essay About Childhood* (New York: William Morrow, 1997).

Jose Luis Gonzalez, *Puerto Rico: The Four-Storeyed Country* (Maplewood, NJ: Waterfront Press, 1990).

Jay Kinsbruner, *Not of Pure Blood: The Free People of Color and Racial Prejudice in Nineteenth Century Puerto Rico* (Durham, NC: Duke University Press, 1992).

Adalberto Lopez, *The Puerto Ricans: Their History, Culture, and Society* (Cambridge, MA: Schenkman Publishing Co., 1981).

Edwin Melendez and Edgardo Melendez, *Colonial Dilemma: Critical Perspectives on Contemporary Puerto Rico* (Boston: South End Press, 1992).

Arturo Morales Carrion, *Puerto Rico: A Political and Cultural History* (New York: W. W. Norton, 1984).

Clara Rodriguez E., Virginia Sanchez Korrol, Jose Oscar Alers, *The Puerto Rican Struggle: Essays on Survival in the U.S.* (Maplewood, NJ: Waterfront Press, 1984).

Roberto Santiago, Ed., *Boricuas: Influential Puerto Rican Writings, An Anthology* (New York: Ballantine Books, 1995).

Juan Angel Silen, *We, the Puerto Rican People: A Story of Oppression and Resistance* (New York: Monthly Review Press, 1971).

Jalil Sued Badillo, *Puerto Rico Negro* (San Juan, Puerto Rico: Editorial Cultural, 1986). Published in English and Spanish.

Karl Wagenheim and Olga Jimenez de Wagenheim, *The Puerto Ricans: A Documentary History* (Princeton, NJ: Markus Wiener Publishers, 1994).

# Lesson 3.1 Race and Identity

**Objective:** To help students explore how identity is constructed differently in distinct cultural environments.

**Themes:** race, culture, identity, ethnicity

The poem "¿Y tu Agüela, a'onde Ejta?"* (And Your Grandmother, Where's She At?) was written by the Puerto Rican poet Fortunato Vizcarrondo (1896–1980). This poem was published in Vizcarrondo's book entitled *Dinga y Mandinga* (1942).

In this poem, Vizcarrondo challenges the constant denial of their African heritage by some people of mixed African and European descent. In essence he is saying, "you call me black, wanting to make me feel ashamed. But I respond that my grandmother sits proudly in the living room when guests visit my home, while you, on the other hand, hide yours in the kitchen."

The predominant conception of race in the United States presumes that different races are distinct groups that can be clearly separated. Individuals (with a few exceptions) belong either to one race or another.

In Puerto Rico, as in some other Latin countries, the conception of race is quite different. Puerto Ricans understand themselves to be the product of centuries of *mestizaje,* or mixing of different groups. As Vizcarrondo's poem indicates, Puerto Rican society is not free of racial prejudice, but such prejudice exists within a different cultural context.

This difference helps to explain why Puerto Ricans, like other Latinos, often feel they do not "fit" within the racial categories of U.S. culture. For many Latinos, their sense of national or ethnic identity (for example, as Puerto Rican) is far more important than their sense of racial identity. As the second poem, "Ode to the Diasporican," reveals, this sense of Puerto Rican identity is also shaped by historical circumstances that shift over time.

## Suggested Activities

1. Tell the students they will be reading a poem entitled, "And Your Grandmother, Where's She At?" Ask them to suggest what they think the poem might be about, based on the title.

2. Distribute the poem and have students read it out loud in class. After the students have read the poem, ask them the following questions:
   - To whom is the author of the poem speaking? Why does he ask, "And your grandma, where's she at?"
   - What do you think the author's views are on the concept of race? What do you think the views are of the person to whom the

*Readers who know Spanish will note the non-standard spelling of many words in this poem. Vizcarrondo was writing in the tradition of *"Poesía Negroide"* or Black Poetry, which sought to give written form to Black Puerto Rican dialect.

poem is addressed? What do these views tell you about the issue of race in Puerto Rico?

- Explain that in the poem, the writer is attacking someone for favoring "light skin" over "dark skin." Ask students to think of ways such favoritism plays out in the United States. What examples can they can give of how concepts of beauty or worth are defined by "white" standards?
- In the sixth verse, the author says "You only like doing the fox trot, I'm about some jitterbug jive." Explain to the students that the author is also making a statement about cultural forms that are associated with different races. What examples can students think of in which European-based cultural forms are more highly valued than forms from other cultures?
- Finally, ask students to consider how they know what is given more value. Where do the messages come from? If these lessons were never taught directly, how have students learned them?

3. Distribute the poem "Ode to the Diasporican." Ask the students to look at the description of the author. What ethnic group does she belong to? If she was born and raised in the Bronx, is she still Puerto Rican? Do they think she could be "as Puerto Rican" as someone born and raised in Puerto Rico?
4. Read the poem out loud in class. Ask them how the author defines what being Puerto Rican is.
5. Ask students to consider their own identities. How would they identify themselves: by race, ethnicity, gender, age, class . . . How do they know what they are? What makes them claim that particular identity?
6. Have students write an "Ode" to their own identity.

# Reading: Two Poems on Race and Identity

## ¿Y tu Agüela, a'onde Ejta?

Ayé mi dijijte negro
Y hoy te boy a contejtá:
Mi mai se sienta en la sala,
¿Y tu agüela, a'onde ejtá?

Yo tengo el pelo 'e caíyo;
El tuyo ej seda namá;
Tu pai lo tiene bien lasio,
¿Y tu agüela, a'onde ejtá?

Tu coló te salió blanco
Y la mejiya rosá;
Loj lábioj loj tiénej finoj...
¿Y tu agüela, a'onde ejtá?

¿Dísej que mi bemba ej grande
Y mi pasa colorá?
Pero dijme, pot la binge,
¿Y tu agüela, a'onde ejtá?

Come tu nena ej blanquita
La sácaj mucho a pasiá...
Y yo con gana 'e gritatte
¿Y... tu agüela, a'onde ejtá?

A tí te gujta el fojtrote,
Y a mí brujca maniguá.
Tú te laj tiraj de blanco
¿Y... tu agūela, a'onde ejtá?

Erej blanquito enchapao
Que déntraj en sosiedá
Temiendo que se conojca
La mamá de tu mamá.

Aquí el que no tiene dinga
Tiene mandinga...! ja, ja!
Por eso yo te pregunto
¿Y tu agüela, a'onde ejtá?

## And Your Grandma, Where's She At?

Yesterday you called me black
And today I answer back:
My mama sits with the family
And your grandma, where's she at?

My hair is coarse and nappy
Yours combs silkily,
Your dad's hair is straight
And your grandma, where's she at?

Your complexion came out white
And your cheeks shine rosily
Your lips are thin and fine
And your grandma, where's she at?

You say I have big lips
And a red and kinky do
But, for the Virgin Mary, do tell,
And your grandma, where's she at?

Since your baby girl is white
You strut her ceaselessly . . .
And me, dying to shout out,
And your grandma, where's she at?

You only like doing the fox trot,
I'm about some jitterbug jive
You will be acting like white folks
And your grandma, where's she at?

You are white painted white
Trying to move up socially
Afraid that they may know
Your mama's mama.

Now, over here, if you an Indian,
You're black . . .! Ha, ha!
That's why I keep asking,
And your grandma, where's she at?

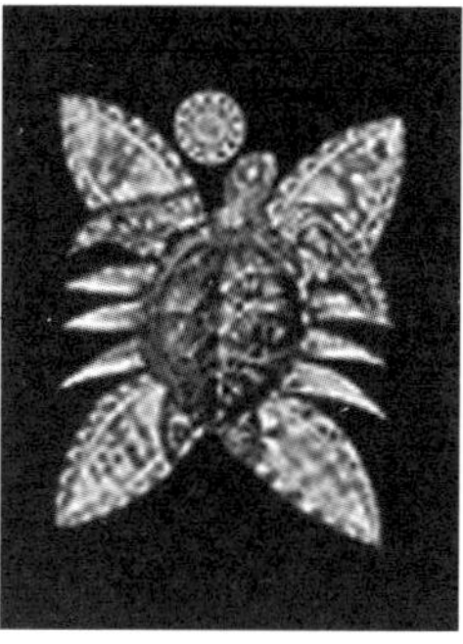

Ayé mi dijijte negro
Queriéndome abochojná.
Mi agūela sale a la sala,
Y la tuya oculta ejtá.

La pobre se ejtá muriendo
Al belse tan maltratá,
Que hajta tu perro le ladra
Si acaso a la sala bá.

¡Y bien que yo lo conojco!
Se ñama siña Tatá....
Tú la ejconde en la cosina
Pocque ej prieta de a beldá

— *Fortunato Vizcarrondo*

Yesterday, you called me black,
As if though trying to embarrass me
But my grandma sits in the living room
And your grandma, where's she at?

Poor old lady, quite naturally,
Is dying of neglect,
Even your dog barks at her
If she comes out to the living room.

And you know I know her story,
Her name is Mrs. Tatá
You hide her in the kitchen
Cause your grandma is sure enough black.

*(English translation adapted from Juan Rodrigo Rojas)*

---

**Source:** *Fortunato Vizcarrondo,* Dinga y Mandinga *(San Juan, Puerto Rico: Baldrich, 1942).*

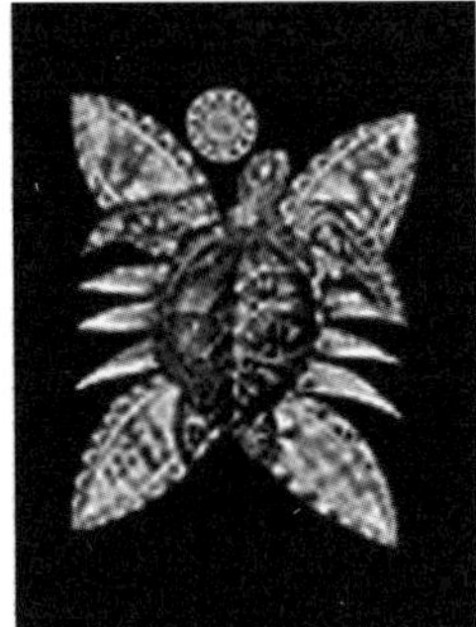

## Ode to the Diasporican

Mira a mi cara puertorriqueña — *(Look at my Puerto Rican face)*
a mi pelo vivo — *(at my lively hair)*
a mis manos trigueña — *(at my dark-skinned hands)*
Mira a mi corazón que se llena de orgullo — *(Look at my heart filling with pride)*
y díme que no soy Boricua — *(And tell me I'm not Puerto Rican)*

Some people say that I am not the real thing
Boricua, that is
cause I wasn't born on the enchanted island
cause I was born on the mainland
north of Spanish Harlem
cause I was born in the Bronx
Some people think I'm not bonafide
cause my playground was a concrete jungle
cause my Rio Grande de Loiza was the Bronx River — *(Great River of Loiza)*
cause my Fajardo was City Island
my Luquillo, Orchard Beach
and summer nights were filled with city noises instead of *coquis* — *(small frogs)*
and Puerto Rico was just some paradise that we only saw in pictures
What does it mean to live in between
What does it take to realize
that being Boricua
is a state of mind
a state of heart
a state of soul

No nací en Puerto Rico — *(I was not born in Puerto Rico)*
Puerto Rico nació en mi — *(Puerto Rico was born in me)*

Mira a mi cara puertorriqueña — *(Look at my Puerto Rican face)*
a mi pelo vivo — *(at my lively hair)*
a mis manos trigueña — *(at my dark-skinned hands)*
Mira a mi corazón que se llena de orgullo — *(Look at my heart filling with pride)*
y díme que no soy Boricua — *(And tell me I'm not Puerto Rican)*

— Mariposa ©1995

---

*Mariposa, Maria Teresa Fernandez, was born and raised in the Bronx. She is a poet, artist, and political activist. She is currently finishing a master's degree in Bilingual Special Education at New York University.*

# LESSON 3.2 La Borinqueña (The Song of Borinquen)

**Objective:** To explore the relationship between art and politics, by comparing the original and revised versions of the song, "La Borinqueña."

**Themes:** independence, propaganda, censorship

The song "La Borinqueña" was originally written in the nineteenth century as the anthem of the Puerto Rican independence movement. The lyrics were revised following the establishment of the Puerto Rican Commonwealth 1952, and the revised version remains as Puerto Rico's anthem today. This lesson examines the nature and implications of the changes.

## Suggested Activities

1. Have students read the introductory paragraphs from the handout at the end of this lesson. Then have them read both versions of the song out loud.
2. With the whole class, ask students to explain the principal differences between the two versions.
3. Tell students they will assume one of two roles: that of Lola Rodriguez de Tió, the author of the original version of "La Borinqueña," or that of Manuel Fernandez Juncos, who wrote the revised version. From within their role, they will write a one-page essay explaining what the words of the song mean to them and how they feel about the changes.
4. With the whole class, ask students whether they believe the words should have been changed. Why or why not? Ask them to defend their views with arguments for or against the changes. Ask students whether they believe the change in the words was a form of censorship. Why or why not?

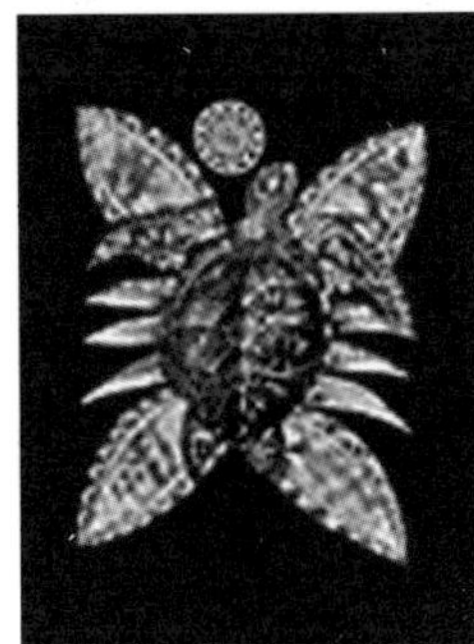

# Reading: "La Borinqueña" (Song of Borinquen)

*Lola Rodriguez de Tió was a famous Puerto Rican patriot of the nineteenth century. She was a fierce advocate for Puerto Rican independence, as well as a prolific writer who wrote the lyrics for Puerto Rico's national anthem, "La Borinqueña" (The Song of Borinquen). As a result of her revolutionary activities, she was exiled to Cuba in 1887. In 1892, she was forced to leave for New York because of her support for the Cuban independence movement. She returned to Cuba in 1898 and died there in 1924.*

*"La Borinqueña" was written by de Tió during a period of intense revolutionary activity in Puerto Rico. "La Borinqueña" was embraced by Puerto Rican freedom fighters during the period leading up to their unsuccessful revolt against the Spanish in 1868.*

*With the establishment of the Puerto Rican Commonwealth in 1952, a new version of the song was published. These new lyrics, written by Manuel Fernandez Juncos, were attributed to Lola Rodriguez de Tió. The revised lyrics have become well known as Puerto Rico's official anthem. Nonetheless, independentistas (those favoring independence for Puerto Rico) still sing the original version of the song to this day.*

## Version 1. By Lola Rodriguez de Tió

Despierta, borinqueño,
que han dado la señal.
Despierta de ese sueño
que es hora de luchar.
A ese llamar patriótico,
¿no arde tu corazón?
Ven, nos será simpático
el ruido del cañon.

Nosotros queremos la libertad,
nuestro machete nos la dará

Vámonos, borinqueño,
vámonos ya.
Que nos espera ansiosa,
ansiosa la libertad.
La libertad, la libertad,
La libertad, la libertad !

Awake, Borinqueños,
for they have given the signal.
Awake from your sleep
for it's time to fight.
At the patriotic clamor
doesn't your heart burn?
Come! the sound of cannon
will be dear to us.

We want freedom,
and our machete will grant it.

Come, Borinqueño
join us now.
Our freedom anxiously awaits us,
anxious liberty.
Liberty, Liberty,
Liberty, Liberty!

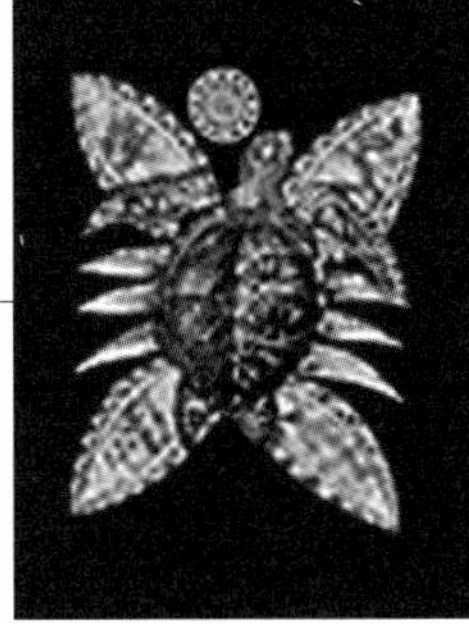

## Version 2. By Manuel Fernandez Juncos

La tierra de Borinquen
donde he nacido yo
Es un jardín florido
de mágico primor.

Un cielo siempre nítido
nos sirve de dosel,
Y dan arrullo plácido
las olas a su pies.

Cuando a sus playas llegó Colón
exclamó de admiración:

O, o, esta es la linda tierra
que busco yo.
Es Borinquen la hija,
la hija del mar y el sol
Del mar y el sol, del mar y el sol,
Del mar y el sol, del mar y el sol.

The land of Borinquen
where I was born
is a garden full of flowers
with magical charm.

A sky always blue
is the canopy above,
and sweet lullabies
sing the waves at its feet.

When on its shores Columbus arrived
he cried, seized with admiration:

Oh! Oh! This is the beautiful land
I'm looking for
Borinquen is the daughter
born from the sea and the sun,
the sea and the sun,
the sea and the sun.

---

**Source:** *Deborah Menkart and Catherine A. Sunshine, Eds.,* Caribbean Connections: Puerto Rico *(Washington: Ecumenical Program on Central America and the Caribbean and Network of Educators on Central America, 1990).*

# Lesson 3.3 Puerto Rico's Political Status

**Objective:** To engage students in a consideration of the economic and social impacts of potential changes in the political status of Puerto Rico.

**Themes:** self-determination, development, democratic decision-making

**Vocabulary:** commonwealth, sovereign

## Suggested Activities

1. As a research project, you may wish to assign students to look up information about the establishment of the state where they live. As a class discussion or a writing assignment, ask them to compare their state's history with Puerto Rico's. What similarities and differences can they identify between Puerto Rico's historical development and the process through which their state became part of the United States? This optional activity will provide a useful background perspective for the other suggested activities in this lesson.
2. Have students read the overview section of this chapter. Then have them review the chart at the end of this lesson on Puerto Rico's political status. You may wish to explain to them that some important questions about political status have not yet been decided. Examples include:
   - What would happen with the use of the Spanish language in Puerto Rico if Puerto Rico were to become a U.S. state?
   - What would happen to the U.S. citizenship of Puerto Ricans if Puerto Rico were to become an independent nation? What about families with some members on the island and some on the mainland — would they be able to immigrate freely if Puerto Rico and the United States were separate countries?
   - How would an independent Puerto Rico develop an independent economy? Would Puerto Rico be able to maintain its infrastructure and build up a range of indus tries? Would it remain economically dependent on the United States?
3. Ask students to answer the following questions:
   - What are the major similarities and differences between the three status options for Puerto Rico?
   - What are the major changes that would occur in Puerto Rico if it were to become another state of the United States?
   - What are the major changes that would occur in Puerto Rico if it were to become an independent nation?
   - In your opinion, what are some of the advantages of Puerto Rico becoming a U.S. state? What are the disadvantages?
   - In your opinion, what are the advantages of Puerto Rico becoming an independent nation? What are the disadvantages?

- In your opinion, what are the advantages of Puerto Rico remaining as a commonwealth of the United States? What are the disadvantages?

4. Have the class hold their own plebiscite on the issue of the status of Puerto Rico. Explain to the students that they should base their vote on what they have researched, read, and discussed in class. They are being asked to assume the role of the Puerto Rican people and vote for the status they believe is the best for Puerto Rico. For the purposes of this exercise, you may wish to limit students to a choice between statehood or independence. Before the vote, you may wish to have the class hold a debate in which they defend their beliefs about which is the best option for the status of Puerto Rico.

5. Now tell the students they must develop a plan of action for implementing the winning option. Their plan should address the following questions:

   - What should be the first actions taken to implement the winning option — in government, the judicial system, citizenship, economics, education, social programs, and cultural and language issues?
   - How will they address the possible political pressure or resistance coming from the people that voted for the opposite status option? For example, if statehood were to win, what would you tell those Puerto Ricans who voted for independence be cause they did not want to be permanent citizens of the United States? Alternatively, if independence were to win, what would you tell those Puerto Ricans who voted for statehood because they did not want Puerto Rico to be an independent nation?

6. As a final activity, have students imagine that the status determined in their plebiscite has now been in operation for fifty years. Ask them to describe the Puerto Rico of fifty years in the future and explain how any changes came about.

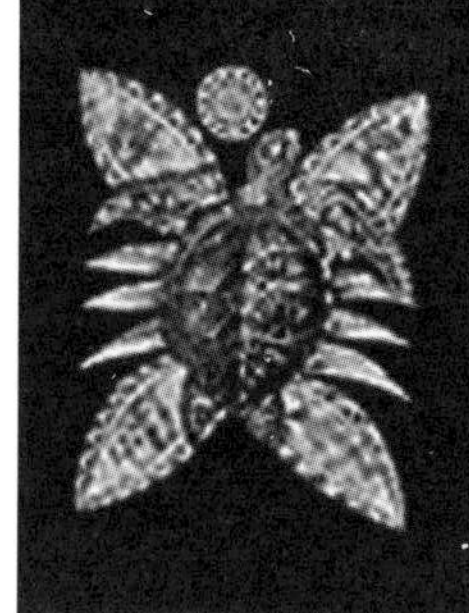

# Chart: Three Options for Political Status

## Commonwealth

**Puerto Rico has commonwealth status today (1998). This status has the following characteristics:**

Puerto Ricans are citizens of the United States and can travel freely within U.S. territory.

Puerto Rico has its own constitution. The Puerto Rican government has control over most domestic affairs, but not foreign affairs. The United States regulates Puerto Rico's contact with other countries.

Puerto Ricans living in Puerto Rico cannot vote for the president of the United States.

If the draft were reinstated, Puerto Ricans could be drafted into the U.S. military.

Puerto Rico sends one nonvoting representative to the U.S. Congress.

The Puerto Rican governor and the members of the Puerto Rican House and Senate are elected by popular vote.

The United States can control the use of the Puerto Rican National Guard.

U.S. environmental laws apply to Puerto Rico. However, they are not enforced as strictly in Puerto Rico as they are in the United States.

The United States controls Puerto Rico's postal and immigration regulations.

Puerto Ricans do not pay federal taxes, although they do pay taxes to the commonwealth government.

The United States provides for Puerto Rico's defense.

The U.S. military uses Puerto Rico as a base in the Caribbean and as a military testing site for weapons.

## Statehood

**If Puerto Rico became a state of the United States, it would have the following characteristics:**

All Puerto Ricans would be U.S. citizens, with the right to travel freely throughout U.S. territory.

In time, Puerto Rico would most likely lose a sense of being its own country. Only the U.S. flag and national anthem would be honored. Schools would teach U.S. history and culture even more than they do today.

People living in the state of Puerto Rico would vote in all federal elections (including for president of the United States). Puerto Rico would have a state constitution, and representatives would be elected to a state legislature.

If the draft were reinstated, Puerto Ricans could be drafted into the U.S. military.

The state of Puerto Rico would have voting representatives in both houses of the U.S. Congress.

The state of Puerto Rico would have a governor like all other states in the United States.

The federal government would control the use of Puerto Rico's National Guard, as it does with all states.

Puerto Rican state laws plus U.S. federal environmental laws would protect the environment.

All U.S. federal regulations would also apply to the state of Puerto Rico.

Puerto Ricans would pay federal taxes, as well as state and local taxes.

The United States would provide for the defense of Puerto Rico, as it does for all states in the United States.

The U.S. military could continue to use Puerto Rico as a base in the Caribbean and as a military testing site for weapons.

## Independence

**If Puerto Rico became independent, it would be a sovereign nation, with the same control of its own affairs as any country. It would have the following characteristics:**

Citizens of both Puerto Rico and the United States would no longer automatically have the right to travel between the two countries. They would be subject to the immigration laws of both countries.

Puerto Rico would have its own constitution with control over domestic and foreign affairs. For example, Puerto Rico might be free to do more trading with countries other than the United States.

Puerto Ricans living in Puerto Rico would no longer be citizens of the United States. They would not vote in U.S. elections, but in their own elections.

Puerto Rico would have its own government, including representative bodies and elected officials.

Puerto Rico would elect a president with more power than the current governor. The House and Senate, or their equivalents, would have more power than the current Puerto Rican House and Senate.

The Puerto Rican National Guard would no longer be controlled by the U.S. government.

Puerto Rico would make and enforce its own laws to protect the environment.

Puerto Rico would develop its own postal and immigration regulations.

Puerto Ricans would pay taxes to their own government.

Puerto Rico would have to develop its own military defense.

The U.S. military would no longer be able to use Puerto Rico as a base in the Caribbean and as a military testing site for weapons, unless a special agreement were negotiated between the two countries.

# THE PACIFIC AND ASIA

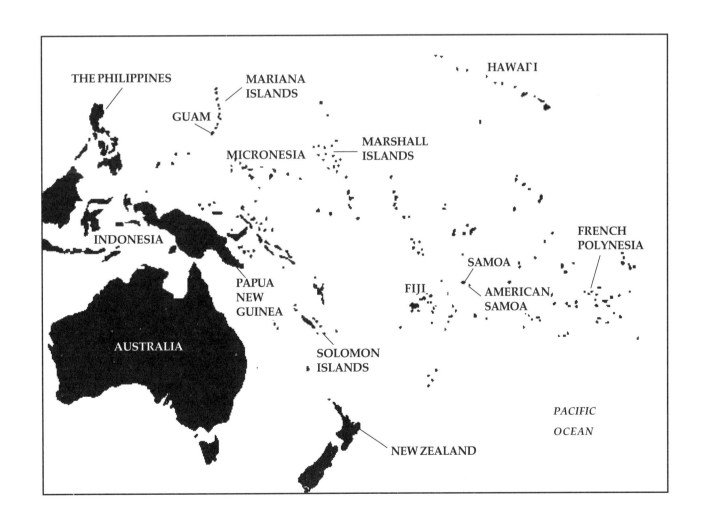

THE PHILIPPINES
MARIANA ISLANDS
GUAM
MICRONESIA
MARSHALL ISLANDS
HAWAIʻI
INDONESIA
PAPUA NEW GUINEA
AUSTRALIA
SOLOMON ISLANDS
FIJI
SAMOA
AMERICAN SAMOA
FRENCH POLYNESIA
PACIFIC OCEAN
NEW ZEALAND

# American Samoa

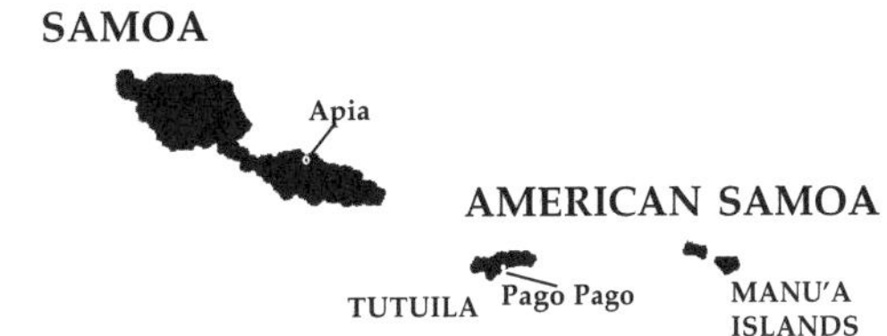


Dan Taulapapa McMullin

SAMOA is an archipelago with twelve principal islands that are united by a common language, history, and culture. It is located in the South Pacific basin, enjoying a central position among the islands and archipelagos of Fiji, Tonga, Tahiti, Tokelau, Niue, and many other island nations, all lying south of the equator and north of Aotearoa (New Zealand).

The Eastern Samoan islands were seized by the United States in the aftermath of the Spanish-American War. Following on the Treaty of Paris of 1898, the Berlin Treaty of 1899 divided Samoa into two colonies, German (Western) Samoa and American (Eastern) Samoa, which was also known as Tutuila Naval Station. Western Samoa, including the islands of Upolu, Savai'i, Manono, Apolima, and others, became a German colony, passing under New Zealand's colonial administration after World War I as a protectorate of the League of Nations. In 1962, Western Samoa became the first Pacific Island nation to gain its independence from Western colonization; it changed its name to Samoa in 1997.

Eastern Samoa, which includes Tutuila Island, several smaller islands, and the Manu'a Group, composed of Ta'u, Olosega, and Ofu islands and some outlying atolls, became a U.S. colony under the Berlin Treaty, and so it has remained to this day. Before colonization, Tutuila was politically allied to Atua in Western Samoa. Manu'a was always its own political body, although linked culturally to the other islands; it is believed to be the first Pacific homeland of the Polynesian people, before they began spreading to Tonga, Tahiti, and elsewhere.

American Samoa (or, as it is known in Samoan, "Amerika Samoa") was administered by the U.S. Navy from the turn of the century until it was transferred to the Department of the Interior in 1951. Since 1977, the governor has been locally elected; previously this post was filled by appointment by U.S. authorities. As with Guam and Puerto Rico, one nonvoting representative from American Samoa sits in the U.S. Congress. Pago Pago Harbor, the capital of American Samoa and a major harbor in the South Pacific, was used as a U.S. naval base from 1904 to 1951. Today, there are no U.S. military bases as such in American Samoa, although the airport in Tafuna serves as a military stopover, since it is the only U.S. territory located south of the equator.

This chapter focuses on the direct effects of colonization in Samoa. Several other key issues that affect Samoa, as well as other Pacific islands, are important to mention, although a full exploration lies beyond the scope of this guide. These include the nuclear issue in the Pacific, the honoring of territorial water rights by other nations, and global warming.

After years of protest by Pacific Islanders, a recent test ban has halted nuclear testing, but nuclear disposal and transport are still a major problem. The United States, France, Japan, and other advanced industrial nations have utilized lands and waters in the Pacific to dispose of radioactive waste, against the wishes of indigenous peoples. Also at issue is the right of indigenous peoples to control the traditional fishing waters of their countries, which have been overfished by mechanized fleets from Japan, the United States, and elsewhere.

Global warming, also known as the "greenhouse effect," poses a major threat to many island nations, including Samoa. Global warming is caused by the generation of excess carbon dioxide through industry and the use of automobiles, with the advanced industrial nations, especially the United States, contributing the lion's share. Most scientists believe that global warming will provoke an overall rise in the sea level as the polar ice caps melt due to an increase in atmospheric temperature.

Islands, especially in the tropics, are the first to feel the effects, and many are already witnessing a rise in water levels, with potentially devastating consequences. American Samoa is currently building ramparts along the shores of Tutuila

***This 1929 photograph shows a traditional Samoan dwelling.***

Island to counter shoreline damage. The Kyoto Treaty of 1997 represents a small first step to control emissions of greenhouse gases, but falls far short of providing an adequate response to the problem (and, at this writing, its ratification by the U.S. Congress is far from certain). Despite making the world's largest contribution to global warming, the United States has failed to take a leadership role in preventing the warming trend.

## Samoa *Vavau*: Old Samoa

Samoa is an ancient country with long traditions. Samoan families can trace their genealogies back a thousand years or more, illustrating the importance of genealogy in maintaining family obligations and communal land rights.

Samoans descend from the Lapita people, who came to the Pacific from the island of Pulotu. The old religion of Samoa teaches that all Samoans return to Pulotu at death. From the easternmost tip of the island of Ta'u, their spirits travel the ridges westward, leaping from sacred rocks into the ocean and scaling the ridges of each island in the Samoan archipelago.

***An 1896 German engraving showing a Samoan warrior.***

Finally, at the westernmost tip of Savai'i, at a place called Falealupo, they descend to the ocean for Pulotu. At the gate waits Pili, a great chief of old Samoa.

Pili, who came from Manu'a, divided Samoa into the confederations of precolonial times. A Pili is mentioned in Hawaiian tradition as an ancestor who came to Hawai'i from Samoa. In the nineteenth century, King Kalākaua, one of Hawai'i's last monarchs, wrote,

> . . . But stronger leaders were soon to follow from the south. Among the first was the high priest Paao, from Samoa. The people were in an unsettled condition politically, and Paao, grasping the situation, either sent or returned in person to Samoa for Pili, a distinguished chief of that island. Arriving with a large following, Pili assumed the sovereignty of the island of Hawai`i and founded a new dynasty. Paao became his high priest . . . and from him the last of the priesthood, 700 hundred years after, claimed lineage and right of place.*

This Pili must have come after the original Pili and may have taken the title with him to Hawai`i. There are many such instances in the genealogies of Polynesian peoples who crossed from archipelago to archipelago, for instance, Lata of Tutuila, who built a great ship and became the Rata of Aotearoa (New Zealand.) For many hundreds of years after the first peoples from Manu'a went to the then-uninhabited islands of the Tuamotus, Tonga, and Tahiti, tributes were still sent to the Tui (ruler) of Manu'a. This sacred and ancient title of Tui Manu'a lasted for centuries, perhaps millennia, until the era

*From King David Kalākaua, *The Legends and Myths of Hawai`i* (Honolulu: Mutual Publishing, 1995) pp. 20-21. First published 1888.

FREE LIBRARY OF PHILADELPHIA

***Snapshot of three Samoan dancers. This photograph was probably taken in the 1940s.***

of U.S. colonial domination. The family of the Tui Manu'a was called "Moa" and the word "*sa*" means "clan," so it is possible that Samoa also takes its name from the Tui Manu'a.

Two of the most important figures in Samoan history are Nafanua and her descendent Salamasina, who lived around the fourteenth century AD (by the Western calendar). Nafanua came from Manu'a and introduced many of the social practices of Samoan society, known as *faasamoa,* the Samoan way. *Faasamoa* is practiced today by Samoan families in Aotearoa, Australia, Hawai'i, and the United States, as well as in Samoa. The *autalavou* or youth groups of Samoan churches are important learning grounds for Samoan cultural practices; there is an active and continual community dialogue about how to blend useful contemporary ways and the *faasamoa.* These customs are especially important in the political life and in oratory and behavior in the *fono* (Samoan family or village meetings). Nafanua became deified after her death and, until Christianity was introduced in Samoa, she took part in political decisions through *taulaitu* or mediums in Savai'i. Even today Nafanua is invoked at important Samoan gatherings. She is the goddess of war, but also of peace.

Nafanua's descendant Salamasina was the greatest ruler of Old Samoa or Samoa *Vavau* (except Manu'a). During her lifetime Samoa enjoyed peace and a general cultural flowering. She was empowered by her own abilities and her familial connections to hold all the most important titles of Samoa.

Samoa has always maintained strong connections with other island nations, especially Tonga and Fiji. For a long time, Tonga controlled Samoa militarily, until an uprising was led from Tuamasaga (c. 1200 AD). Forced to flee, the king of Tonga, the Tui Tonga, from his ship praised the Samoan leaders of the uprising, saying *"Malie tau. Mailie toa!"* (brave fight, great warrior). Since that time the ruler of Tuamasaga as been known as Malietoa. When John Williams, an English missionary, arrived in Samoa in 1830, the current Malietoa was engaged in another war to gain power over the greater part of Samoa. Williams the missionary and Malietoa became allies, and since that time the title of Malietoa has gained ascendancy in the western islands of Samoa. The current Malietoa is the head of state of (Western) Samoa, which uses a parliamentary form of government. In general, decision making in Samoa, like land ownership, tends to be a communal process, although there are several high titles besides Malietoa.

## Samoa's Communal Land System

Although Samoa and American Samoa are divided politically, the people of Samoa have always considered all these islands to be one homeland. Democracy has many forms and not all of them are Western. Samoans have maintained their culture in part by maintaining *faasamoa,* the Samoan way. *Faasamoa* includes communal land ownership: almost all of the land in Samoa is owned by *aiga* (family groups) and is administered by *matai* (family chiefs). The *matai,* however do not make decisions without meeting in *fono* (community meetings).

In maintaining land ownership by *aiga,* Samoa ensured that it would not be entirely dispossessed of its sovereignty. For example,

American Samoa's park lands are the only ones in the U.S. National Park system that are not owned by the U.S. government: they are leased. In other parts of Polynesia, the forced privatization of land has led to land becoming a commodity, that is, something that can be bought and sold. This "commodification" has led in turn to the loss of indigenous lands, for example, in Hawai`i, where in the 1800s settlers from the United States forced the traditional chiefs to privatize communal lands. The privatization of land represents a fundamental departure from the Polynesian communal land system, which for thousands of years has maintained a stable social and political system of indigenous sovereignty. More recently, ecologists have recognized that indigenous stewardship ensures the most long-lasting preservation of land, while the Western system of private land ownership has resulted in widespread degradation of the environment, not only in the Pacific but worldwide, especially in those areas that have historically been subjected to colonization.

## Nonviolence and the Mau

Even before Gandhi's nonviolent protests freed India from British colonial rule in 1947, the Samoan people were engaged in nonviolent protest against the administration of New Zealand in Western Samoa and the U.S. Navy in American Samoa. Although the colonial administrations in both instances sought to suppress these movements, which were known as the Mau, they eventually led to independence for Western Samoa. American Samoa remains a colony, but the Mau succeeded in winning the replacement of the U.S. Navy with a civilian U.S. administration.

The Mau was influenced by the belief in peacemaking, common to Samoan Christianity and traditional Samoan culture, as well as the traditional Samoan belief in *malo,* strong government that attends to the needs of the people. The Mau began in Western Samoa following the global influenza epidemic of 1918, which killed 20 or 25 percent of the Samoan population. Many Samoans died because of racist policies exercised by New Zealand, including the colonial administrator's refusal of medical help offered from Pago Pago.

The Mau began with nonpayment of taxes and a series of nonviolent marches, mostly in Apia, the capital of Western Samoa. Violent responses by the New Zealand military caused the death of Tupua Tamasese, an eloquent high chief and a leader of the movement. Tamasese was shot in the back while encouraging his people to refrain from killing in reprisal (see Lesson 5.4).

The Mau was a nationwide movement by men and women of Samoa, many of whom were killed or exiled. In American Samoa the U.S. Naval Administration imposed martial law, effectively preventing an uprising of the Mau. Several U.S. naval officers, both active and retired, supported the Mau movement; these sympathizers, as well as Samoan Mau supporters of mixed blood, were transferred or exiled to the U.S. mainland or refused re-entry to Samoa when returning from foreign travel.

For native Samoans, the racial prejudice, limitations of civil rights, and lax moral standards of the U.S. Navy were antagonistic to their way of life. The *palagi* (whites) introduced to Samoan society the racial segregation they were familiar with in the United States. For example, when the first movie theater opened in Samoa, a rope separated the front seats, which were reserved for *palagi* families, from the back seats, where native Samoan families were to sit. The Amerika Samoa Mau wanted a civil government and a return to the spirit of the Deeds of Cession of 1900 and 1904, which the chiefs of Samoa were originally made to sign. From the viewpoint of Samoans, these documents guaranteed U.S. protection of Samoan sovereignty and *faasamoa.* It should be noted that these treaties are interpreted differently by Samoans and the United States, based on

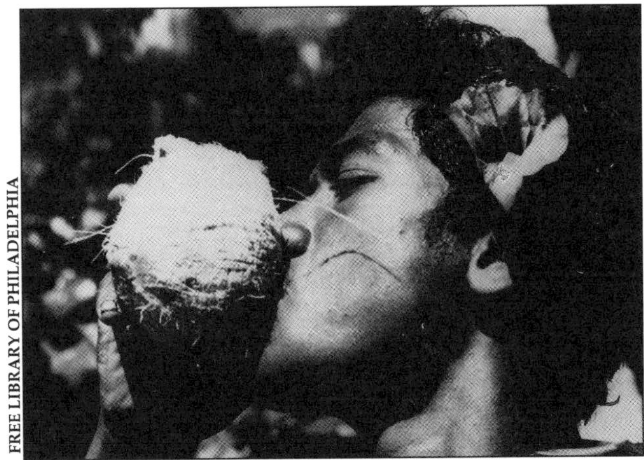

FREE LIBRARY OF PHILADELPHIA

***Still photographs from a 1972 documentary on public television, "American Samoa: Paradise Lost?" Images like these offer rich opportunities for discussion of Western perceptions of Pacific Islander cultures as "primitive" and idyllic.***

differences between the Samoan-language version and the English version.

## Whose Education?

In Old Samoa, education was transmitted through the oral tradition, which is still greatly respected in Samoa. Since the first arrival of Western missionaries in the 1830s, however, foreign educators have sought to indoctrinate Samoans with a belief in the superiority of their

FREE LIBRARY OF PHILADELPHIA

***Another still from the 1972 public TV documentary. The original caption for this photo reads as follows: "Samoan children, docile by habit, are being encouraged to develop their independence through Western influences." Lesson 4.3, "Whose Education?," explores the Samoan experience of attempts to "Americanize" their culture.***

written culture over Samoan oral culture, especially Samoan spiritual and historical traditions. Nonetheless, Samoans have kept much of the old oral culture alive and have adapted Western and Christian beliefs to their own culture.

During the 1960s, American Samoa was used by the United States as a testing ground for television education. For many Samoans this represented their introduction to electronic media as well as consumer culture. Recently, due to community complaints about a decline in traditional Samoan courtesies among the young, Samoan educators have reinstituted a Samoan-language curriculum for the first four years of schooling. Previously, all education was conducted in English. Overall policy for Samoan education is influenced by the Pacific Regional Education Laboratory, a U.S.-based nonprofit organization. Currently there is no policy mandating the education of Samoan students in Samoan history and literature, while U.S. history and literature are taught.

Samoans and other Pacific Islanders are greatly concerned with attaining access to higher education, to enable the people to make personal, family, village, and national decisions based on a thorough understanding of the contemporary world. Many more powerful nations, including the United States, France, the United Kingdom,

Australia, New Zealand, China, and Japan, are interested in the resources and labor of Pacific Island nations, as well as their strategic location. Often, however, they would rather not see Samoa, Tahiti, Hawai`i, Guam, or Tonga as independent self-managing Pacific nations. Teresia Teaiwa, a poet and professor at the University of the South Pacific in Fiji, has said,

> In the South Pacific, the curricula are decided by the [colonial] governments through their ministries of education. Emphases in the curricula are often determined by the governments' development interests — often called "needs" — and also the aid donors' interests. What is needed is more Pacific Islanders in higher education; more enlightened Pacific Island leaders who will value education and not just training, and who will take the risk of rejecting unjust demands for conforming to an economic order determined by the World Trade Organization and the World Bank, which are partially responsible for the poverty of our education system.*

## Economic Dependency

The three greatest sources of income for American Samoa are funds from the U.S. federal government for infrastructure and territorial administration, remittances from family members living on the U.S. mainland, and a U.S.-owned Star-Kist fish cannery in Pago Pago.

The traditional economy of the islands was based on local farming and fishing. Marketing of U.S. goods, including cheap consumer products and dried, canned, and frozen foods, has undermined trading in these areas, causing declines in production by farmers and fishers. As a result, the practice of these skills has also declined, especially on Tutuila, where the colonial presence has created a population boom, and also on Manu'a, where local farming and fishing were banned in most areas by the U.S. government in the 1990s, when large tracts of land were declared to be U.S. national parks.

An industrial park was created on Tutuila in the 1980s to facilitate the sale of imported consumer goods from the United States and Japan. A clothing factory has been built there, but the majority of its labor force is from China. Support for an independent local economy would lead to greater political independence for Samoa.

---

**Vocabulary:** archipelago, protectorate, colonization, atolls, genealogies, dispossessed, sovereignty, martial law, remittances

## References

*The information in this chapter draws extensively on Samoan oral tradition. Below are some additional published sources for this material.*

*O le Mavaega i le Tai* (Apia, Samoa: Malua Printing and Publishing, 1988). A collection of traditional Samoan oral history and belief.

E. Schultz, Ed., *Alaga'upu Fa'aSamoa— Samoan Proverbial Expressions* (Auckland, New Zealand: Polynesian Press, 1994).

King David Kalakaua, *The Legends and Myths of Hawai`i* (Honolulu: Mutual Publishing, 1995). First printed 1888.

Michael Field, *Mau, Samoa's Struggle for Freedom* (Honolulu: University of Hawai`i Press, 1990).

Augustin Kramer, *The Samoan Islands* (Honolulu: University of Hawai`i Press, 1994). Originally published 1901.

Richard Moyle, *Traditional Samoan Music* (Auckland, New Zealand: Auckland University Press, 1988).

*Cited in Dan Taulapapa McMullin, "Education as Elision," presented at XCP Poetics Conference, University of Minnesota, Minneapolis, 1997.

# LESSON 4.1 The Oral Tradition

**Objective:** To introduce students to Samoa's oral tradition by presenting a creation story from a Pacific Islander perspective.

**Themes:** oral tradition, religion, creation stories

**Vocabulary:** appendage

## Suggested Activities

1. Hand out the excerpt from "O le Solo o le Va" included at the end of this lesson. Explain to students that this is a creation story from Samoa. They will need a vocabulary list to help them understand the Samoan names:

   **Tagaloa:** A great god who created Samoa and the Samoan people

   **Manu'a, Upolu, Tutuila, Atua, Aana, Tuamasaga:** Islands and districts in the Samoan archipelago

2. Ask students to tell the Samoan creation story in their own words. Ask them to compare this story with other creation stories they might be familiar with (for example, the Garden of Eden or classical Greek mythology). In what ways are these stories the same? In what ways are they different? What role does the poem say "the soul" has for people?
3. Ask students to use their imagination, depicting the Samoan creation story by drawing pictures, composing a song, or creating a dance or dramatization.

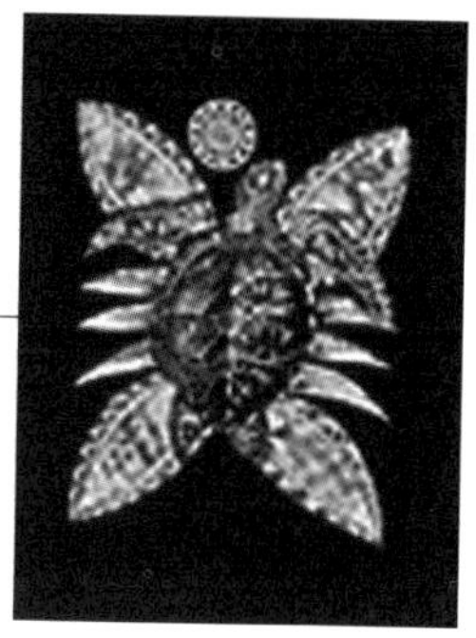

# Reading: Excerpt from "O le Solo o le Va"

*This excerpt presents part of a creation song from Manu'a, in which the great god Tagaloa brings the islands of Samoa up from the sea. Tagaloa creates the first people from grubs climbing out of decayed creeper vines and gives them souls to illumine their bodies.*

He flew across his islands in the west,
He weighed and measured,
If the space between the islands were the same.
Tagaloa climbed upon your mountains,
But stayed on the mountain of Manu'a.
Unthinkably long the island sea lay under the winds,
And Tagaloa was startled by the terrible waves.
He called to heaven for a few small pebbles;
Upolu was only a small rock,
Tutuila was a small pebble,
He enlarged the islands by lifting them up
As a resting place for the chiefs,
All of whom look towards Tagaloa.
Tagaloa sent down the creepers
To populate Tutuila with them,
And Upolu, Atua, and Aana
Together with Tuamasaga.
But soulless moved their bodies,
They could not sit and had no heart.
Tagaloa heard up above
That human beings had come into being from the creepers
That they moved in the sun,
But without feet and without hands,
Without head, without face
And without heart.
Tagaloa came down in the west
That he might bring them speech and form.
The fruits of the creepers were grubs,
He pulled out the limbs and showed the appendages.
He brought down your soul,
That it might illumine your body,
And that you might await Tagaloa when he descends to walk about.

---

**Source:** *from "O le Solo o le Va o le Foafoaga o le Lalolagi," a traditional song from Manu'a. English translation by Theodore Verhaaren from a German translation by Augustin Kramer. Quoted in A. Kramer,* The Samoan Islands *(Honolulu: University of Hawai`i Press, 1994), Vol. I, pp. 541-42. Originally published 1901.*

# Lesson 4.2 Economic Dependency

**Objectives:** To introduce students to the dynamics of economic dependency in a country like Samoa; to have students explore the use of drama and symbolism to express political concepts.

**Themes:** economic dependency, self-reliance, literary expression, art and politics

**Vocabulary:** outrigger, rudder, wake

## Suggested Activities

1. Review the background of the Mau movement with students. Explain that the play *The Demon Anchors* takes place during the period when this movement was active.
2. Hand out the excerpt from *The Demon Anchors* at the end of this lesson and have students take turns reading the roles out loud. After the students have read through the excerpt, ask them to describe Uncle Eliko and Young Lolo, taking into consideration the political turmoil occurring in Samoa during the time of this play.
3. Examine the passage below and ask them what the fog might be symbolic of. How does Uncle Eliko's view of the fog differ from Young Lolo's? Why does Uncle Eliko feel it is so important to teach Young Lolo to fish?

   *Uncle Eliko:* Don't worry, boy, this fog will let up or we can find our way back if it doesn't.

   *Young Lolo:* It's been two days. I can't see the water. I can hardly see you.
4. What do students believe motivated Uncle Eliko to stop Lolo from seeking help from the U.S. naval patrol boat and make him swim home? Is Uncle Eliko being unkind, or is there a loving purpose behind his stern behavior? (If students ask, you may wish to tell them that Lolo does make his way home safely, and that this play is based on true stories.)
5. What is Uncle Eliko trying to teach Lolo? Is it merely a lesson on fishing? Ask students to consider other questions about economic independence, tradition, culture, and resistance that might be embedded in the fishing lesson.
6. How do students think tradition and culture are affected by economics? What do they believe might have happened to traditional practices like shark fishing as the Samoan economic base of fishing and farming has been undermined?

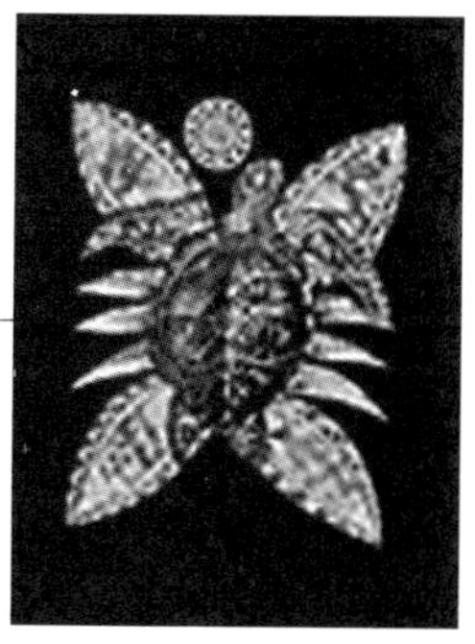

# Reading: "The Shark"

*"The Shark" is a scene from the play The Demon Anchors by Samoan-American playwright Dan Taulapapa McMullin. The scene takes place during the 1920s at the time of the Mau movement, a nonviolent protest movement seeking an end to colonial rule in Samoa. An old Samoan* tautai *(the head of a family's fishing outrigger) named Eliko tries to instill a sense of self-sufficiency in his young relative, Lolo. In Samoan society both past and present, the young are expected to respect and serve their elders, during ceremonies, at work, and in everyday life. At sea, with its many dangers, the* tautai *holds complete authority. In Old Samoa, sharks were caught by dropping a noose over the side of a canoe into the sea. A special shark rattle was shaken in the water to attract the shark; when it swam into the noose the shark was jerked out of the water and clubbed.*

*Uncle Eliko:* Lolo!

*Young Lolo:* Yes, Uncle Eliko!

*Uncle Eliko:* Lolo!

*Young Lolo:* Yes, Uncle?

*Uncle Eliko:* Stay awake and keep paddling or I will knock your head off with the rudder!

*Young Lolo:* Yes, sir.

*Uncle Eliko:* Don't worry, boy, this fog will let up or we can find our way back if it doesn't.

*Young Lolo:* It's been two days. I can't see the water, I can hardly see you.

*Uncle Eliko:* Keep paddling. There are bonito here.

*Young Lolo:* Listen!

*Uncle Eliko:* Keep paddling.

*Young Lolo:* Listen!

*Uncle Eliko:* Shut up.

*Young Lolo:* Look! Lights! I bet it's the patrol boat! Hey!

*Uncle Eliko:* Shut up.

*Young Lolo:* But . . .

*Uncle Eliko:* Quiet.

*Young Lolo:* Uncle . . .

*Uncle Eliko:* I'll be damned if the U.S. Navy is going to help me find my own island.

*Young Lolo:* But . . .

*Uncle Eliko:* Quiet, my boy.

*Young Lolo:* They're leaving. They're gone.

*Uncle Eliko:* Samuelu is your second name. After your Uncle Samuelu. He was stupid enough to write to the President of the United States.

*Young Lolo:* I know he was.

*Uncle Eliko:* Asking that he remove the U.S. Navy from Eastern Samoa. And what was the answer to Samuelu? They ship him out. As though this was not his home. This place. Tutuila.

*Young Lolo:* Yes.

*Uncle Eliko:* We will never see him again. And

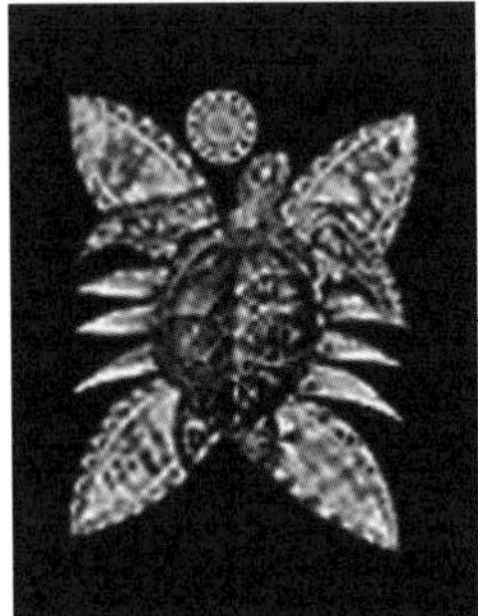

now they want soldiers for their own wars. I'll be damned if the U.S. Navy will take me home. Keep paddling.

*Young Lolo:* Yes, Uncle Eliko.

*Uncle Eliko:* There's bonito here. They are here! Faster. Faster! Your poles now! Your poles!

*Young Lolo:* Shark! A shark!

*Uncle Eliko:* Put the shark rattle in the water. The noose! Hold the noose open in the water, Lolo! On my signal raise it and I'll club the shark! Let it swim into the noose. On my signal!

*Young Lolo:* Its teeth!!

*Uncle Eliko:* Wait! Ah! Damn you! Look! It tore the shirt off my back! On my signal, I said!

*Young Lolo:* I'm sorry! I'm sorry, Uncle Eliko!

*Uncle Eliko:* Get out of my boat! Get out!

*Young Lolo:* Uncle . . .!

*Uncle Eliko:* Get out, damn you! You can swim back!

*Young Lolo:* Uncle. The fog.

*Uncle Eliko:* Swim, Lolo! The fog is letting up. You can follow our wake.

---

**Source:** *from Dan Taulapapa McMullin,* The Demon Anchors. *"The Shark" has been published in* Folauga, A Samoan Language Journal for Young People, *Vol. 2, 1998, published by Learning Media Ltd., Wellington, New Zealand.*

# LESSON 4.3 Whose Education?

**Objective:** To help students reflect on the purposes of education, by exploring the impact of U.S.-oriented education on the people of Samoa.

**Themes:** cultural differences, identity, individualism, socialization

## Suggested Activities

1. Pass out the excerpt "We," which appears at the end of this lesson, and have students read it over.
2. Ask the students why they think Alofa had a problem writing the essay in the way that Miss Cunningham required. Was it a language problem, a lack of motivation, a cultural problem?
3. The reading ends with the sentence:

   "I" is "we" . . . always.

   How do the students understand the meaning of this statement? Can they suggest ways in which Samoan culture might be different from mainstream U.S. culture?
4. Ask the students to focus on the second part of the excerpt, entitled "Girl Lessons." Do the "lessons" described here convey Christian or Old Samoan values? (Some background on Old Samoan values is provided in the overview to this chapter on p. 89.) Do they draw on both? In what ways do these two value systems seem compatible? In what ways might they differ?
5. Ask the students to draw a picture of their home. Which are the "I" areas, and which are the "we" areas? Now ask them to write down everything they have done so far today. Which are the "I" activities, and which are the "we" ones? Is there more "I" or more "we" in their lives? Do they wish the balance were different? In what ways?
6. Ask the students why they think the passage is entitled "Girl Lessons." What would "boy lessons" consist of? Do males and females have a similar experience with the balance between "I" and "we" in their lives?

# Reading: "We"

*The excerpts below are from Samoan novelist Sia Figiel's book,* Where We Once Belonged, *which tells the story of a Samoan girl named Alofa. Note the clash between the expectations of the teacher, who is from the United States, and the culture of her Samoan student. The second part of the excerpt, "Girl Lessons," takes place in Alofa's Sunday school class. In Samoan, the* malae *is the village green, the* faifeau *is the pastor, the* autalavou *is the youth group, the* aoga *is the school, and the* nu'u *is the village.*

When I was in Standard Three the American peace corps, Miss Cunningham, gave the class an essay writing assignment.

Write an essay on one of the following topics:

1. My village.
2. My pet.
3. On my way to School today I saw a . . .

Half the class wrote on "My village." I belonged to the other half who decided to write on topic two, "My pet."

> My family has a pet. His name is Piki. Piki is born last week. Piki is white and is black too. He likes eating pegu. My sisters and me loves him. We loves him because he is good. He is a good piki and he likes to play with us. He is a good piki and we going eat him when he grows up.

"Who does the piggy belong to?" asked Miss Cunningham, as she handed me back my essay.

"He is belongs to me, and to my sisters, and to my brothers, and to my 'aiga. He is our piki," I replied.

"Oh!" said Miss Cunningham, with a smile on her face and her pimples turning red. "I thought you were going to write about *your* pet, *your* piggy? Do you have anything else that doesn't belong to your sisters too? Something *very special* that doesn't belong to your brothers? Like your toothbrush here at school with *your* name written on it? You know, no one else is allowed to brush their teeth with *your* toothbrush, because it has *your* name written on it. Do you have something at home that's the same as *your* toothbrush here at school?"

"Yes, Miss Cunningham," I said proudly. "I have ten sene. It is hiding in a hole under a rock in the garden. No one knows . . . only Piki and me."

*

The next time we had essay writing Miss Cunningham narrowed the range of topics to one. The first time, the whole class had written their essays on "My village" and "My pet." Everyone had avoided writing on "What I saw on my way to school." I didn't know then why I didn't choose essay topic three. I knew only that it was hard to witness something — anything — alone.

You were *always* with someone. I didn't go to school alone. I went to school with Moa and five, maybe even ten other girls at the same time. We all woke up then the sun woke up . . . rolled our sleeping mats . . . washed our faces . . . kae le paepae . . . put on our school uniforms . . . ran to the store to buy bread . . . made tea . . . drank tea . . . carried our books on our right hands while a large piece of buttered bread (with jam, if it was pay day) was attached to our left. We all took the same road to school . . . rode the same bus . . . snuck out of the back of the bus to avoid paying bus-fare . . . teased the old fool, Siniva . . . teased Siniva's dogs . . . threw stones into the Vaipuga . . . played a game of hairpins . . . before we entered the gates of Falelua Primary School.

Nothing was witnessed alone. Nothing was witnessed in the "I" form — nothing but penises and ghosts.

"I" does not exist, Miss Cunningham. "I" is "we" . . . *always.*

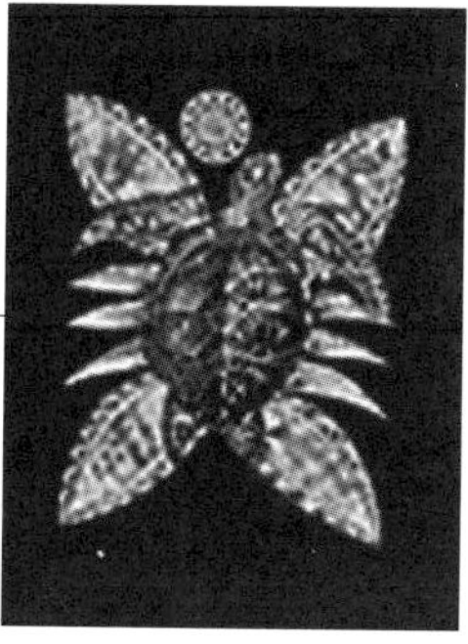

## Girl Lessons

"I" does not exist.

I am not.

My self belongs not to me because "I" does not exist.

"I" is always "we,"

is a part of the 'aiga

a part of the Au a teine,

a part of the Aufaipese

a part of the Autalavou,

a part of the Aoga a le Faifeau,

a part of the Aoga Aso Sa,

a part of the Church,

a part of the nu'u,

a part of Samoa.

*

Girls should come straight home from school, take off their uniforms and hang the bats out — fa'aea le pepe'a. After this ritual of chasing away the scent of flying foxes from the underarms of our uniforms, we were then supposed to have a little something to eat . . . a piece of bread with coconut, if there was any bread, or anything else lying around the sefe.

The bell for the Aoga a le Faifeau or pastor's school rang, rang, and rang around three in the afternoon which everyone under sixteen had to attend — except for Meleane who is eighteen, and all the mothers call fa'akamakama and kids call ai valea, and will probably be in Vasega Ogo for the rest of her life . . . for the rest of her life, re-e-eally!

At the fale o le faifeau we were taught by the pastor to read the Bible correctly. That is, with meek and humble voices. We were taught also to recite passages from the Bible, to recite all the books of the Bible, from Creation to Revelation where the dragon with ten heads lived. Children were asked to recite creation again and again.

"O ai na faia oe?" (Who made you?)

"O ai lou fa'aola?" (Who is your savior?)

"Name all the twelve apostles."

"Which book does one find the wedding in Cana in."

. . . and so on.

The pastor's faletua taught us girls how to sew, how to dress, how to behave. Whenever we didn't behave, she would pull our ears or pull our hair or slap our faces . . . no matter how tall we were, no matter how tall we became.

We were not allowed to laugh too much or too loudly.

We were taught to be meek.

We were taught to be humble, again.

We were taught also to offer our seats to anyone older than us, regardless of location — may it be a crowded bus, a crowded public toilet in Apia, a crowded anything.

Don't walk *and* eat.

Only pigs walk and eat.

Only pigs stuff themselves and walk.

Always take a shower twice a day, once when you wake up and once in the evening — and three times when you are sick from the moon.

Never wear the same panty twice when you have the moon sickness.

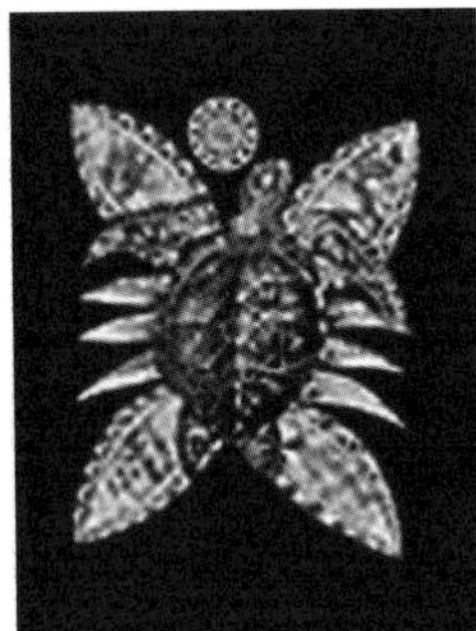

Never laugh at blind people or deaf people . . . or palagis.

Never walk around alone at night — only bad girls and teine o le po walk around that late.

Never wear anything exposing your knees.

Never wear pants on the malae or at the pastor's house.

Never wear high heels.

Never wear make-up.

Never go to church without a hat.

Never go bra-less to church.

Never speak with the "k" in your mouth.*

Never pray for yourself — you should pray for the whole village and for the whole of Samoa.

"We" were taught to mimic Jesus Christ in all that he was, so that "we" too could be good examples of his life.

"We" were young ladies, and "we" should handle ourselves as such.

Therefore:

"I" am "We."

"I" does not exist.

---

*This statement refers to a more casual form of speaking in the Samoan language, as distinct from more polite speech.

---

**Source:** *from Sia Figiel,* Where We Once Belonged *(Honolulu: University of Hawai`i Press, 1997).*

# Lesson 4.4 The Influenza Epidemic of 1918

**Objective:** To help students understand how a serious epidemic became a devastating tragedy for the people of Samoa, owing to the indifference and discriminatory treatment of the colonial administration.

**Themes:** racism, discrimination, cultural memory

**Vocabulary:** influenza, scourge

## Suggested Activities

1. Have the students read the excerpts included at the end of this lesson. Explain that both readings describe an influenza epidemic in Samoa in 1918.
2. Ask students to discuss the attitudes toward the Samoan girls displayed by Colonel Logan, the colonial administrator in the first excerpt. Do they believe that Colonel Logan treated the Samoans fairly? What attitudes do they believe might have underlain his behavior? What differences can they observe in the attitudes and behavior of Moore (the school teacher)?
3. Ask the students to consider everything they have learned about the colonization of Pacific Island and Caribbean nations, in this chapter and the others included in this guide. What attitudes do colonizers typically display toward their colonial subjects? In what ways is this similar to the students' understanding of racism within the United States? In what ways is it different?
4. Ask your class to imagine that they are students at the girls' boarding school. Have them write a letter to a U.S. newspaper describing the influenza epidemic in Samoa and its effect on their families. In their letters they should describe how they have been treated by the colonial administration on the island.
5. The song "Faanoanoa" recalls the grief of Samoans at the loss of 20 to 25 percent of their entire population during the influenza epidemic, which took place eighty years ago. Ask students why they think this epidemic is still recalled. Can they remember any disasters that took place in their community (or their country) a long time ago? Ask them to describe any such events. How does it make them feel to think about it today?

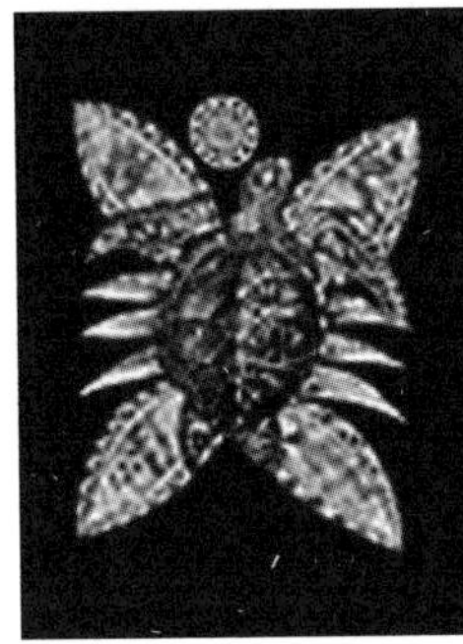

# Readings: The Influenza Epidemic of 1918

*The following excerpt is from* Mau, Samoa's Struggle for Freedom *by Michael Field, which recounts the efforts of the Mau to free Samoa from the colonial administration mandated by the League of Nations. It presents an account by a teacher at a girls' school at which all but one of 120 girls caught influenza. The colonial administrator, Colonel Logan, wanted the ailing girls to help bury the dead in Apia, and threatened the teacher with punitive actions.*

## Papauta Girls' School

When Moore [the school teacher] heard that meat would be distributed at the market hall, she sent a request for ten kilograms of beef so she could have soup made for the 150 sick people [under her care]. Logan was outraged at the request. Moore related what happened next:

It was about 10 am Sunday, November 24 — on the ninth day after the appearance of influenza in our school. About eighty girls were lying ill in the various dormitories, Miss Small was going about among them attending to their wants, while I, with two girls, was on the balcony preparing for burial the girl who had died the day before, when I was summoned below by the loud voice of the administrator calling my name. Scarcely waiting for a greeting, he began — as far as I remember — by saying in a voice which became louder and more angry, "Miss Moore, I believe you have sent down this morning for meat. I wish to inform you that no meat will be given you. I consider this the most disgraceful institution in Samoa, and I intend to inform your headquarters in London of the fact. Send them food! I would rather see them burning in Hell! There is a dead horse at your gate — let them eat that! Great, fat, lazy, loafing creatures" (waving his hand towards the dozen or more miserable convalescents sitting huddled up in their wraps in the native houses). "Send them down to the public burial ground to dig graves! A disgrace to Christianity! I should like to see them all in Hell," etc. etc.

When I remonstrated with him by saying that they were ill, "Let them come and bury the dead!" I told him I was at that moment trying to find any who were strong enough to bury our own dead, but he kept on, "If you do not send me twenty-five girls to help dig graves, I will come back this afternoon and burn down the school," etc.

The proposition being impossible of fulfillment, I said, "Of course, as you know Colonel, they won't come, and if you burn down the school, I can't help it."

At this he became more angry than ever, and shook his stick threateningly, and shouted, "Won't come! I'll see about that I'll make them come," etc., etc., and went away reiterating that he would return in the afternoon and burn down the school.

---

**Source:** *from Michael Field, Mau,* Samoa's Struggle for Freedom *(Honolulu: University of Hawai`i Press, 1990).*

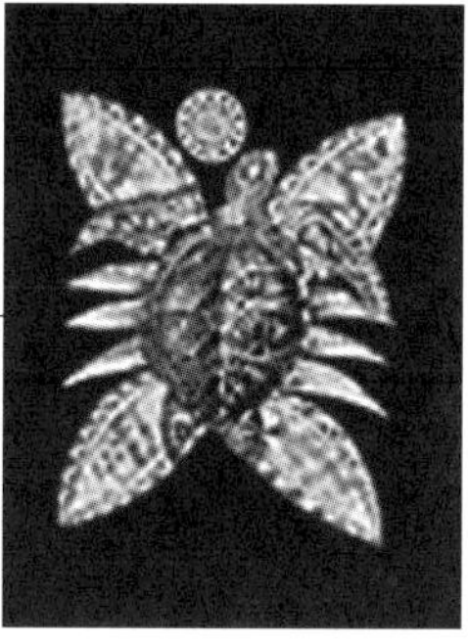

## Faanoanoa

*The song below laments the 1918 epidemic, in which 20 to 25 percent of all Samoans lost their lives. It was sung by Taua Fatu, Paipa So'o, and Matila Logona of Sale'a'aumua village, Upolu, when first recorded; and is quoted in Richard Moyle's Traditional Samoan Music. (The version used here is translated by Dan Taulapapa McMullin.)*

| | | |
|---|---|---|
| **Leader:** | Faanoanoa | *Sorrow,* |
| **Response:** | Faanoanoa e | *Grief!* |
| **Leader:** | Faanoanoa | *Sorrow,* |
| **Response:** | Faanoanoa | *Sorrow.* |
| **Leader:** | Lou alofa i Samoa e | *My love is for Samoa* |
| **Response:** | Talofa i Samoa e | *Alas for Samoa* |
| | Ua maua i le mala | *Caught by the scourge* |
| **All:** | Ua uma e le oti ni aiga | *Entire families dead* |
| | A ua i Vaimea. | *And buried together in Vaimea.* |

---

**Source:** *Richard Moyle,* Traditional Samoan Music *(Auckland, New Zealand: Auckland University Press, 1988).*

# Lesson 4.5 Black Saturday

**Objectives:** To help students reflect on nonviolent resistance as a strategy for winning social change and to introduce them to the Mau movement, which won independence for Western Samoa and a change from a military to a civilian administration in American (Eastern) Samoa.

**Themes:** nonviolence, resistance, social change

## Suggested Activities

1. Ask students if they have ever heard about the use of nonviolent resistance or of some of the leaders of nonviolent resistance movements. In particular, they may be familiar with Gandhi, who led India's movement for independence from Britain in the late 1940s, or Martin Luther King, Jr., a central leader of the U.S. civil rights movement of the 1950s and 1960s.
2. Have students read the excerpt at the end of this lesson. Divide them into small groups and ask them to discuss the ways in which nonviolent movements are effective. What have been some of the achievements of such movements, and what have been their limitations? Do they believe that participants in such movements are wise or foolish? Encourage them to reflect on the experience of the civil rights movement in the United States, as well as on the information provided about Samoa.
3. Write the following phrases from the passage on the board:

   *Uma, uma . . . onosa'i, onosa'i.*
   Finish, finish, be patient.
   They are few, we are many.
   They are guests in our country.
   He called out "keep the peace."

   Ask students to use these phrases in a poem that expresses their response to the reading on the Mau movement.

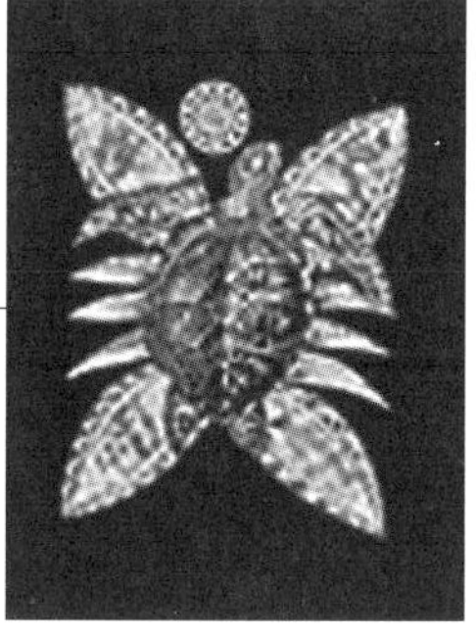

# Reading: "Black Saturday"

*This excerpt from* Mau: Samoa's Struggle for Freedom *recounts the death of independence leader Tupua Tamasese during a nonviolent march by the Mau through Apia, in the aftermath of the influenza epidemic.*

Tupua Tamasese arrived at the 'Ifi'ifi-Beach Roads junction as Waterson began using the machine-gun. Frightened Mau supporters were still walking into the intersection, exposing themselves to machine-gun and rifle fire. Dressed in a white jacket and white lavalava, carrying a rolled-up umbrella and holding both his arms high in the air, Tupua Tamasese walked into the open calling out in both Samoan and English, "Filemu Samoa, peace Samoa."

Standing between a lamp post and the administration offices in 'Ifi'ifi Road, just back from the intersection, he called up each road to the oncoming Mau, "Uma, uma . . . onosa'i , onosa'i." "Finish, finish, be patient." Another witness said he called out to the Mau, "They are few, we are many. They are guests in our country . . ."

Standing virtually alone in the open and on occasion with his back to the police station, Tupua Tamasese was dangerously exposed to the hail of bullets. Over the noise his strong, clear voice could be heard by both the police and the Mau as he called for peace. With his arms high in the air, his actions were anything but aggressive. As he made his desperate appeal, McMillan, Cahill, or Spark — we will never know who, nor whether they were acting on orders — aimed a Lee Enfield rifle at his back and pulled the trigger. The .303 bullet struck him in the upper right thigh, chewed its way through the muscle and shattered the femur and pelvis. Tupua Tamasese collapsed to the ground in great pain.

Su'a remembered events clearly: "He called out — to the west and to the east — "keep the peace." . . . He was walking; he was calling out and raised his hands, saying "stop — keep the peace" . . . One shot was fired before the machine-gun fired; that was the shot which hit Tamasese."

Su'a, Faualo and Tufuga were standing nearby when he fell, and they ran to his aid, despite the continuing rifle and machine-gun fire. Tufuga was the first to reach him. "I tried to lift up Tamasese's head, and as I was doing that I was hit in both legs."

Su'a tried to shelter the wounded chief with his own body and was hit as well. So was Faualo. Two others, Migao and a youth, Tu'ia, ran after the other three towards the chief and were seen by Avea, the woman in 'Ifi'ifi Road, as they were hit by what she said was machine-gun fire. They were dead within minutes . . .

Eventually the firing stopped as the police realized they were not, and had never been, under attack. The Mau began to pick up their dead and wounded and head back to Vaimoso. As they did the police re-emerged from the police station armed with rifles and bayonets and the machine gun. They followed the Mau to the outskirts of Vaimoso.

A visitor from Suva, Miss A. Cross, told how the mortally wounded Tupua Tamasese was rushed away in a car with Mau police on the running board shouting to the driver to go quicker.

Another car drew up where I was standing, with blood trickling from under the door. In it was one of the men supported by wailing women, who begged for water to try to revive him with, as they thought he had fainted. Willing hands brought the water, but he was quite dead, and they drove madly on.

---

**Source:** *from Michael Field,* Mau, Samoa's Struggle for Freedom *(Honolulu: University of Hawai`i Press, 1990).*

# 5.

# Guam, Mariana Islands

Anne Perez Hattori
Keith Lujan Camacho
Erwin Bordallo Manibusan
Joaquin Cepeda Sablan
Mary Perez Hattori Sasaki

GUAM is an island in the western Pacific that has been held as a colony of the United States since 1898. Also referred to as Guahan, Guam is one of the islands in a chain known as the Mariana Islands. The fourteen islands of the Marianas chain form the homeland of the indigenous Chamorro people. Throughout the island chain, the Chamorro people speak a language known as *fino' Chamorro,* which translates as "the language of the Chamorro people."

Guam is the southernmost of the Mariana Islands, lying only 1,500 miles southeast of Tokyo and approximately 6,000 miles west of San Francisco. Guam occupies approximately 212 square miles; it is about 30 miles in length with a width ranging from 12 miles to 4 miles at its narrowest point. Although Guam is located far from the U.S. mainland, its people, land, and seas have been held as a possession of the United States for the past century. Guam has been used as a military port for U.S. ships, airplanes, and employees traveling in the Asia-Pacific region.

The resident population of Guam numbers close to 150,000, an increase of nearly 600 percent since 1940. Today the indigenous Chamorros are only about 43 percent of the total. By contrast, in 1940 Chamorros made up more than 90 percent of the island's population. After the 1940s, and especially since the 1960s, the United States decided to open up Guam for settlement by people from outside. This decision was made without the approval or even consultation of the Chamorro people. Because of this policy, today the indigenous people of Guam face the challenge of increasing numbers of settlers whose presence threatens their political and cultural sovereignty. Today, Chamorros face the daily fear that the arrival of more and more settlers will mean the total loss of Chamorro control in their own homeland.

## Maintaining Chamorro Culture

Many Chamorros believe that these fears about losing control over their homeland are legitimate and important concerns. Chamorros have lived in these islands since the dawn of history, and their love for their islands cannot be measured. In the Chamorro world view, the Mariana Islands lie at the center of the universe and all human life began in Guam. This belief is expressed in the Chamorro creation story of Puntan and Fu'una, which says that:

> In the beginning of time, before the creation of the earth and the sky, there lived a powerful being named Puntan. After a long period of time, Puntan felt himself about to die, so he called his sister, Fu'una. Puntan gave her explicit directions as to the disposal of his body. He decreed that upon his death his eyes should become the sun and moon. Fu'una turned his breast into the sky, and his back into the earth. Puntan's eyebrows formed the rainbow, and the rest of his parts shaped the lesser things of the world.
>
> When Fu'una contemplated the beautiful earth that had been brought into being, she decided that it should be peopled with men and women created in the likeness of her brother and herself. So, to this end, in order to best accomplish her purpose, she turned herself into a large rock, and situated herself in the southern part of Guam. The rock soon split open and out came hundreds of people who looked just like Fu'una and Puntan.[1]

Outsiders have dismissed the Chamorro creation story in favor of the Christian story, which asserts that the Christian god created the world in seven days and seven nights. Nonetheless, the Chamorro people have preserved the Puntan and Fu'una account for centuries. Despite the problems posed by foreign domination on Guam, the Chamorros continue to practice their own cultural traditions and maintain their cultural values.

One key aspect of Chamorro culture is the concept of *inafa'maolek,* or the idea that, through cooperation and interdependence, the Chamorro people can coexist peacefully and productively. Inafa'maolek reminds Chamorros that the clan or extended family, and *not* the individual, serves as the core of society. As a clan member, each Chamorro learns from childhood the importance of knowing his or her familial relationships. Knowing one's extended family teaches Chamorros to be aware of the duties and obligations that are a part of daily life. Bonds among extended families are a key part of what enables Chamorro culture to survive in the modern era. Each Chamorro clan, though distinct, is related to other clans in many different ways, through webs created by bonds of marriage, childbearing, work, friendship, and more.

The Chamorro clan structure remains in place today, despite a history of more than 300 years of foreign rule. In 1521, navigator Ferdinand Magellan dropped anchor on Guam en route to the Philippines. Though Portuguese by birth, Magellan sailed under the Spanish flag, and his landfall marked the beginning of Guam's historical relationship with Spain. Spain claimed the entire island chain and named it the Mariana Islands, in honor of the Spanish queen, Maria Ana. The Spanish established their first colony in the Mariana Islands in 1668. By 1672, the Chamorro people were engaging in open rebellion against these foreign colonizers.

The Chamorro revolt against Spain lasted nearly thirty years, and this long war took a heavy toll on the Chamorro people. By the early 1700s, Spanish accounts report that the population of the Mariana Islands had dropped from an estimated 50,000 to only 3,500, with most deaths attributed to warfare and diseases brought by the Spanish. Today's modern Chamorros owe their continued existence to the determination and bravery of those who survived this invasion. The survivors found ways to continue practicing their cultural values and beliefs despite the genocidal policies of the Spanish government and forced conversion by the Catholic Church. While contemporary Chamorro culture shows the influences of Spain's culture and history, many of the underlying values and social structures remain Chamorro in essence.

FREE LIBRARY OF PHILADELPHIA

*Weaving palm leaves, Guam, 1930s.*

Quite often, mainstream history books portray the last years of the Spanish period as a peaceful time. Evidence exists, however, that the Chamorro people never really accepted their colonized status. Toward the end of Spanish rule in the Marianas, on August 2, 1884, Spanish governor Angel de Pazos was assassinated by a Chamorro palace soldier named Jose de Salas.[2] The Spanish feared at that time that a Chamorro uprising might take place. An investigation revealed that a large group of Chamorro soldiers planned to overthrow the government. Forty-seven suspects, all Chamorros, were arrested and sent for trial to the Philippines (also under Spanish rule at the time). Thirty-one of them were found guilty and sentenced to prison terms. Four others were sentenced to death, and these men were brought back to Guam in 1885 and killed by a firing squad. Spanish colonial officials ordered that the four be killed in front of an audience of Chamorros, to teach a strong lesson against rebellion.

## "Americanization"

By 1898, Spain had colonized the Mariana Islands for more than 200 years. Although Spanish domination ended with the outbreak of the Spanish-American War, once again the Chamorros of the Marianas were deprived of their sovereignty. The Marianas became a pawn of Western politics, this time falling under U.S. domination. Because of the U.S. government's ignorance and seeming lack of concern for the indigenous people of the Mariana Islands, the Chamorros were divided into two groups. Guam was colonized as a territory of the United States, while the rest of the Mariana Islands remained under Spanish rule. These islands are referred to today as the Northern Mariana Islands. Though Guam was politically severed from the rest of the Chamorro people, strong familial and cultural ties still connect Chamorros throughout the Marianas. The Mariana Islands remain two separate political entities today. Both are now under U.S. domination, as the

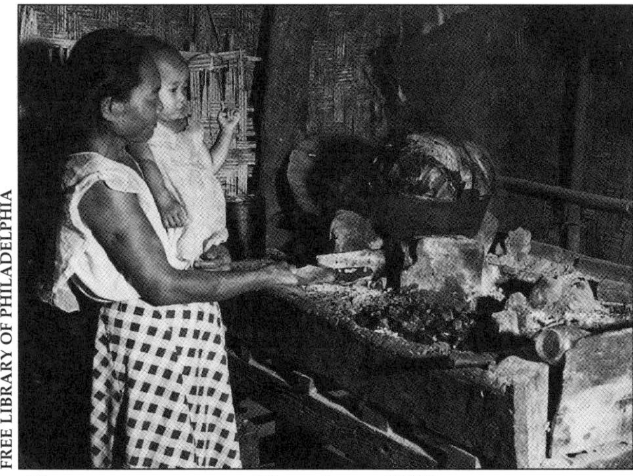
FREE LIBRARY OF PHILADELPHIA

*Chamorro woman at her stove, 1930s.*

FREE LIBRARY OF PHILADELPHIA

*When this 1957 news service photograph was taken, Guam was home to 30,000 Chamorros and 25,000 U.S. military personnel. Notes the original caption, "in the words of one high-ranking Navy officer, 'it's one place in the Far East we can't get kicked out of.'"*

Territory of Guam and the Commonwealth of the Northern Mariana Islands.

The Treaty of Paris, which ended the Spanish-American War, passed control of Guam from Spain to the United States. In 1899, the United States established its first colonial outpost on Guam. Those sent to Guam were U.S. Navy officials who treated the entire island as a naval base and ran the government of Guam in military fashion. Naval officers were appointed to serve as governors of Guam, while Chamorros were treated as noncitizens. These military governors passed laws on Guam that regulated everything from the length of women's dresses to the number of pigs and chickens that each Chamorro man was required to own. Naval officials inspected the homes and lawns of

Chamorro families. Literally every aspect of Chamorro life came under scrutiny by naval officials who sought to "Americanize" the people. In the schools, children's fingernails, hair, and clothing were inspected for cleanliness as the navy defined it. Official navy policies, as well as the ways in which Chamorros were treated in the schools and villages, reveal that many U.S. officials on Guam considered the Chamorro people to be dirty, ignorant, and childlike. Most navy officers were never interested in learning about Chamorro culture and history. They simply wanted to change the Chamorro people into "Americans."[3]

Despite U.S. government attempts to mold the Chamorro people into something that would be acceptable in the United States, Chamorros of that period were able to maintain their cultural practices and values. Before World War II, the U.S. presence on Guam was never more than a small settlement that exercised little actual power over Chamorro villagers. Chamorros were able to adopt those U.S. customs that they felt were beneficial and profitable. They were also able to ignore other laws and policies that they felt were trivial or interfering. For example, naval governors repeatedly passed laws commanding the Chamorro people to register their land holdings. To this day, however, a full century after the United States began attempting to enforce this policy, land titles are legally unclear and the island has never been satisfactorily surveyed. Chamorro resistance to such laws can be attributed in part to the fact that the navy taxed people for the lands they registered. Some people who did not want to pay these taxes or who could not afford to simply avoided the situation entirely. The navy, for its part, never had enough personnel to enforce the law over every single Chamorro.[4]

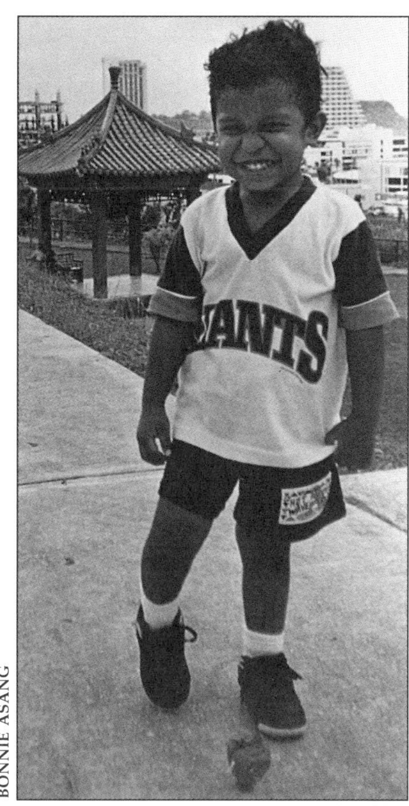

BONNIE ASANG

*Guam, 1990s.*

The U.S. Navy's rule over Guam was nondemocratic: the Chamorro people were not allowed to participate in their government. The Guam Congress was instituted in 1917, but it was only an advisory body whose members were appointed by the naval governor. Even so, the naval governor rarely even paid attention to the concerns raised by the Guam Congress. Local courts were composed mainly of naval officials who acted as judges. Until World War II, the Chamorro people had little or no involvement in the operation of the island's government.[5]

With the coming of World War II, however, things changed once again for Guam. This time, Japan was the invader. While many people are familiar with Japan's bombing of Pearl Harbor in Hawai`i, fewer know that Guam was also attacked the following day. Guam was invaded and occupied by Japanese forces during the war. The two-and-a-half year period of Japanese rule was a time of great fear and uncertainty for the Chamorro people. Their lives were disrupted as they were forced to provide food and labor for the Japanese military. Many Chamorros today remember that time as a period of torture, death, and hunger.

These wartime experiences help explain why, in July 1944, the returning U.S. military forces were met with enthusiasm. This excitement, however, did not last long, especially once the U.S. military began seizing large portions of the island for its own use. By 1948, the U.S. military and other parts of the federal government had taken 42 percent of Guam's land. These lands were used primarily for military bases. Some lands, however, were taken from Chamorro families simply to be used as military parks and recreational areas. For the Chamorros, it was painful to observe how lands that once fed their families were now being used as recreational areas by the military. Even beachfront areas were taken for the exclusive use of the military families, and Chamorro landowners were sometimes arrested by the military for fishing in those waters. Though the military has returned some of its land holdings, it still controls more than one third of Guam's land.[6]

Unresolved land problems on Guam are but one of the issues that cause dissatisfaction among Chamorros today. The repeated refusal by the United States to allow the Chamorro people to govern themselves is another important issue. To this day, the Chamorro people have never had the opportunity to decide for themselves what their political status should be. Though they have been ruled by the United States for a century, their struggle for self-determination continues. Throughout their long history of foreign rule, the Chamorros have proven themselves to be a strong, durable, and flexible people who can survive under even the most difficult conditions.

## Notes

[1] There are many different versions of this creation account, though all are in agreement on the major details. For example, see Laura Torres Souder, *Daughters of the Island: Contemporary Chamorro Women Organizers on Guam* (Lantham, MD: University Press of America, 1992). Also, see *Hale'-ta, Hestorian Taotao Tano': History of the Chamorro People*, Elementary Course, Political Status Education Coordinating Commission, Agaña, Guam, 1993.

[2] Robert Rogers, *Destiny's Landfall: A History of Guam* (Honolulu: University of Hawai`i Press, 1995), pp. 101-102.

[3] For a detailed discussion of naval efforts to "Americanize" the Chamorro people of Guam, see Anne Perez Hattori, "Bodily Harm: Rereading Naval Discourses on Guam, 1898-1941," forthcoming in *Isla: A Journal of Micronesian Studies*, Mangilao, Guam, 1998.

[4] For other examples of naval policies on Guam and Chamorro resistance to them, see Anne Perez Hattori, "Bodily Harm," *op. cit.*

[5] For additional information on the U.S. administration of Guam and Chamorro acts of resistance, see Penelope Bordallo, *A Campaign for Political Rights on Guam, Mariana Islands, 1899–1950*, unpublished master's thesis, University of Hawai`i at Mānoa, 1982.

[6] Pedro C. Sanchez., *Guahan Guam: The History of Our Island* (Agaña, Guam: Sanchez Publishing House, 1988).

---

**Vocabulary:** clan, colonial, colony, conversion, genocidal, homeland, indigenous, interdependence, self-determination, sovereignty

# Lesson 5.1 Land Seizures

**Objective:** To sensitize students to the impact of land seizures on the population of Guam.

**Themes:** militarism, land tenure, territorial expansion

**Vocabulary:** colonized, liberation, condemned, genocidal, indigenous, oppressed, acculturate, assimilate, supplanted, legacy, colonialism, dictatorship

## Suggested Activities

1. Distribute the worksheet at the end of this lesson with a map of the continental United States. Ask students to follow the directions on the worksheet, then have the entire class discuss the questions included on the worksheet.
2. Have the students review the readings at the end of this lesson, either in class or as homework.
3. Divide the class into small groups. What possible solutions can students think of to resolve the land crisis on Guam? Each group should write a letter to a U.S. senator or representative, urging him or her to consider the group's proposals for Guam's land crisis.

# Worksheet: Military Land Seizures

The map below shows the continental United States. Shade in one-third of the land mass, including most of the coastal regions. Discuss what the United States would be like without the use of those regions. Where would everyone relocate? Where would you move to if you lived in one of the condemned regions? What would be the impact upon the U.S. economy? On the culture and identity of people in the United States?

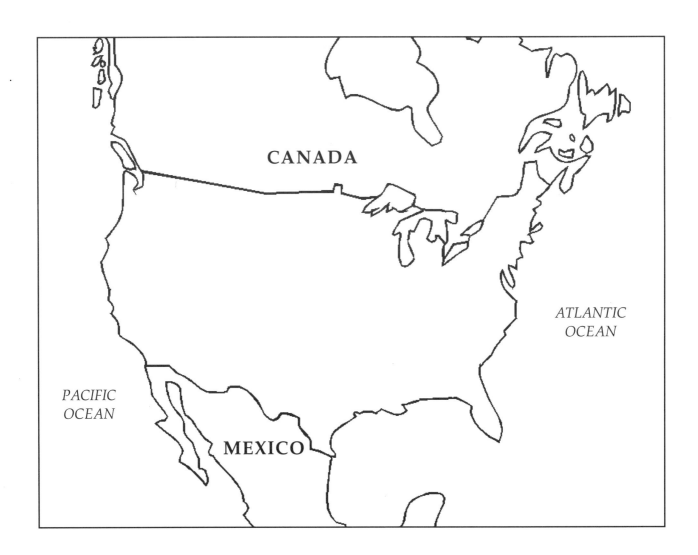

CANADA

ATLANTIC OCEAN

PACIFIC OCEAN

MEXICO

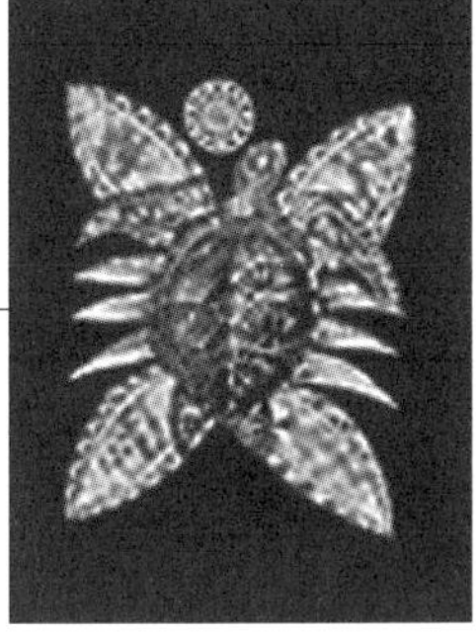

# Reading: Righting Civil Wrongs

By the time of the outbreak of World War II, Guam had been colonized by the United States for almost a half century. Concerns expressed by the Chamorro people for political change on Guam, however, remained unaddressed by the U.S. Congress at the time of Japan's World War II attack on Guam on December 8, 1941. Guam was to be occupied by Japan for almost three years, and the Chamorros suffered terrible cruelties at the hands of the Japanese military. In the last month before the United States returned to reoccupy Guam, Chamorros were made to walk out of their villages and move into concentration camps where they were forced to provide labor and food for the Japanese military population. Men, women, and children worked on huge agricultural projects and on military construction projects, such as building airfields, bunkers and gun emplacements. Executions, beatings, and rapes were bleak aspects of the war experience.

But even Guam's so-called "liberation" by the U.S. military had its horrors. The island's villages were devastated by the effects of American bombardment. All across Guam, about 80 percent of the island's homes, buildings and permanent structures were destroyed. The capital of Agaña, home to over half the Chamorro population before the war, was almost completely destroyed by the bombardment. Sumay, the second largest village before the war, was completely condemned for use by the military. By 1947, 1,350 families had lost their land and homes due to wartime bombings and military policy.

Military land grabbing was *the* critical concern of the postwar Chamorro population. The loss of land to the military touched Chamorro lives unlike any other imposition of U.S. colonialism. In the villages of Agaña and Sumay alone, approximately 11,000 of the island's 20,000 inhabitants were moved out, and other Chamorros in different areas all over the island suffered the same fate. By 1948, the naval government was condemning lands just for the recreational use of military dependents. In Agaña, roughly 500 people were evicted when 82 lots were condemned for a park and in Tamuning, 60 hectares of Tumon Beach were condemned for another military recreational center. Today, Chamorros are still not allowed to fish or swim in several beach areas which are controlled by the military for the exclusive use of their personnel.

---

**Source:** *Anne Perez Hattori, "Righting Civil Wrongs: The Guam Congress Walkout of 1949,"* Isla: A Journal of Micronesian Studies, *Vol. 3, No. 1 (Rainy Season, 1995), pp. 1–27.*

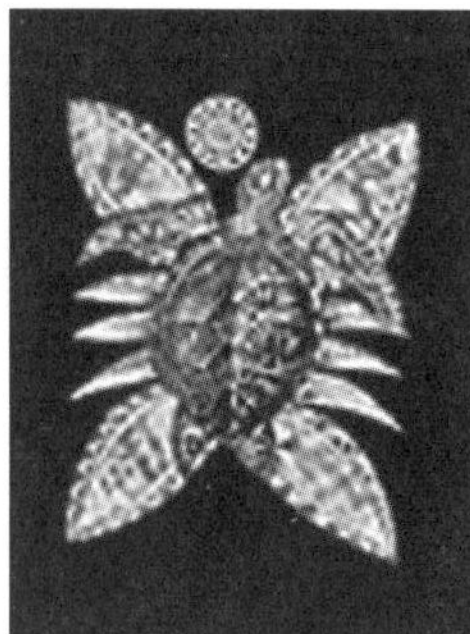

# Reading: Land and Culture

Guam is not just a piece of real estate to be exploited for its money-making potential. Above all else, Guam is the homeland of the Chamorro people. That is a fundamental, undeniable truth. We are very profoundly *"taotao tano"* — people of the land. This land, tiny as it is, belongs to us just as surely, just as inseparably, as we belong to it. No tragedy of history or declaration of conquest, no legalistic double-talk can change that fact. Guam is our legacy. Is it for sale? How can one sell a national birthright?

— Governor Ricardo J. Bordallo

. . . The intentional separation of Chamorros from their land base is an unjust policy at best. At worst, this process has had a genocidal effect on a distinct, dynamic cultural group of indigenous Pacific Islanders, the Chamorro people of Guam. For more than 400 years, the Chamorros have been a people oppressed by policies meant to convert, acculturate, assimilate, conquer, or otherwise stamp them out, promulgated by imperialist nations such as Spain, Japan, and America. . . .

When the U.S. occupied our island, it took more than our land; it took away our culture, our way of life, and supplanted these with its own imported values. In this way, the entire Chamorro population of Guam was injured, not just the property owners. Consequently, a complete remedy must involve all Chamorros of Guam and their descendants.

Whether that remedy will ever come to the people of Guam remains to be seen. What is clearly evident is that the U.S. practice of land grabbing leaves a legacy of colonialism that far exceeds any actions practiced by England upon the U.S. Taxation without representation, no human rights, no legal rights, no independent judiciary, dictatorship — all were, and in some respects, still are present on the island of Guam.

---

**Source:** *Mike F. Phillips, "Land," in* Kinalamten Pulitikåt; Siñenten I Chamorro *(Issues in Guam's Political Development: The Chamorro Perspective), Political Status Education Coordinating Commission, Agaña, Guam, 1996, pp. 2–16.*

# LESSON 5.2 The Sovereignty Movement

**Objective:** To introduce students to Guam's sovereignty movement.

**Themes:** sovereignty, national identity, nationhood

**Vocabulary:** indigenous, strategic, export, inalienable, perpetuate, colonial domination, civil disobedience, nonconformity, bondage

## Suggested Activities

1. Have students review the readings at the end of this lesson, either in class or as homework the night before.
2. Ask the entire class to discuss how they understand the concept of sovereignty. Ask them whether they are familiar with related terms that are usually applied to individuals, such as independence, autonomy, or self-determination. How would they extend these terms to the level of a cultural group (such as women, African Americans, young people, or the like)? What do such terms mean when applied to a nation such as Guam?
3. Now ask students to consider obstacles and limitations to self-determination. What are some of the things that prevent individuals from being fully autonomous? What do they think prevents nations such as the Chamorro nation from attaining their sovereignty?
4. Ask students to imagine that they are the leaders of Guam's sovereignty movement. They have been successful in winning their independence. Now they are the government of a new nation. What are the first three things they would do?

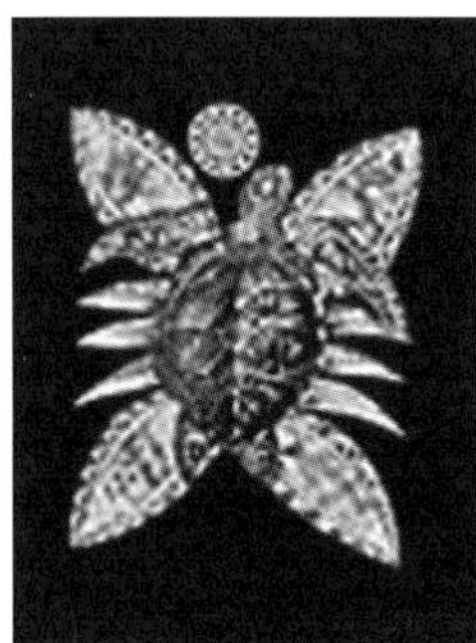

# Reading: Hotels and Military Bases

*Guam is an island where the old adages "behind every palm tree there is a military base" and "behind every military base there is a tourist hotel" ring true. Hotels mesh with military bases, leaving little room for the people. In the extract below, writer Laura Souder describes the situation on Guam:*

On Guam, which is a piece of land 212 square miles total of land area, we have eleven military establishments, and those establishments are distributed throughout the island from the northern tip to the southern tip; they are typically located in beachfront areas, prime land areas.

*One-third of Guam's land is controlled by the U.S. military. Attempts to regain control of the land have long been on the agenda of the Organization of People for Indigenous Rights (OPI-R), as Hope Cristobal explains:*

After World War II there was a lot of land-grabbing and as a result one-third of our island is in the hands of the military.

Much of the [indigenous rights activism] that has to do with land is the result of military takings. It all started back in the early seventies when people started questioning. You know, someone started a land claim, a legal suit, and then all of a sudden it popped open and everyone started looking at their lands. They started checking their roots, finding out that all that land was theirs at one time and taken from them. It seems a lot of people, especially throughout the Pacific, have had a lot of land taken away from them for strategic reasons, for military reasons . . .

I think that to be independent is not to have this military on our lands. There is a lot we can do with our lands. Much of the land they have is fertile land, farming land. Fena Valley (a nuclear weapons storage site), with the only lake on this island, is being held by them. We can't touch it. I've never been to it. I can only see it from fifteen miles away. The only deep harbor, where the naval ship repair facility is, is held by the military. All the flat land to the north; Andersen Airfield. So, much of the area that we could use for farming, for export, is being held by the military. It wasn't an accident that they got all of this. I'm sure it was well thought out.

---

**Source:** *Statements by Chamorro activists Laura Souder and Hope Cristobal of Organization of People for Indigenous Rights. Quoted in Zohl de Ishtar,* Daughters of the Pacific *(Melbourne, Australia: Spinifex Press, 1994), pp. 74-75.*

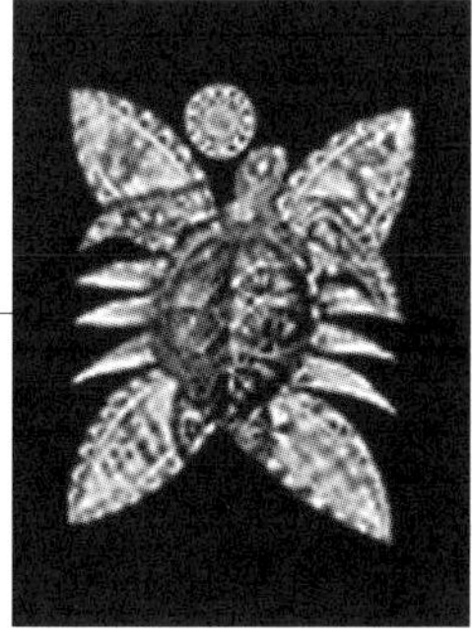

# Reading: The Existence of a People

On 21 July 1991, the Chamoru Chelus* proclaimed the existence of a people. Our right to exist as a nation of people. Just like the nation of Korea for the Koreans, a nation of the Philippines for Filipinos, Japan for the Japanese. We felt that we had the inalienable right to proclaim to the world that we are a People. . . . Then we had to ask ourselves: "Great, now that we have proclaimed the Chamoru Nation, where do we go from here? How do we define the Chamoru Nation? What constitutes the Chamoru Nation?" . . .

We found that we had to define the word "sovereignty" — the right for us to control our destiny — before we could plan a course of action of how to perpetuate a nation. We came onto the concept that no nation can survive without protecting the six elements: the *tano*, land; the *hanom*, water; the *aire*, air; *hinnenghe*, spirituality; *linguahe*, language; and *kottura*, culture. That is our responsibility: to protect these six elements in order to survive as a peoplehood. We established working committees accordingly. They are responsible for identifying what it is that threatens our nation, our sovereignty, our right to exist.

We were considered radical at the beginning. Our people are not accustomed to standing up against the government, to speaking out. You have to understand four hundred years of colonial domination of our people. They have been intimidated to the point that what you tell them, they'll do. So people are not used to protest; civil disobedience; nonconformity; challenging the system. The seeds of loyalty have been planted in the minds of our people. . . .

We have been taught that we are not-Chamoru. That there are no more Chamorus any more — they're all dead — and that we are Americans. In 1922, naval governor Dorn imposed the California school system, he wanted to make Guam a loyal possession of the United States. I can see how they set out to do that. At the age of five or six, when we entered school, we were immediately taught to memorize the Pledge of Allegiance to the United States; we were taught to identify the four seasons (which we don't have in Guam); we were taught American history. The United States methodically set out to destroy our culture, our language, our identity. . . .

We're hoping to draft up a constitution that would protect the indigenous rights of Chamorus while, at the same time, safeguarding the civil rights of the non-Chamoru. We have to find a happy medium. We cannot kick out foreigners. So, there is still a lot of work to do, things to iron out. Still, I thought it was going to be more difficult than this. I'm not saying that there's no valleys and troubled times — we have a lot of work ahead of us. We know what we have got to do, and we're doing it step by step. We will free our people from the bondage of colonial slavery. It is now or never. It is almost too late. We have to save what's left.

---

**Chelu* is the Chamorro word for brother or sister and "Chamoru" is an alternative spelling for Chamorro. The Chamoru Chelus were an indigenous rights activist group led by Angel Santos, which later evolved into the group known today as the Nasion Chamoru, or Chamorro Nation.

**Source**: *Statement by Chamorro activist Angel Santos of Nasion Chamoru (Chamorro Nation), in Zohl de Ishtar,* Daughters of the Pacific *(Melbourne, Australia: Spinifex Press, 1994), pp. 80-81.*

# Lesson 5.3 Domination and Disrespect

**Objective:** To illustrate how U.S. military officials in Guam perceived the Chamorro people and their own role as an occupying force.

**Themes:** cultural domination, prejudice, discrimination

**Vocabulary:** sanitation, hygiene, economic development, progenitors, industry, Americanized, remnants, detrimental

## Suggested Activities

1. Pass out the readings at the end of this lesson. Direct the students' attention to the cartoon that is included in the handout and ask them what this image says to them. What is its literal meaning? What is it trying to convey? How is Guam represented and why might that be? How is the United States represented and why might that be? What relationship is suggested between Guam and the United States? Whose perspective is being represented? Whose perspective is being left out — and why is that an important issue to consider?
2. Divide the class into groups. Have each group analyze one of the extracts included in the readings. What change is the author trying to encourage? Come up with a list of qualities or conditions that would result if this change were made. Discuss the validity of the writer's argument. Whose voices are left out? What impact do these "missing voices" have on how the story is heard?
3. Ask the students to draw their own cartoon depicting the relationship between Guam and Uncle Sam as they understand it. Would it have been published in 1925? Today? Why or why not?

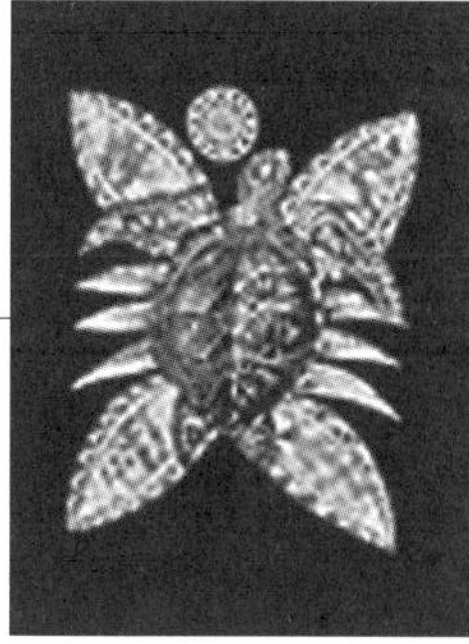

# Readings: Three Images of Guam

*In the September 1925 issue of the naval publication,* The Guam Recorder, *an anonymous naval officer wrote:*

English will bring to the people of Guam, through the public schools, a knowledge of sanitation and hygiene, which will enable them to live in a correct manner. This will result still more favorably in the increase in population. Along with such increase will come further and enforced economic development. With economic development will come more of the real pleasures of life. Through English will come a knowledge of fair play and a keen sense of honor such as the progenitors of Americans had at the time of the origin of the language and such as is practiced by the American nation at the present time. With a knowledge of English under American tutorship will come a natural love for labor and industry by those who come to think themselves educated.

---

**Source:** *"English in the Schools of Guam,"* The Guam Recorder, *Sept. 1925. Quoted in Katherine B. Aguon, "The Guam Dilemma: The Need for a Pacific Island Education Perspective," Amerasia, Vol. 6, No. 2, 1979, pp. 77–90.*

---

*This excerpt is a 1935 editorial from* The Guam Recorder:

. . . [U]ndoubtedly all of us are united in speeding the day when in thoughts, language, and ideals the people of this lovely island are thoroughly Americanized and may truly enjoy the full benefits of an American form of government. It is a fact that inasmuch as the United States governs here, the Chamorro people should make a determined effort to throw off the last remnants of customs, languages, and ideas which are detrimental to their advancement. . . . To assist in the process is the duty of every American on the Island. . . . Take into your confidence the Chamorro people who work with and under you. They are in your hands and are a kindly and worthwhile people. Help them in their struggles.

---

**Source:** *Jack Flynn, "Over the Editorial Desk,"* The Guam Recorder, *Nov. 1935, p. 202.*

---

More Like His Dad Every Day.

**Source:** The Guam Newsletter *(published by the U.S. Navy), Vol. 4, No. 1, July 1912.*

# Lesson 5.4 Culture and Resistance

**Objective:** To explore the role of language in cultural identity.

**Themes:** cultural identity, cultural resistance, art and politics

**Vocabulary:** imprisoned, degradation, uncivilized, dispossession, decolonization, independence, exterminated, half-caste, infantile, wards, contemptibly, theologized, forefathers, delusive, diplomacy, conquistadorial, manifestos

## Suggested Activities

1. Pass out the reading entitled "I Was Imprisoned for Twenty-One Years." Split the class into five groups and have each group discuss one section of the reading, either the introductory paragraph or one of the four sections. Ask students to discuss what the section means. What is being described? What experiences are being expressed? What images are being used by the author? What is the prison being discussed? At the end of this exercise, have the groups come together and share their thoughts on their particular section.
2. Ask students to imagine their own "prison of language." Have each student write a paragraph to describe a special family occasion. Pair students off and have them trade paragraphs. Each student should cross out eight key words in their partner's paragraph. Have them return the papers and then attempt to tell their story without using those key words. Discuss the impact of language and the feelings which result from one's inability to use it fully and freely.
3. Divide the class into groups and pass out the reading at the end of this lesson entitled "A Song and Two Poems." Ask each group to work on either the song lyrics or one of the poems. Ask them to discuss the following questions: What issues are addressed by the author? What is being criticized? What does your reading say about Chamorro peoples' attitudes toward themselves, their culture, and the U.S. colonial presence?
4. Ask the class to examine the cartoon presented at the end of this lesson. What does the image of the prison say to you? Now ask them to compare this cartoon with the one in lesson 5.3. What are the cartoons trying to convey? How is Guam represented in each and why might that be? How is the United States represented and why might that be?

# Reading: I Was Imprisoned for Twenty-One Years

*The following essay was presented as a speech at the Inetnon Para Ni Libre (Gathering for Freedom) held on Guam on July 4, 1997. The Chamorro activist group, the Ancestral Landowners' Coalition, under the leadership of Señora Patty Garrido, sponsored and organized this event. At the time he gave this speech, Keith Camacho was a 23-year-old native Chamorro with extended family from both Guam and Saipan in the Mariana Islands and a student in the master's program in Pacific Islands Studies at the University of Hawai`i at Manoa.*

*Buenas yan hafa adai todus hamyo. Guahu si Keith Camacho.* [Hello and thanks to all of you. My name is Keith Camacho.] Today, July 4, 1997, marks America's Independence Day. This gathering, *Inetnon para ni libre* [gathering for freedom], challenges America's call for justice and freedom. We, *i manchamorro* [the Chamorro people], are an oppressed people under the mask (and it is an ugly one) of so-called American democracy. My talk is about one aspect of this oppression felt among many of *i manhoben* [the young people] — the degradation of *fino' Chamorro* [the Chamorro language] by the elevation and imposition of the English language on Guam. The title of this speech comes from the song of the same name, written by the late Chamorro musician, J. D. Crutch. His music says much about the pains and joys of growing up in Guam. Songs like his tell the histories of our people. *Bente unu yu gi presu* [I was imprisoned for 21 years] reminds me, *kada diha* [every day], that we are in prisons. Some call these prisons the federal government or the United States military, and, let us not forget, even shopping malls and hotels — places and peoples who often treat *i manchamorro* with little or no respect. This is my story about slowly breaking out of one prison — *fino inglis* [the English language].

*Lay the foundation*
*Raise the walls*
*Install the rebar*
*Enclose the prisoner*

## Agaña Heights Village in Guam

A - B - C - D - E - F - G — Already by the age of five I was being taught how to sing the English alphabet, how to pronounce the letters correctly, and how to spell and write words such as "cat" and "dog." My parents were so proud of me. They would ask me to sing the alphabet in front of our relatives at fiestas and other familial gatherings. I did. I did sing. Once I sang at a preschool somewhere in Agaña Heights, and I remember this because of the big hill with the big GUAM sign labeled on it. At the school, everyone was smiling at me. Their faces were bright. They would speak in Chamorro to each other, on the side, away from me, saying stuff like, *"Hey Ba'bara, esta sotteru I patgon-mu"* [Barbara, your child is already mature]. I was never involved in those conversations because my *familia,* whether they were in Agaña Heights, Barrigada, or Santa Rita, were always happy, always content, almost unaware that America's education system, specifically its practice of the English language on Guam, would soon transform those smiling faces into confused ones.

*Paint everything white*
*Weld stainless steel bars*
*Speak only English*

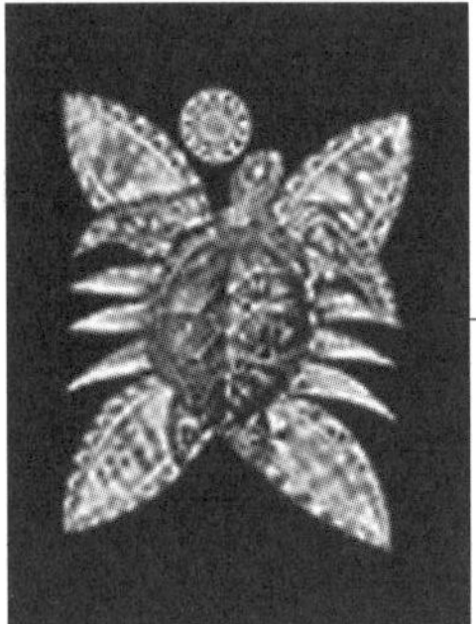

## Chalan Piao Village in Saipan

*"Hayi na'an-mu? Haaaaa yi naaaa' aaaan muuuu?"* [What's your name?] Standing. I was just standing . . . still. I'm about twelve years old now. Brain going at one thousand miles per hour trying to understand what my cousin just uttered to me in Chamorro. I replied, "uh, my name is Keith." Eyebrows bent, looking straight at me, and twitching his smile just a little bit, my *primu* [cousin] remained standing — confused as to why I responded in *fino' inglis.* Then he stopped smiling. "Let's go play pickle war," he said. We did play. And all of Chalan Piao echoed with our laughter. I came home smelling like a pickle. Even my *primu* smelled sour. As I arrived back in Guam I began to wonder why most of my *familia* continued to speak in English to me.

*Limit visitors*
*Segregate the Chamorros*
*No free time whatsoever*

## University of Guam in Mangilao, Guam

I was twenty-one years old at the time. Western education has taught me well. "Well, well, well, what do we have here?" I thought to myself. Hmmmmmmmmm . . . more American documentation about Guam in the early twentieth century. "The Chamorro language is a backward one, something inferior to the English language, something uncivilized." Furthermore, there were rules and laws during the post–World War II American reoccupation of Guam that punished Chamorros for speaking our language in public. *Baba este na klasen* rules and regulations [these kinds of rules are bad].

*The prisoners are out of control!*
*Quickly, chain them up!*
*Beat them down!*
*Teach them to obey*
*and not to question authority!*
*Their spirits must be broken!*

## Village of Harmon, at the Cliffline, Guam

*Ahe* [No]. Our spirits are not broken. We are a strong people. (Sing) *Benti unu yu gi presu ti siña humuyong* [For twenty-one years I could not get out of prison]. In the process of my education, I've come to realize the importance of J. D. Crutch's music and the music of others as well. J. D. Crutch reminds us that we are all in some kind of prison cell. Some of us speak Chamorro fluently. Some of us understand our cultural values and beliefs. Some of us live with the Land. And then there are those, like myself, who want to share and learn, how to protect, promote, and preserve *i kottura-ta, i lenguahi-ta, i tano-ta, i tasi, i guma yu'us, yan i manchamorro* [our culture, our language, our land, the ocean, the church, and the Chamorro people]. We all have keys — *meggai na yabi* [many keys] — to open these prison doors that bind us. Then again *ti guaha yabi-mu, umbre nai, u'usa i* crowbar or bulldozer [if you do not have your key, then use a crowbar]. Whatever choice of keys or tools we have let us play *active* roles in freeing our people. For me, *chagi kumentos fino' Chamorro pot fabot* [please try speaking our Chamorro language]. For others, let us share our beliefs, our wisdom, our experiences about education, about our histories, about respecting *i manamko* [our elders], about land dispossession, about decolonization. Now that is Liberation. That is Independence. That is *Biba Chamorro! Biba!* [Long live the Chamorro people!]

---

**Source:** *Keith Lujan Camacho, "Bente Unu Yu Gi Presu" (I was imprisoned for 21 years), unpublished address, 1997.*

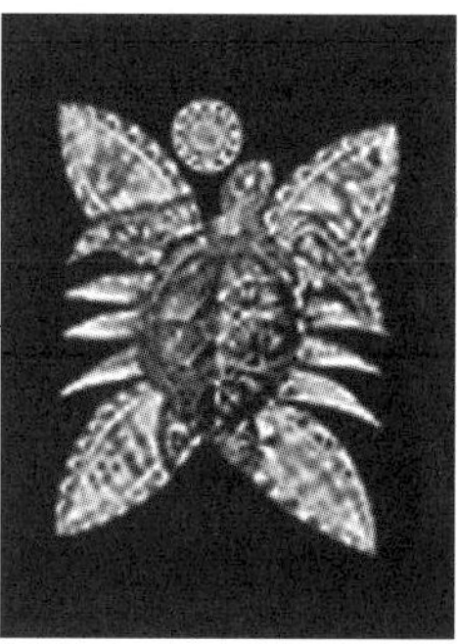

# Reading: A Song and Two Poems

## Munga Yu Ma Fino Inglisi
## *(Don't Speak English To Me)*

*chorus:*

| | |
|---|---|
| Munga yu' ma fino' Inglisi | *Don't speak English to me.* |
| Ke lao hafa hinasso-ku | *What are you thinking of?* |
| Malago' hao umotro klase | *You want to be somebody else* |
| Lao Chamorro i rasa-mu | *But Chamorro is your race.* |
| | |
| Si tata-mu sen Chamorro | *Your father is very Chamorro* |
| Si nana-mu tuma'lo | *Your mother is also* |
| Hafa na para un amerikanu | *Why are you trying to be an American?* |
| Kao oson hao nu hagu | *Are you tired of yourself?* |
| | |
| I palabra an un prununsia | *The words when you pronounce them* |
| Un usa i banida | *You use boastfully* |
| Nisisita un ripara | *You need to notice* |
| Hayi un keke fa'baba' | *Who you are trying to fool.* |
| | |
| I patgon-ta para hu | *Our children will* |
| Fino' English fine'nana | *Speak English first.* |
| Yan umamko' siempre ma chatgi | *When they get older, they'll be laughed at* |
| sa' ti ha tungo' | *Because they won't know* |
| I lengguahi-ña | *Their very own language.* |

---

**Source:** *Excerpt from "Munga Yu Ma Fino Inglisi" (Don't Speak English To Me), a song popularized in the 1960s by the Chamorro musician, Johnny Sablan. Lyrics by Jesus "Chamorro" Charfauros, a popular disc jockey. English translation by Fermina Perez Hattori.*

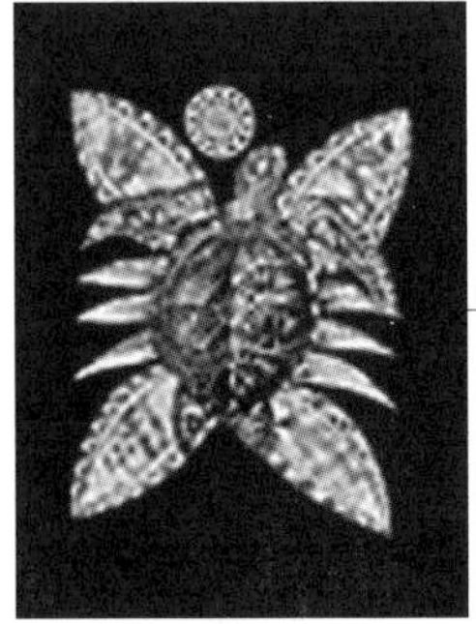

## thieves

Thieves, they called us.
Religious converts, they made us.
Said we were sinful,
naked, savage, primitive.

Exterminated, they called us.
Half-castes, they branded us.
Said we were impure,
racially — culturally — spiritually.

Infantile, they called us.
Wards of the state, they made us.
Said we were immature,
**UN**educated, **UN**developed, **UN**civilized.

Now they tell us,
we are simply, sadly, contemptibly

OVER-developed
OVER-modernized
OVER-theologized
OVER-Americanized

UNDER-CHAMORICIZED.

— *Anne Hattori*

## foreFathers

Our foreFathers
with their white-wigged hair
and exquisite accents
With their delusive diplomacy
and quieted conquistadorial cruelty

our foreFathers
like washington and jefferson
franklin and lincoln,
who are these gentleMEN anyway
whose faces flatter bulletin boards
and whose manifestos are memorized
by school children islandwide

did they sweat sweet tropical perspiration
did they plant *suni* and pick *lemmai*
and beseech the blessings of *guelas yan guelus*
under the sweltering sun of latitude 14

so why do We
yes, WE
teach that They
are everything
or something
or even anything
to us brown-skinned natives
who work the soil,
ride the sea,
inhale our exhalations,
and inherit the land
immortally.

— *Anne Hattori*

---

*suni:* taro
*lemmai:* breadfruit
*guelas yan guelus:* male and female elders

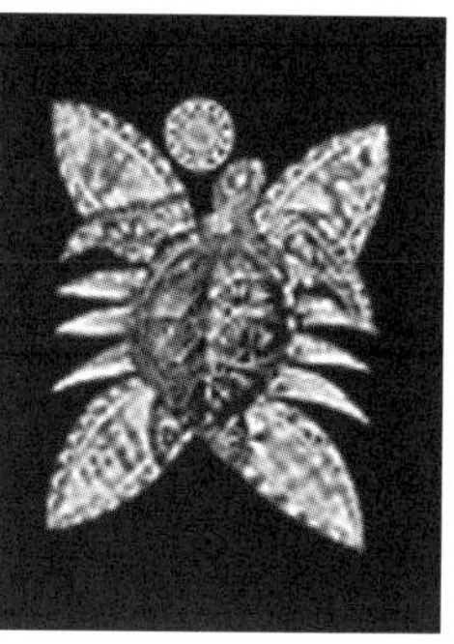

# Cartoon: A Political Prisoner

CELL BLOCK
FEDERAL
SYSTEM

OP

GUAM: A POLITICAL PRISONER

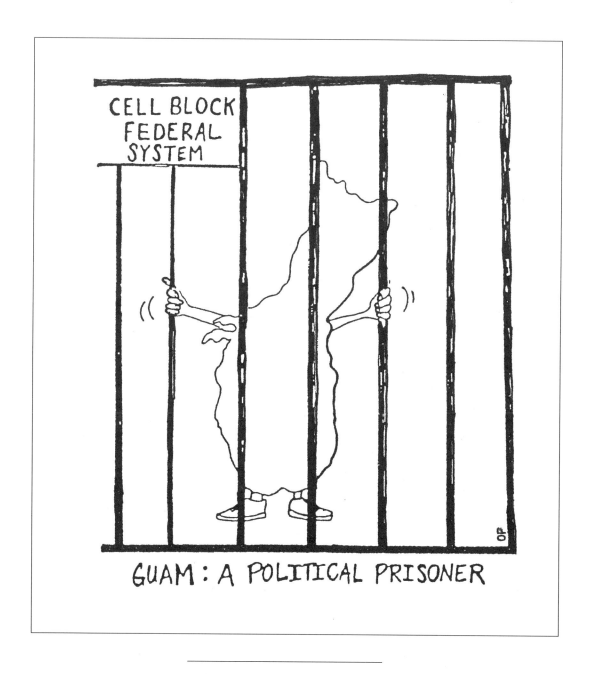

**Source:** *Political Action Committee, Organization of People for Indigenous Rights, P.O. Box 7932, Tamuning, Guam 96911.*

# 6.

# Hawai`i

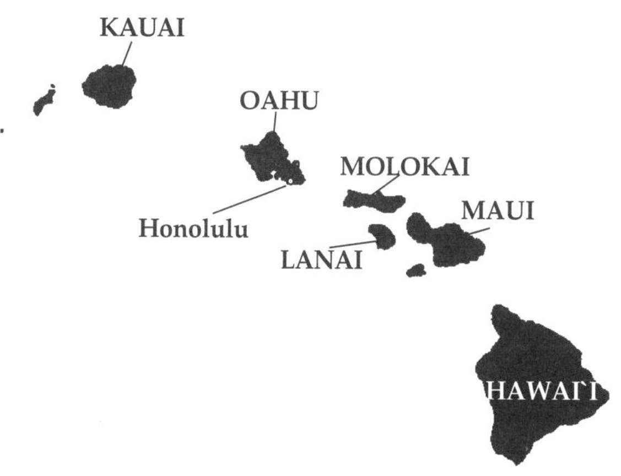


*Overview*
**John Kamakawiwo`ole Osorio**

*Lessons*
**Wayne Au, Noenoe Silva**
**Nancy Aleck, Bonnetta Adeeb**

THE first arrivals in the Hawaiian Archipelago probably arrived more than 2,000 years ago and were Polynesian voyagers from more southern islands. Over the next millennium settlers and explorers sailed between the northern islands and the southern islands with great frequency, exchanging ideas, technologies, new religions, and possibly even certain kinds of diseases. In short, Hawai`i was a distant but participating partner in a regional community that included most of Polynesia.

Hawai`i's distance as well as its ecological wealth did, however, impel the growth of certain unique characteristics. Most significant, perhaps, was that the population came to depend on labor-intensive agricultural development of the inland valleys, involving the construction of irrigation ditches that fed a network of taro gardens (the traditional staple crop) and fish ponds. This agricultural society depended, in turn, on an increasingly complex system of social and political divisions. Hawai`i was also densely populated; recently, historians and other scholars have estimated a population of 800,000 or more when James Cook, a British adventurer, sailed into Hawai`i in 1778.

## The Arrival of the *Haole*

Cook's arrival heralded that of an increasing number of foreign explorers, traders, missionaries, and settlers at the dawn of the nineteenth century. Referred to as *haole*, these foreigners from Europe and the United States brought new technologies, ideas, and economies that competed with the traditions of the Kānaka Maoli, or Native Hawaiians. They also brought fierce epidemic diseases. Syphilis, gonorrhea, tuberculosis, cholera, typhoid, mumps, measles, smallpox, and leprosy reduced the Hawaiian population to a tenth of its former size by 1850, and halved it again over the next forty years.

FREE LIBRARY OF PHILADELPHIA

***This painting shows a traditional Hawaiian chieftain.***

As the Hawaiian population plummeted, the number of foreigners increased. The *haole* population, though still small, had an increasingly large influence on culture, government, and economics throughout the nineteenth century. In 1820 Calvinist missionaries arrived from Connecticut and Massachusetts to begin what proved to be their most successful mission anywhere. By 1850 virtually every Hawaiian was said to be enrolled as a member of some Christian church. These missionaries came to be even more influential in the political arena than in religion. They wrote a constitution for Hawai`i, creating government positions at the highest possible level (just below the king), which they proceeded to fill with their own members. From the mid-1830s on they continually pressed for economic and social "reforms" that privatized land traditionally held in common, thus destroying the relationship between the ruling chiefs and their people.

The first commercial sugar-planting operation was formed by a missionary on Kaua'i in 1835. By the 1880s, *haole* plantation owners and corporations owned or leased the bulk of private lands in the Hawaiian Kingdom, close to a million acres in all. The crucial event in this development was the 1848 *Māhele* (division) of lands, promoted and designed by *haole* missionaries, in which the ruling families registered claims to the 4.2 million acres of the archipelago. When the final act of the *Māhele* was completed in 1852, the majority of Hawaiian farmers and fishers were landless and compelled to leave the lands on which they had subsisted for millennia. In the same year, the government passed a series of vagrancy acts designed to force the now landless Native Hawaiians into labor on government projects and sugar plantations.

The sugar industry grew by fits and starts over the next twenty-five years, until by the 1880s it was a multimillion-dollar operation. The demand for cheap, dependent labor could not be met by the dwindling population of Native Hawaiians, so immigrant labor was brought in from China, Japan, and, later, Korea and the Philippines. In the process, the Native Hawaiians came to be outnumbered by the foreign population even as they erected, on missionary advice, a constitutional government that allowed universal male suffrage from 1852 to 1864.

Concerned over the still-diminishing Native Hawaiian population and the enormous political and economic power wielded by *haole*, the Hawaiian monarchs from 1864 until 1893 sought constitutionally acceptable ways of strengthening Hawai`i's political independence. One such measure was a requirement that voters and political candidates be true citizens, either native-born or naturalized by taking an oath of allegiance solely to the Kingdom of Hawai`i. In this period, Hawai`i was as liberal as any nation in the world in its extension of citizenship. Chinese and Japanese immigrant laborers and merchants took advantage of the country's hospitality and pledged their allegiance to the Hawaiian kings.

Meanwhile, the Kānaka Maoli (Native Hawaiians) continued to struggle with disease and dispossession. While some families clung to lands that they had wisely claimed during the *Māhele*, even these fertile taro lands began to lose their productivity as privately funded water projects began to divert water from upland streams to sugar plantations in the more arid areas of the central plains on Maui and O'ahu islands. The government supported by law and subsidy any measure that promoted the production and sale of sugar — but sugar grew at the expense of Native Hawaiian agricultural production. Native Hawaiian voters became increasingly hostile to *haole* business owners, whom they characterized as arrogant, uncharitable opportunists. The slogan "Hawai`i for Hawaiians" became both a moral and political statement in the 1880s, and the term "missionary party" became an insult.

## From Annexation to the Sovereignty Movement

The *haole* were stung by the growing criticism of their leadership and worried about continued government support of their industry. They were also concerned about the increasing confidence and competence of Native Hawaiian legislators and their electorate. In 1887 a small group of *haole* business owners and lawyers, backed by their own private paramilitary force, coerced King Kalākaua into abrogating the Hawaiian Kingdom's constitution in order to replace it with one they themselves had drafted. This constitution, known as the Bayonet Constitution, eliminated the king's power and undermined the Native Hawaiian–controlled legislature by making the House of Nobles accessible only to those with large incomes or land holdings. This constitution also ended citizenship for hundreds of Asian immigrants who, in the eyes of the *haole*, were not considered trustworthy.

From 1887 until 1893, Native Hawaiian and *haole* legislators sympathetic to Native Hawaiian control continued to lobby both Kalākaua and his successor, Queen Lili`uokalani, to reinstate the older constitution. The *haole* supporters of

NANCY ALECK

***This statue commemorating Queen Lili`uokalani was built in 1993, on the hundredth anniversary of her overthrow.***

the Bayonet Constitution grew uneasy and began to openly support annexation by the United States. In 1893, when Lili`uokalani declared her intention to abrogate the Bayonet Constitution, these annexationists conspired with U.S. ambassador John Stevens to overthrow the queen. In the third week of January 1893, U.S. troops aboard the U.S.S. *Boston* disembarked in Honolulu to protect the conspirators while they declared themselves to be a provisional government. The queen, unwilling to commit her police and guard to a bloody confrontation with U.S. soldiers, abdicated while lodging a formal protest with the U.S. government. In 1898, the United States annexed the Hawaiian Islands by a joint resolution of the U.S. Congress.

The annexation of Hawai`i accelerated the domination of the island's economy by five interconnected companies. These companies, often referred to as the Big Five, were Castle and Cooke, C. Brewer, American Factors, Theo H. Davies, and Alexander and Baldwin. Most of the leadership of the Big Five were descendants of *haole* missionaries to the islands. The Big Five controlled most of the economic life of the Hawaiian Islands. Beginning with their control of the sugar and pineapple industries, the Big Five branched out to control transport, communications, banking, insurance, and retailing in Hawai`i. This economic domination was also linked directly to political control by the Republican Party, which lasted until the 1950s.

The ultimately successful process of unionizing sugar and pineapple workers on the plantations and longshoremen on the docks, begun in the 1930s, resulted in major shifts in political power in the territory. The interlocking power of the Big Five lessened with the rise of Japanese Americans and others into political power. Their growing influence was consolidated within the ranks of the Democratic Party and marked by the party's victory in the 1954 territorial elections. The turn away from an agricultural economy had also begun, with tourism becoming the major industry. This economic shift picked up rapidly with the admission of Hawai`i as the fiftieth state in 1959.

What had not changed for the better in this dynamic period was the status of the Kānaka Maoli (Native Hawaiians). Their position was one of continuing marginalization in their own country in economic and political terms, as land loss continued and power remained out of their hands. Many Native Hawaiians opposed statehood when given the opportunity to express their sentiments. Among other sectors of the population, however, support for statehood was overwhelming. This was particularly the case with the now dominant Asian communities in the islands, for whom statehood symbolized racial equality and acceptance by the U.S. mainstream. The Big Five, for their part, saw statehood as the best way to protect traditional agricultural interests.

In 1993, President William Clinton signed a joint resolution (PL 103-150) that acknowledged the illegality of the U.S. role in the loss of Hawaiian independence. Committing the United States to seeking reconciliation with the Hawaiian people, this "Apology Bill" has provided a new legal foothold for the Native Hawaiian sovereignty movement, now more than ten years old. Citing not only the illegal overthrow and annexation of Hawai`i, but also persistent social and economic ills that plague Hawaiians up to the present, many Native Hawaiian leaders have come to believe that only sovereign control of their land and resources will prevent their culture from disappearing altogether. Native Hawaiians lead every other ethnic group in Hawai`i by large margins in the incidence of heart disease, diabetes, and alcohol and drug abuse. As a result, they also face much greater risks during childbirth and child rearing. Native Hawaiians, who constitute about a fifth of the population of Hawai`i, are underrepresented in the college population, where they are one in ten students, and overrepresented in the state's prisons, where they make up more than half of incarcerated felons.

CORBIS-BETTMAN

*In 1898,* **Harper's Weekly** *published this drawing showing crowds in Honolulu cheering the news of the U.S. annexation of Hawai`i. Lesson 6.1 presents the reactions of Native Hawaiians to this news.*

Before the rise of the sovereignty movement, Native Hawaiians were treated as a minority group; like Native Americans, they were considered to be wards of the government. They could look forward either to complete assimilation into U.S. society and gradual distancing from their ancestral culture, or to fruitless and pitiful defiance, usually accompanied by poverty and persecution. Meanwhile, tourism, which has overtaken sugar as the principal industry of Hawai`i, has brought nearly seven million visitors a year into the islands, creating tremendous pressure on once lavish resources of water, land, and sea. As ancient sacred lands are turned into resorts and golf courses, Native Hawaiian culture and arts are taken over and reissued as attractions for tourists from the United States, Japan, and Europe.

The natural resources of Hawai`i have also been taken for use by the U.S. military, which holds some of the choicest lands in the islands. Hawai`i's strategic location in the Pacific makes it particularly attractive to the United States. The Pacific Command, with control over U.S. armed forces operating in more than half of the world, is headquartered in Hawai`i.

Nonetheless, Native Hawaiians are still here, defiantly optimistic. The Hawaiian language is making a comeback and is now one of the most popular language courses in the university. Hundreds of young people are being educated in Hawaiian language immersion schools and the number may grow into the thousands over the next decade. Many sovereignty initiatives are

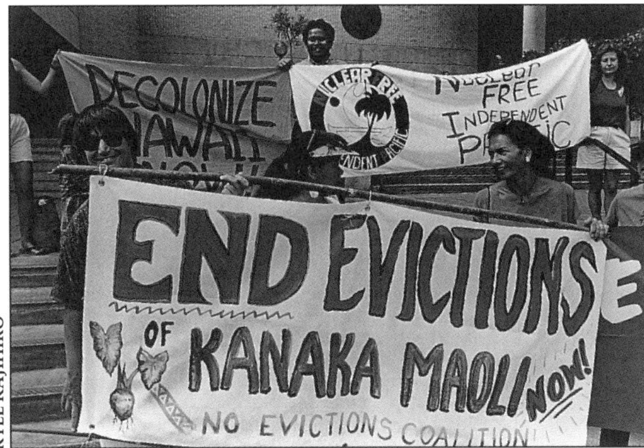


KYLE KAJIHIRO

***A 1997 rally protesting the eviction of a Native Hawaiian family.***

on the table and a high percentage of the Native Hawaiian population believes that sovereignty is attainable in their lifetime.

If Hawai`i should be sovereign again, it would demonstrate to the world that self-determination is a universal value that is available to even the smallest and most vulnerable of peoples. For too long, the message given to the nations of the world has been that only the militarily and economically powerful could assert their independence. In Hawai`i, people without land or weapons have quietly and determinedly asserted their sovereignty in the face of the most powerful nation in the history of the world. Whether or not they prevail should be of some interest to humanity.

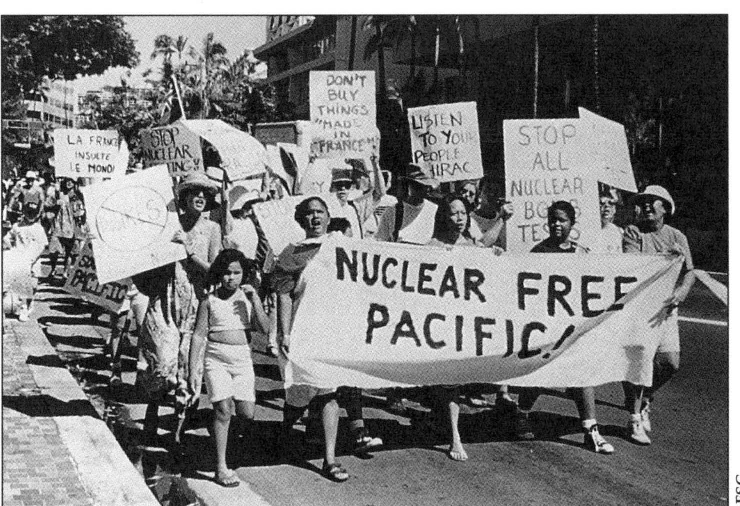


AFSC

***This 1995 march in Hawai`i protested French nuclear tests in Tahiti.***

# References

*"He Alo Ā He Alo"* (Face To Face): Hawaiian Voices on Sovereignty," Hawai`i Area Office, American Friends Service Committee, Honolulu, 1993.

D. N. Hall (Ed.), *Mālama: Hawaiian Land and Water* (Honolulu: Bamboo Ridge Press, 1985).

G. Kealoha, "Aloha `āina: Native Hawaiians Fight for Survival," *Civil Rights Digest*, Fall 1976, pp. 52–57.

R. Morales, *Ho`Iho`I Hou: A Tribute to George Helm and Kimo Mitchell* (Honolulu: Bamboo Ridge Press, 1984).

Na Māka o ka `Āina, *Act of War: The Overthrow of the Hawaiian Nation* (video cassette), Na Maka o ka `Āina in Association with the Center for Hawaiian Studies, University of Hawai`i, Mānoa, 1993.

---

**Vocabulary:** abrogate, annexation, archipelago, bayonet, immersion, naturalization, sovereignty, vagrancy, wards, natural resources

# Lesson 6.1 Annexation: Support and Opposition

**Objective:** To enable students to contrast how the annexation of Hawai`i was perceived by the mainstream U.S. media and by Native Hawaiians.

**Themes:** protest and resistance, media racism, indigenous perspectives

**Vocabulary:** autonomy, provisional, annexation, canvass, dilatory, deprecate

## Suggested Activities

1. Have students review the readings at the end of this lesson, either in class or as homework the night before.
2. Ask students to think about how differing views of annexation are portrayed in the *New York Times* article of March 15, 1898. What do they think the article means by the term "intelligent natives?" How does the perspective underlying the *New York Times* articles differ from that given in the reading "Hawaiian Resistance to Annexation?"
3. Have students read aloud selected parts, or even just the headlines, of the July 7 article from the *Times.* What do they think that Senator Pettigrew meant when he said that "annexation would be a violation of our national honor?"
4. Have students divide into small groups of four or five. Each group should prepare a news article for a Hawaiian-language newspaper that will report on the U.S. annexation of Hawai`i from the Native Hawaiian point of view. Have the groups present their articles to the entire class.
5. Following the presentations, ask each student to write a one-page discussion of how these presentations are similar or different from the *New York Times* articles.

# Reading: Hawaiian Resistance to Annexation

The Hawaiian government was overthrown by U.S. businessmen on January 17, 1893. Immediately, the Kānaka Maoli (Native Hawaiians) organized to protest. They formed an organization known as Hui Hawai`i Aloha `Āina, from the Hawaiian phrase *aloha `āina,* which means "love of the land." A branch for women was also formed, the Hui Hawai`i Aloha `Āina no Nā Wāhine. The object of the association was "to preserve and maintain, by all legal and peaceful means and measures, the independent autonomy of the islands of Hawai`i."

The Native Hawaiians who wanted to retain their own government called themselves *ka po`e aloha `āina,* the people who love the land. Both branches of the Hui Aloha `Āina prepared testimony for a commissioner sent by U.S. President Grover Cleveland to investigate both the overthrow of the Hawaiian nation and the new government the that was set up in its place. The Native Hawaiians asked for the assistance of the U.S. president in the restoration of the Hawaiian government, and said they were waiting in "simple faith in the generosity and honor of the most liberal and honorable Government of the world [for] justice."

The women's petition read, in part:

> We, the women of the Hawaiian Islands, for our families and the happiness of our homes, desire peace and political quiet, and we pray that man's greed for power and spoils shall not be allowed to disturb the otherwise happy life of these islands.

Some of the women of the Hui Aloha `Āina were married to *haole* (U.S. or European) men. However, their love for their land and nation was apparently greater than their worry about political disagreement with their husbands.

The report of the commissioner led President Cleveland to announce that the overthrow and formation of a provisional government had been illegal. But Cleveland's power at that time was not great enough to persuade Congress to allow the restoration of Hawai`i's Queen Lili`uokalani. Some members of Congress favored the annexation of Hawai`i because they believed that the health of the economy depended on continuous expansion of their country's territory.

When William McKinley was elected president in 1896, the debate over annexation in the U.S. Congress had not come to a conclusion. In June 1897, McKinley submitted for congressional approval a treaty of annexation. It was time for the *huis,* as the Native Hawaiian activists were known, to take decisive action. The Kānaka Maoli wanted the U.S. government to live up to its stated principles of justice. They hoped that once the president and members of Congress saw that the great majority of Hawaiian citizens opposed the annexation, the principles of fairness would prevail and the Hawaiian government would be restored.

On September 6, 1897, the Hui Aloha `Āina held a meeting at the Palace Square in Honolulu which was attended by thousands of people. The association's president, James Kaulia, gave a rousing speech, saying, "We, the nation, will never consent to the annexation of our lands." He said that agreeing to annexation was like agreeing to be buried alive. He predicted that annexation would open the door for many foreigners to come and take jobs and resources away from the Native Hawaiians. He asked, "Then where will we live?" Kaulia asserted that "if the nation remains steadfast in its protest," annexation could be prevented.

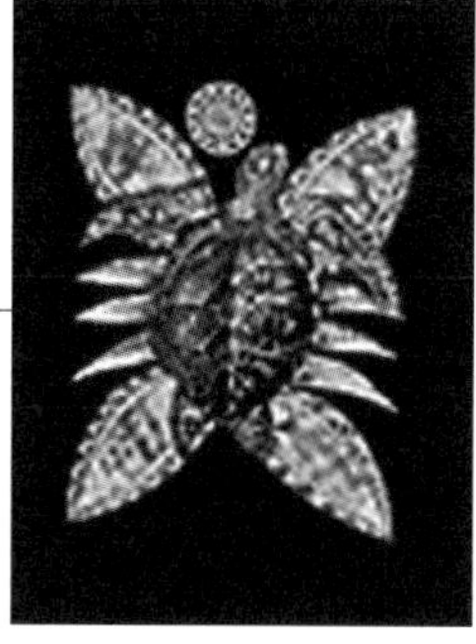

At this meeting, the Hui Aloha `Āina began to organize mass petition drives. The heading on the petition was in the Hawaiian language only. It said, *Palapala Hoopii Kue Hoohui `Āina,* which means "Petition Protesting Annexation." The women's branch of Hui Aloha `Āina also took action, traveling by ship to each island to gather signatures against annexation. When all the work was done, there were more than 21,000 signatures — about equal numbers from men and women. When one considers that the population of Native Hawaiians at the time was less than 40,000, this is an overwhelming number.

The Hui Aloha `Āina held another mass meeting on October 8, 1897, where they decided to send delegates to Washington, DC, to present their petitions to President McKinley and the Congress. The petitions and the lobbying by the Kānaka Maoli delegates succeeded in killing the annexation treaty in the U.S. Senate in February 1898. The original petitions are now held in the National Archives in Washington, DC. A few months later, in the midst of the war fever stirred up by the Spanish-American War, a joint resolution was passed by Congress supporting the annexation of Hawai`i. In today's movement for Hawaiian sovereignty, there are many who say that annexation was never really legal, since a resolution is not binding as law.

## Hawaiian Terms and Phrases Used in This Reading

*Kānaka Maoli* — Native Hawaiians

*aloha `āina* — love of the land

*ka po'e aloha `āina* — people who love the land

*Hui Hawai`i Aloha `Āina* — Native Hawaiian group opposed to annexation

*Hui Hawai`i Aloha `Āina no Nā Wāhine* — women's branch of the anti-annexation group

*huis* — members of the anti-annexation group

*haole* — foreigners who came to Hawai'i from the United States or Europe

*Palapala Hoopii Kue Hoohui `Āina* — Petition Protesting Annexation.

**Source:** *Based on original research by Noenoe Silva.*

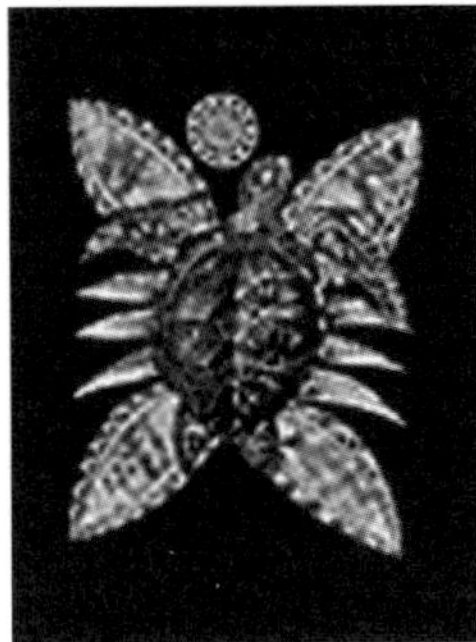

# Readings: The *New York Times* on Annexation

## Hawaiians On Annexation

**Half the Intelligent Natives Said to be Eager for it.**

**SAN FRANCISCO March 14.**

Ben Cluff, Jr., the President of the Brigham Young Academy at Provo, Utah, has returned from a visit to the Hawaiian Islands, where he went, at the solicitation of United States Senator Frank J. Cannon, to determine the strength of the annexation sentiment. He made a thorough canvass among the natives on the Islands of Oahu , Maui, and Hilo. He said:

Probably one half of the intelligent natives of the islands are pronounced advocates of the annexation. Of the remaining half the great majority are, primarily, in favor of the restoration of the monarchy, and, secondly, they much prefer annexation to the United States to a continuation of the present Government.

**Source:** New York Times, *March 15, 1898*

## Hawaii - Almost Ours.

**Senate Passes the House Resolution by a Vote of 42 to 21.**

**PRESIDENT'S ACTION FOLLOWS**

**Amendment After Amendment Was Offered and Rejected.**

**Twelve Pairs Announced — The Vote Unexpected — Not Strength Enough to Pass the Treaty.**

**WASHINGTON July 6.**

The annexation of Hawaii now is accomplished, so far as the legislative branch of the Government is concerned.

Unexpectedly, the resolution providing for the annexation of the islands was brought to a vote in the Senate late this afternoon, and it was passed by the decisive vote of 42 to 21.

Early in today's session of the Senate, conferences of the leaders on both sides of the chamber were held, and an agreement was reached that a vote should be taken tomorrow or Friday, at latest. The opponents of annexation practically had concluded their arguments and as they had no desire to keep the Senate in session by purely dilatory tactics, they announced their willingness that a vote should be taken as soon as Mr. White, Mr. Pettigrew, and Mr. Allen should have finished their speeches.

Neither Mr. White nor Mr. Pettigrew spoke at great length, but Mr. Allen thought when he began that his speech might occupy the remainder of the day and a part of tomorrow. However, he concluded to eliminate a part of the matter he had prepared, and at 4:15 o'clock completed his speech.

It was evident instantly that a vote was at hand. The word was passed swiftly through the corridors and committee rooms and in a few minutes every senator at the Capitol was in his seat. The galleries filled rapidly, and members

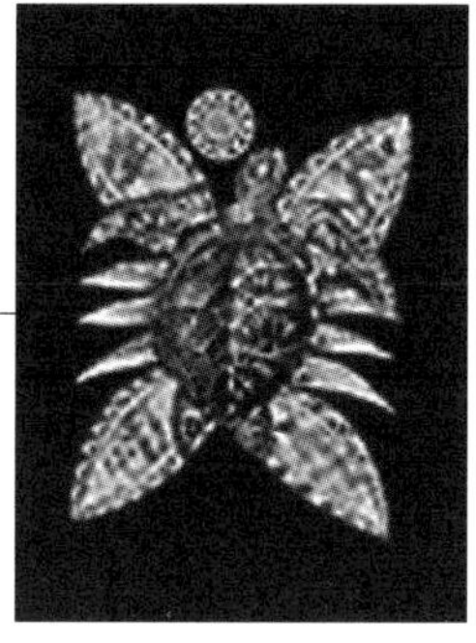

of the House of Representatives, learning that a vote was to be taken, came hurriedly to the Senate side of the building to witness proceedings that will be historic.

### Test Vote on an Amendment

The test vote came upon an amendment offered by Mr. White of California. It was offered with no expectation that it would be adopted, but merely to place ideas and opinions of the opponents of annexation on record. It was rejected by a vote of 40 to 20, indicating that the annexationists were strongly in the majority.

Amendment after amendment was offered, but the advocates of the resolution stood solidly together, gaining rather than losing strength on successive voices.

Finally, at 5:30 p.m. the resolution in precisely the form in which it was received from the House of Representatives was reported in the Senate and the roll call began. Intense interest was manifested by every spectator. Not a sound was to be heard in the chamber except the call of the Clerk and the response of the Senators. When the Vice-President announced the vote by which the resolution was passed, a tremendous wave of applause swept through the galleries, which the Vice-President made no effort to check.

Those who had advocated the resolution expressed their pleasure by shaking hands with one another, and on all sides evident relief was seen that the end had come. For a few minutes so much good-natured confusion existed that the dignity of the Senate was threatened, but Vice President Hobart quietly reminded the Senators that the session was not yet at an end....

When the Hawaiian resolution was laid before the Senate today, Mr. White (Dem., Cal.) resumed his speech in opposition.

He addressed the Senate only briefly, urging strongly that the question of annexation ought to be submitted to the Hawaiians themselves. He thought it was not good policy or evidence of broad and enduring statesmanship to adopt the resolutions in their present form, and although he realized fully that they would pass, he believed the future would justify the action of those opposed to them.

Upon the conclusion of Mr. White's speech, Mr. Pettigrew resumed his remarks, dealing at length with the methods employed in the erection of the present Hawaiian Republic.

Mr. Pettigrew spoke for about an hour and a half. He said the United States was paying an awful price for the Hawaiian Islands. "Independently of the assumption of the Hawaiian debt, independently of the assumption of immense Governmental responsibilities," he said, "we are paying a terrible price in the violation of our National honor which will be a black page in our history, and a blot upon our civilization." He deprecated the policy of imperialism, upon which, he said, the United States was entering, and concluded by saying that after the acquisition of Hawaii, the Philippines, Cuba, and Puerto Rico, the conquest of the countries of South America would begin....

**Source:** *Excerpted from* New York Times, *July 7, 1898.*

# Lesson 6.2 A Cause for Celebration?

**Objective:** To help students imagine how "patriotic" celebrations might seem from the perspective of colonized peoples.

**Themes:** patriotism, militarism

**Vocabulary:** allegiance, unalloyed, sanction, commemorate

## Suggested Activities

1. Before distributing the reading at the end this lesson, ask students what the Fourth of July means to them. How is it observed in their community? Is it an opportunity for seeing fireworks and partying, or is it an occasion for celebrating patriotism?
2. Have students review the reading. Ask them what happened on July 3, 1894. Divide the students into groups of three or four. Each group should take one of the passages quoted in the reading from Hawaiian newspapers (there are three passages altogether). Each group should restate in their own words what the passage is saying.
3. Have students share their versions of the passages with the class.
4. Tell the students to imagine that they are Kānaka Maoli — Native Hawaiians. Ask each student to write a poem entitled "July 4, Independence Day." In writing the poem they can assume the character of a Native Hawaiian person from either the past or the present.
5. With the whole class, ask students to discuss the concept of patriotism. Were Native Hawaiians who opposed annexation patriotic? What about in the United States, where there were people who both supported and opposed the annexation of Hawai`i (and the other countries discussed in this guide)? In the opinion of the students, who was more patriotic? Why? (Note that there are no "right" and "wrong" answers to these questions. Their purpose is to help students critically analyze history and develop their own sense of the meaning of "patriotism.")

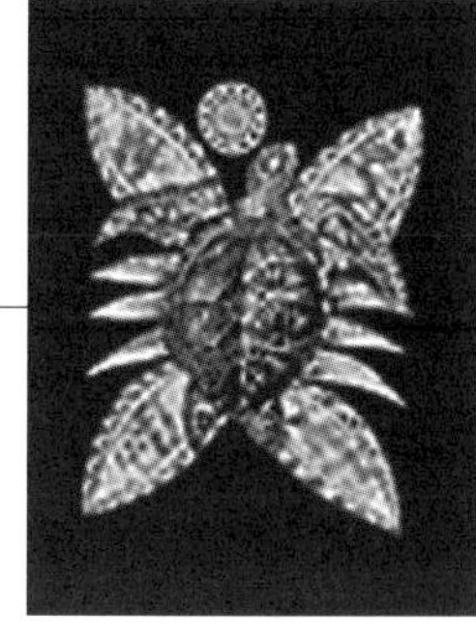

# Reading: Hawai`i and the Fourth of July

U.S. Marines landed in Hawai`i to overthrow the Hawaiian monarchy in January 1893. This invasion resulted in the formation of a provisional government of U.S. businessmen, headed by Sanford B. Dole. The United States did not immediately give its support to this government, so "President" Dole created a new constitution. The constitution declared the new Republic of Hawai`i controlled Hawai`i's lands, waters, and citizens.

Eighteen of the delegates to the constitutional convention held in May 1894 were elected. Nineteen others, however, were appointed by Dole himself, guaranteeing a majority. To qualify for election, delegates and voters had to swear allegiance to the newly formed Republic of Hawai`i, thus eliminating most of the Kānaka Maoli (Native Hawaiians). On July 4, 1894, settlers from the United States were celebrating their Independence Day by firing cannons from their warships in Honolulu Harbor. Dole stood on the steps of `Iolani Palace and said:

> [B]y virtue of the charge to me given by the Executive and Advisory Councils of the Provisional Government and by the Act dated July 3, 1894, [I] proclaim the Republic of Hawai`i as the sovereign authority over and throughout the Hawaiian Islands from this time forth. And I . . . now assume office and authority of President thereof.

After Dole's proclamation, 300 people signed an oath of allegiance to the new republic. The next day, the *Pacific Commercial Advertiser,* a locally published newspaper, called July 4, 1894 "the greatest day in Hawaiian history" and declared a "new life for Hawai`i." But Hawaiian newspapers tell another story. On July 2, four Hawaiian papers announced a public meeting. Seven thousand Hawaiian citizens and their supporters turned out to protest the constitution and the coming announcement of the Republic of Hawai`i. On July 3, the newspaper *Hawai`i Holomua* said this about the Fourth of July:

> In every country in the world, Americans living away from home celebrate the glorious day and demonstrate their unalloyed devotion to the Stars and Stripes. . . . But let us remember that the Fourth of July is a day on which we all who remember the many benefactions of America can celebrate and show our respect to the great republic, the justice of which we never doubt, . . . and of which Hawai`i will never become a member. Ho! for the Fourth.

Coverage of Dole's proclamation in the *Hawai`i Holomua* on July 6 read:

> In spite of the official statement that the ceremony would be purely civilian and that no military display would be made, the basement was filled with armed men . . . Most of the councilors and delegates carried pistols . . . The hurry was so great that our "missionary" friends even forgot to open the proceedings with prayers . . . No blessing will come to this government . . . And so the Hawaiian republic was declared without the sanction of people, without prayers, but with display of pistols and rifles.

On June 22 of the following year, in anticipation of celebrations of the Fourth of July, the Hawaiian language paper *Ke Aloha `Āina* reminded its readers of the differences in the meaning of this date:

> The glory of the Fourth of July was that it was established by Americans to commemorate the independence of America from Great Britain. That is in no way similar to the Republic's choice of July 4 as a day of independence for itself . . . They should not be confused.
>
> (Translation by Noenoe Silva.)

---

**Source:** *Based on original research by Noenoe Silva.*

# LESSON 6.3: Tourist Hawai`i

**Objective:** To decode the hidden messages underlying tourist industry advertising and interpret the relationship between promotional images and reality as it is understood by Native Hawaiians.

**Materials needed:** Enough tourist brochures for small groups to examine. These are available free and in large quantities from any travel agency. The best are those with lots of pictures of people and landscapes.

**Vocabulary:** commodify, dispossess, *haole*

Many people in the continental United States have preconceived notions of what Hawai`i looks like. In particular, people maintain a false idea of Hawai`i that reflects the images the tourist industry churns out in endless amounts: hula dancers, surfing, palm trees, sun, fun, beautiful women, and friendly natives, to name a few. This lesson is aimed at using this image of Hawai`i, which so many share, as an entry point into thinking about Hawai`i. The focus here is for students to arrive at a critical reading of tourist brochures.

## Suggested Activities

1. Ask the class what images, sights, smells, or sounds come to mind when we say the word "Hawai`i." Allow the students to be frank, for some of the images may be sexual. Keep a list of their answers.
2. Have students discuss the following questions with a neighbor: What would you include if you were designing a tourist brochure for your town? Would you feature the poorer neighborhoods or omit them? Why?
3. Divide the students into small groups. Pass out the worksheet, "What The Tour Guide Tells Us," to every student and go over it. Give each group a few tourist brochures — one to each person if you have enough. The students' job is to examine their brochures as a group, answer the questions on the handout, and do the short writing assignment.
4. After the students have finished, gather the whole class together and ask them about the information they have prepared. Record on the chalk board the demographic data that they have found and have the class share their descriptions of "Tourist Hawai`i."
5. Ask the class to discuss some of the questions below, using the information they have gathered and their writing assignments from suggested activity 3 as background.
   - How is Hawai`i depicted?
   - What does the land look like?
   - To whom are these brochures supposed to sell Hawai`i?
   - Whose point of view is represented in the brochures?
   - Who and what is being sold as an attraction?
   - How are Pacific Islanders depicted in the brochures?
   - Are these positive or negative images? Could they be both?
   - Do you think the images in the brochures are truthful? Why or why not?
6. Hand out the reading at the end of this lesson entitled "The Aloha Industry" and have students list five effects of tourism on Native Hawaiian women.
7. Using both cartoons presented at the end of this lesson, have students develop captions for each that describe the effects of tourism.

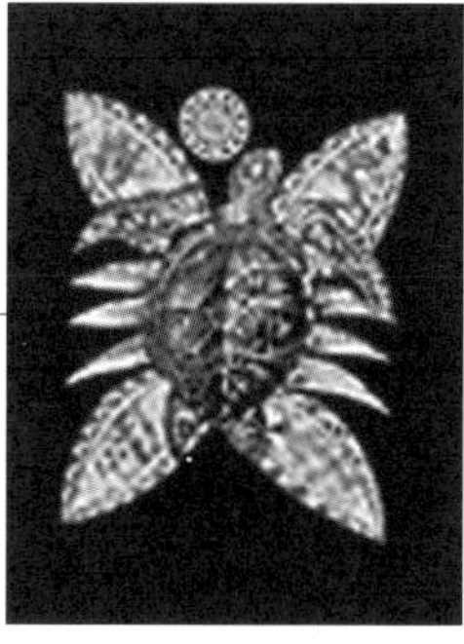

# Worksheet: What the Tour Guide Tells Us: Defining "Tourist Hawai`i"

As a group, your job is to interpret what tourist brochures about Hawai`i are saying to you.

1. Flip through the brochures. Develop a feel for what they are offering you. Look at the pictures and read some of the captions. How do they make you feel? Do they entice you to go to Hawai`i? Or do they look unappealing and uninviting?
2. Examine the pictures of people included in the brochures and answer the questions on the box at the bottom of this page.
3. Using only the information in the brochures, give a written description of a new country that we will call "Tourist Hawai`i." Include the climate, geography, population (including dress, racial or ethnic characteristics, gender, temperament — is everybody happy? — and overall physical appearance), architecture, plants, animals, and culture (what do people like to do there? What do they eat?). Write your impressions of the Hawai`i that the brochure has defined for you. Feel free to be creative with your writing. Use poetry, prose, fiction, or fact, but make sure you base what you write on the information provided by the brochures.

a. Out of all of the people, how many of them look European or European-American? _______

Of these, how many are female? ____ Male? _____

b. Now answer the same questions about other ethnic or racial groups :

| | | | |
|---|---|---|---|
| African Americans: | M ______ | F _______ | Total _______ |
| Asian Americans: | M______ | F _______ | Total _______ |
| Latinos: | M ______ | F _______ | Total _______ |
| Hawaiians or other Pacific Islanders: | M ______ | F _______ | Total ______ |
| Native Americans: | M_______ | F _______ | Total _______ |

c. How many of the pictures portray couples? ______ Singles? ______

d. How many of the people depicted are poor? ______ Middle class? ______ Rich? _____

# Reading: The Aloha Industry

Tourists flock to our native land for escape, but they are escaping into a state of mind while participating in the destruction of a host people in a native place. To Hawaiians, daily life is neither soft nor kind. In fact, the political, economic, and cultural reality for most Hawaiians is hard, ugly, and cruel.

Today, glass and steel shopping malls with layer parking lots stretch over what were once carefully irrigated taro (the staple from which poi is made) lands that fed millions of Hawaiians over thousands of years. Large bays, delicately ringed for generations with well-stocked fish ponds, are now heavily silted and polluted with jet skis, wind surfers, and sailboats. Multistory hotels flood over six million* tourists onto our beaches annually, closing them off to locals.

The true impact of tourism on the Hawaiian people and the land is devastating. Thirty years ago, at statehood, Hawai`i residents outnumbered tourists by more than two to one. Today, tourists outnumber residents six to one, and they outnumber Native Hawaiians thirty to one.

The problem is that we are an island, and there is only so much land to go around. Hawai`i has the lowest rate of owner-occupied housing in the nation outside New York, and probably the tightest rental market anywhere.

The real scandal of Hawai`i is the dispossession of the native people. In 1920, the United States provided 200,000 acres for homesteading of Native Hawaiians . . . Since 1920, the state has settled fewer than 6,000 natives on their homestead land . . . Since 1959, the state has refused to provide a single acre of ceded land to Hawaiians.**

For decades, the Hawaiian people have fought this dispossession, through courts, through continuing to practice their spiritual beliefs, through active reclamation of lands, and through constant occupations. Hawaiians have "occupied" trust lands, built homes, and lived on beaches. The state has evicted them and destroyed and burned their homes. Hawaiian people have fought to protect the rain forest of the major island, Hawai`i, from exploitation. More plants and animals from Hawai`i are now extinct or on the endangered species list than from all the rest of the United States.

## An Ornamental Hoax

Tourism is not here to sell *haole* (white) culture. It is here because we are the native people of this *`āina* (land). It is our culture that tourists come to see. It is our land the tourists come to pollute. Without beautiful Hawaiian women dancing, there would be no tourism.

Our *`āina* are no longer the source of food and shelter, but rather the source of money. Land is now called real estate, rather than *papa*, our word for mother. Beautiful areas, once sacred to my people, are now expensive resorts. Now, even access to beaches near hotels is strictly regulated or denied to the local people altogether.

Tourism displaces Hawaiians, and those who work do so at the lowest level. According

*The latest available figures, from the Visitors Industry Education Council, show 6.8 million visitors to Hawai`i each year, as of 1996.

**As of 1998, the state government has begun to make retroactive payments amounting to millions of dollars to the Office of Hawaiian Affairs for the use of ceded lands.

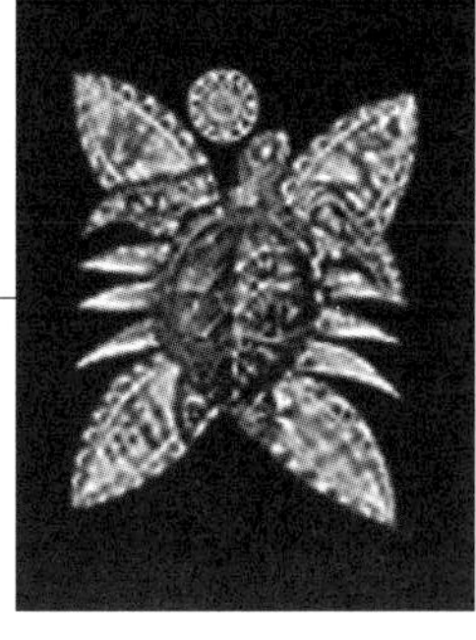

to David Stannard, who teaches American Studies at the University of Hawai`i, "A family of four with one full-time, average-pay hotel worker at its head lives permanently mired in an official state of poverty . . . The tourist industry, in fact, is not for the Hawaiians."

The commodification of Hawaiian culture includes marketing native values and practices on *haole* terms. These talents, in Hawaiian terms, are the hula, the *aloha* — generosity and love — of our people, the *u`i* or youthful beauty of our men and women, and the continuing allure of our lands and waters. Tourism converts these attributes into profit.

Hula dancers wear clown-like makeup, don costumes from a mix of Polynesian cultures, and behave in a smutty manner, rather than in a powerfully erotic manner. The hula is erotic because it depicts the energy of life force — in the earth and among the people of the earth. This life force or *mana* (energy) is sensual. In the hotel version of the hula, the sacredness of the dance has disappeared and been replaced with an ornamental hoax.

In the native tradition, the hula was performed: (1) as a *mōhai* (sacred offering); (2) to transmit knowledge as a component of the oral traditions; and (3) as a vehicle for providing social and cultural cohesion. Tourism commodifies hula for the lurid gratification of the *haole.*

## Undoing Images

Tourism deforms the culture so much that young Hawaiians grow up thinking that our culture is a *haole* interpretation of our culture — to dance the hula is to dance for tourists. The point is that everything in Hawai`i "can be yours" — the place, the people, the culture, and even the identity as native are for sale.

We are working to undo this image. As Hawaiians, one of the first steps is to look at it ourselves and think about the impact of tourism on our culture. Unfortunately, many of our people, and Hawaiian women in particular, don't agree that tourism prostitutes our culture. This is a measure of the depth of our mental oppression: we can't understand our own cultural degradation because we are living it.

We have a long way to go. We also need to educate others and join with them. This problem is not unique to Hawai`i. It is suffered by peoples as far away as Tahiti and the southwestern United States. Tourism is not a neutral industry, and as indigenous women, we need to look at it especially carefully.

---

**Source:** *Excerpted from Haunani-Kay Trask and Mililani Trask, "The Aloha Industry,"* Cultural Survival Quarterly, *Winter 1992.*

# Cartoons: Views of the Tourist Industry

**Source:** Awake: Asian Women and the Struggle for Justice *(Sydney, Australia: Asian Partnership for Human Development, 1985).*

# Lesson 6.4 Protest Poetry: A "No Fight" Fight Poem

**Objective:** To enable students to write a poem about personal struggles, using Native Hawaiian resistance to foreign domination as a model.

**Themes:** cultural resistance, cultural identity, oppression

**Vocabulary:** displaced

Poetry can be a powerful witness to struggle and social change. In Hawai`i, Native Hawaiians have been using poetry for thousands of years, including ancient chants and family lineages that they have carried in memory since their origin as a people. This lesson is designed to use the issue of the mistreatment of Native Hawaiians as a catalyst for students to write protest poetry about issues that concern them in the United States.

## Suggested Activities

1. Read the poem, "No Fight Hawaiians" (provided as a handout at the end of this lesson) aloud as a class. Ask the students whether the poem is about not fighting or whether it is really about fighting. What do they believe that Hawaiians are fighting (or not fighting) against?
2. Ask students to choose a group (or person) who they believe has been harshly treated by this society and write a "no fight" fight poem about them. The subject can be any kind of grouping: homeless people, single mothers, poor people, people of color, immigrants, youth/kids, or they themselves. The first line can be "No fight _____ ." Make sure that the students find ways to describe why and how the group or person they have chosen is being mistreated. Indicate to the students they should not feel bound to follow the format used in the handout.
3. When the poems are done, arrange the room in a big circle and ask all the students to share their work.

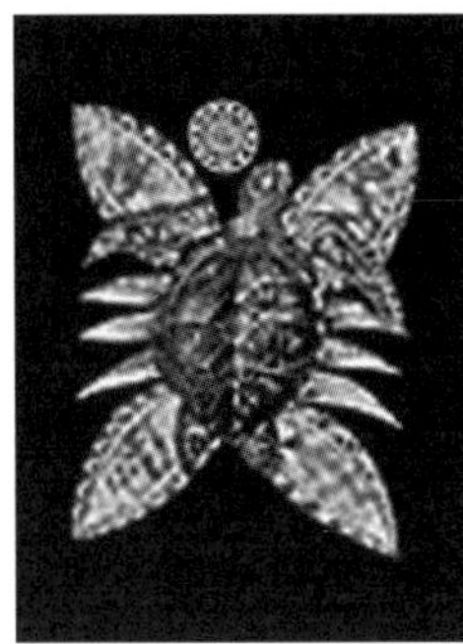

# Poem: No Fight Hawaiians

Eh, Bra,
check it out.
I met
this Brada
the ada day,
suckin Brada
blow my mind!

Everything he
said was
"No fight Hawaiians."

I ask him
What his name?
He said,
"No fight Hawaiians."
I said wea you
from?
He said,
"No fight Hawaiians,
Bra."
Everything I said,
he said,
"No fight Hawaiians."
I asked him
where he work?
He said,
"No fight Hawaiians."
"No fight Hawaiians."
"No fight Hawaiians."
Afta half hour,
Bra,
I start going
nuts!

"No fight Hawaiians."
Man!
I tired hear that
already!
"What?
Wow, Bra, what
talking?
What's the trip?"
"No fight Hawaiians.
wat sa mada wit that?"
Brada wen
look at me and said:
"Too many things to
change,
too many people to
teach
and too much to
do."

"Poverty fights Hawaiians:
the baiting of us out of
the lo'i*
into the Big
City,
Dozens of families
raised in rooming houses
above bars, stores
and more bars.

"A generation of gardeners
starving in
the Big City.
So, Bra,
No fight Hawaiians."

Homelessness.
Homelessness fight
Hawaiians.
A people that
went back in
the same place
hundreds of years
now
find themselves
three generations
of displaced
nomads.
Caught in a web
of evictions
and homelessness.
No fight Hawaiians.
"Having a
confused identity
fights Hawaiians.
Families after families
being raised
to believe
Hawaiians no good.
Hawaiians in the joint.
Hawaiians stupid.
No fight Hawaiians.
Too many things
to fight, Bra.
No fight Hawaiians."

The more I thought
the more it made
sense.

No fight Hawaiians.
The more I thought
the more important
it became.
No fight Hawaiians.
No
fight
Hawaiians!
Heavy.

— *Imaikalani Kalahele*

*Traditional taro gardens

# LESSON 6.5 Pele vs. Progress:
## The Wao Kele o Puna Rain Forest and Geothermal Power Plants

**Objective:** To develop an understanding of the debate over the geothermal plants in the Wao Kele o Puna rain forest and its implications for financial, industrial, cultural, and environmental interests.

**Themes:** environment, development, coalition building

**Vocabulary:** adaptation, niche, conservation, electromagnetic radiation, geothermal energy, greenhouse effect, megawatt, rain forest

**Materials Needed:**

Construction paper or poster board for group name placards

Large pieces of butcher paper

Crayons or markers

Since the late 1970s the energy industry has been discussing the possibility of using geothermal energy from the volcanoes in Hawai`i as a safe, viable energy source in the islands. The first drilling experiment came to fruition in the early 1980s near Pahoa, a small town on the big island of Hawai`i. Due to toxic fumes, complaints from the neighborhood around the drilling sites, and the immediate death of the vegetation surrounding the geothermal vent, this initial experiment was closed down.

The specter of geothermal energy came to life again in 1989. More electric power was sorely needed to sustain the tremendous economic and industrial growth in the state of Hawai`i, on the island of O`ahu in particular. In order to meet this need, Hawai`i has had to import oil to generate almost 90 percent of its electricity. Since Hawai`i sits on top of what geologists consider to be a volcanic hot spot, where molten lava comes to the surface and is constantly creating new land in the islands, the state seems to be a perfect place to develop geothermal energy plants that can harness this energy to generate electrical power.

Some, however, warn of dangers to the environment, as well as threats to Native Hawaiian culture. The site where the True Geothermal Energy Co. placed its first geothermal drilling rig, with the state's permission, was in the middle of the Wao Kele o Puna rain forest near Puna on the island of Hawai`i. Wao Kele o Puna is the last lowland tropical rain forest in the United States. It is also sacred to Native Hawaiians, who use its resources to meet their traditional medicinal and cultural needs. In addition, many Native Hawaiians worship the goddess Pele, the goddess of the volcano who can both create and destroy. To drill into her body would be sacrilegious to native spirituality.

Should we or shouldn't we drill for geothermal energy in the Wao Kele o Puna rain forest? This lesson offers a role play that is designed to introduce students to the specific debate at hand, as a way of understanding the conflicting interests that can arise between development, environment, and culture. Background information is provided in the reading at the end of this lesson, "Hawai`i's Natural Heritage." Five role statements are given following the reading. All of these roles represent real people or organizations and their actual positions on the issue at hand (note that as of 1998, many of those listed are no longer in the positions given in this role play).

# Suggested Activities

1. Have students read the handout at the end of this lesson entitled "Hawai`i's Natural Heritage," either in class or as homework, to prepare for the role play.
2. Break students into groups of five. Each group member takes one of the position readings. Each group should understand that its ultimate goal is the creation of posters expressing the group's position.
3. Have the students reshuffle themselves into "expert groups," where all of the students with the same role come together to read, discuss, and analyze their position. Each member of these groups should develop individual notes on the group's shared position.
4. Have students return to their original groups to present their positions to each other. A recorder should keep a list of arguments that are in support of and against geothermal drilling in the rain forest.
5. Each group should try to arrive at a consensus position, either supporting or opposing geothermal drilling. The group should then prepare a poster expressing its point of view. The posters should include a slogan, a graphic image, and bulleted notes explaining the group's position.
6. The groups should chose spokespeople to present their posters to the class.

## Resources for More Information

J. Borg, "Geothermal Energy Dispute Erupts in Hawai`i," *Washington Post,* Sept. 22, 1990, p. A3.

S. J. Bowman, "Hawaiians Try to Preserve a Rain Forest," *Christian Science Monitor,* Jan. 3, 1991, p. 10.

"Hawai`i Hotspot," *American Forests,* Vol. 97, Nos. 7 and 8, July-Aug. 1991, pp. 45, 76.

T. Egan, "Hawai`i Debates Peril to Rain Forest As Energy Project Taps a Volcano," *New York Times,* Jan. 26, 1990, pp. A13, B8.

S. Essoyan, "Blowout Shuts Geothermal Unit in Hawai`i," *Los Angeles Times,* June 15, 1991, p. A19.

"Battle Over Hawai`i Geothermal Plant Heats Up," *Los Angeles Times,* Dec. 10, 1989, p. A48.

B. Finney, "The Dragon Within," *Mother Earth News,* May-June 1990, pp. 14-15.

S. Kelly, "Conservationists Question Hawai`i Thermal Project," *Washington Post,* Dec. 17, 1989, p. A3.

M. D. Lemonick, "Hot Tempers in Hawai`i: Exploiting Clean Geothermal Energy Could Threaten a Rain Forest." *Time,* Vol. 136, No. 7, Aug. 13, 1990, p. 68.

M. Mardon, "Steamed up over Rain Forests," *Sierra,* Vol. 75, No. 3, May-June 1990, pp. 80-81.

B. McKibben, "Power Play Endangers Hawai`i's Rain Forest," *Rolling Stone,* May 31, 1990, pp. 41-42.

W. S. Merwin, letter to the editor, *American Poetry Review,* Vol. 19, No. 2, Mar.-Apr. 1990, pp. 43–45.

J. Seed, "Last Rain Forest in US Is Threatened," *Christian Science Monitor,* Dec. 1, 1989, p. 18.

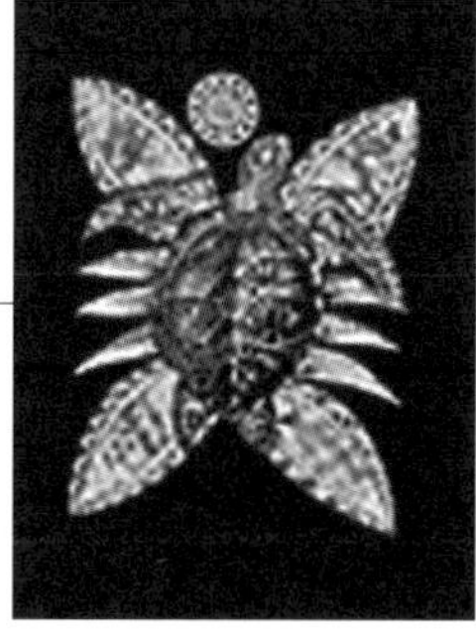

# Reading: Hawai`i's Natural Heritage

*Ke ewe hanau o ka `āina*
The lineage born of the land

The Hawaiian Islands are unique. The most remote island chain in the world, Hawai`i is the site of the world's largest mountain, most active volcano, and highest rainfall. It is also home to over 10,000 unique plants, animals and insects, which populate environments as different as coral reefs, rain forests, and alpine deserts. The fact that many of Hawai`i's plants and animals are extinct or critically endangered is a forceful reminder that adaptation has limits, and that in remaking Hawai`i, one species — humans — has destroyed paradise for many others.

Hawai`i's natural heritage represents millions of years of evolution. The isolation of the islands, which are 2,300 miles from the nearest continent, kept all but the best plant and animal travelers from colonizing Hawai`i. Many came by air, carried by the wind or by birds; some came by water, swimming or in some cases floating, driven by wind and currents. Not many made the journey, with a total estimate of 1,000 ancestral species arriving at the rate of one every 70,000 years.

These native organisms — which arrived without the aid of humans — encountered a landscape that provided a variety of environmental niches. Climate, soil, and temperature ranged widely over the islands. Plants, animals and insects moved into different niches, producing a variety in forms. This led to the development of many species that are found only in Hawai`i. In other instances, single species have slowly changed into many separate species that can no longer interbreed.

Many streams are fed by Hawai`i's rains, including 376 that flow all year around. Hawai`i's streams are generally "flashy," rising and falling quickly in response to rainfall. Many streams are partially fed by groundwater flowing from springs, and there are direct links between ground and surface waters in some areas.

The main Hawaiian islands stretch from Kauai (approximately five million years old) southeast to Hawai`i Island (less than one million years old). The islands have formed as the Pacific plate that supports them moves over a "hot spot," where lava from deep within the earth is able to reach the surface. Today the southeastern portion of the island of Hawai`i is centered over the hot spot, causing frequent eruptions of Mauna Loa and Kilauea volcanoes.

Of all the various influences, change is the defining factor in Hawai`i's environment, for individual species, ecosystems, and entire islands. The native plants and animals never adapted to the presence of either large mammals, such as cattle, or smaller predators, such as rats. These and many other plants and animals were then absent from Hawai`i. Plants that came to these islands lost natural defenses which they had when they arrived (like thorns), while some birds lost the ability to fly. These adaptations were successful only before the arrival of humans, who brought new foreign species and have effected extensive environmental change. The changes that humans have brought to Hawai`i's environment have been so rapid that adaptation has been impossible for most species, and as a result many have become extinct or endangered. The task we now face is to save those unique and irreplaceable species that still exist, before they too become victims of the remaking of Hawai`i.

---

**Source:** *Adapted from "Natural History of the Hawaiian Islands," Sierra Club Legal Defense Fund, 1995.*

# Pele vs. Progress Role Play

## Role: Pele Defense Fund

You represent the position of the Pele Defense Fund (PDF). You are a group of Native Hawaiians who strongly oppose the geothermal drilling in the Wao Kele o Puna rain forest for cultural, political, and religious reasons. Your group was started in 1983 as a response to increased interest in geothermal energy exploration in your home, the big island of Hawai`i.

The Wao Kele o Puna rain forest is in many ways sacred to you. It has supplied traditional Native Hawaiian doctors with the special herbs and medicines they have needed for thousands of years. Henry Auwae, a traditional practitioner of herbal medicine, has stated, "Wao Kele produces these plants with a quality and potency I have found nowhere else." In addition, Hawaiian wood carvers come to the forest to gather special materials for their craft, and practitioners of the sacred hula visit the Wao Kele for the materials they need for their traditional performances. Indeed, the rain forest is of extreme cultural importance to you.

In addition, scientists recently found dried lava tubes beneath the forest. These ancient tubes represent a cave system that is more than ten miles long, and ancient burial sites and religious structures have been found there. Would all of the drilling destroy this special place? What if there are more burial grounds?

Many of the PDF worship the goddess of the volcano, Pele. She is all-powerful, for she is the goddess who has the power to both destroy and create, much like the figure of Mother Earth. The volcano where True Geothermal Energy is drilling is the home of Pele. You consider the land to be her body. To drill into Pele's body would be a severe violation of your religious practices and might constitute a physical affront to your culture.

Politically speaking, you feel you were duped by the State of Hawai`i. Originally the geothermal wells were to be dug on a different piece of land. When they began those wells, the volcano erupted and Pele spoke; the original drilling areas were covered with fresh lava. In order to facilitate the progress of the drilling, the state decided to abandon its plans for the piece of land that was covered with lava and substitute the Wao Kele o Puna rain forest. You know, however, that the government had designated this land as a natural reserve more than twenty years ago. Further, it was supposed to be given to the Native Hawaiians in the first place. Of course, nobody asked you whether this substitution was okay. Besides, why should people who live here on the big island of Hawai`i have to sacrifice your health and culture, just so the people on the island of O`ahu can have electricity for all of their big, fancy hotels?

Drilling in Wao Kele cannot be good or right. It just plain hurts the environment. Palikapu Dedman, a founder of your group, has said, "Our religion is a healthy environment . . . That's our life, our customs, our medicine." The sulfuric gases that the geothermal vents spew out are toxic to all forms of life. Surely the construction of these plants would hurt and even destroy the Wao Kele o Puna rain forest.

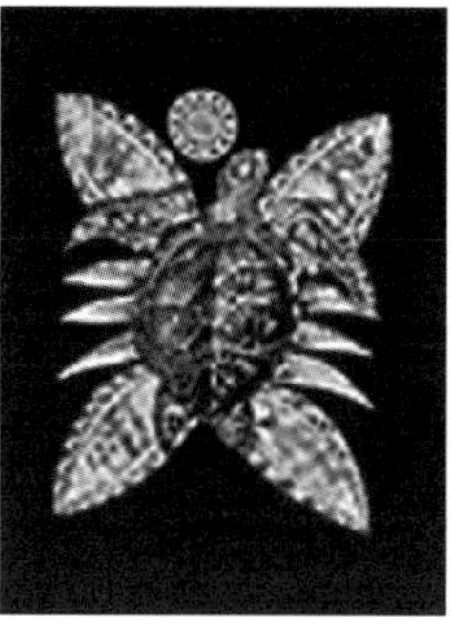

# Pele vs. Progress Role Play

## Role: Rain Forest Action Coalition

You represent the position of the Rain Forest Action Coalition. Your group is mostly made up of middle class European-Americans who are concerned about the environment. Your coalition came from the continental United States to join in the struggle against the geothermal plants in Wao Kele o Puna rain forest, and you have developed a broad base of support in Hawai`i.

Wao Kele o Puna is very important to you for a number of reasons. It is the only lowland tropical rain forest in the United States. That alone should make it a national treasure. Environmentally speaking, Wao Kele holds extreme importance. Ninety-five percent of the flowering plants and 97 percent of the animals there are found nowhere else in the world. For instance, the forest is home to the world's only carnivorous caterpillar; `ie`ie vines grow in this forest that will grow nowhere else. The Hawaiian hawk and happy-faced spider inhabit the forest as well. Think of all of the species that would become extinct if the forest were destroyed by endless geothermal drilling. Further, what about the plants there? Many tropical plants have been found to provide cures for diseases. If the forest were destroyed, how many cures would we lose?

Although the proposal says that it is only going to clear 300 out of 27,000 acres, that could be devastating. Most of that acreage will come in the form of roads criss-crossing and cutting through the rain forest. These roads provide perfect avenues for alien plants and animals to invade the forest and kill the indigenous wildlife. Even though wild pigs do spread some harmful plant species right now, the rate at which alien wildlife spread through the forest would be greatly increased through roads.

The sulfuric gases that are released by the wells are very toxic. In an older drilling experiment in Pahoa, the plants around the well all perished because of the fumes. People living around the drilling sites had to be evacuated a number of times because of problems with the toxic gases. Also, sustainable geothermal drilling has never been proven to work on an active volcano. Who knows, maybe they will start drilling and their well will dry out! Then they would have to destroy more forest just to make more wells to pay off their debts.

The plan also calls for huge power lines to be strung out over the island and then into the water so the power can reach the island of O'ahu. You are sure that the electromagnetic radiation emitted by these lines is extremely harmful to all life. In this case it will cross the path of humpback whales that migrate through the Hawaiian islands every winter. What effect will it have on them?

Why this new idea for geothermal energy anyway? What about conservation? Robert Mowris, an energy efficiency expert from University of California at Berkeley, says Hawai`i could reduce its consumption of electricity without the geothermal plants being needed at all. He has designed special light bulbs that conserve electricity and special glass that will help reduce the need for air-conditioning in the fancy hotels. These are just two of many gadgets Mowris has designed that he says could cut Hawai`i's electricity consumption by 40 to 60 percent. Instituting conservation measures could cost five to seven times less than building the new geothermal supply. Also, what about solar power? After all, Hawai`i has plenty of sun.

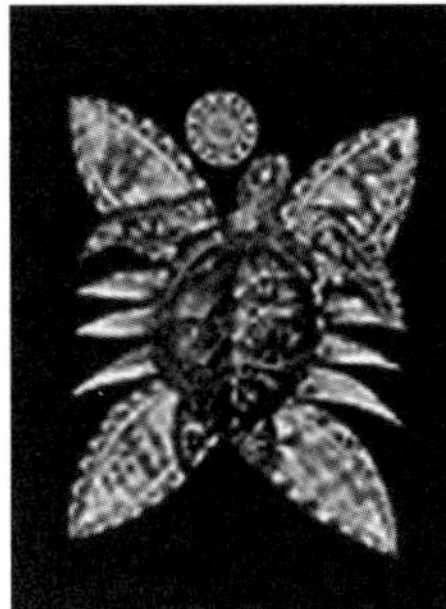

# Pele vs. Progress Role Play

## Role: Hawai`i Department of Land and Natural Resources

You represent the position of the Hawai`i Department of Land and Natural Resources. Technically, you are responsible for the care and management of Hawai`i's resources. Geothermal energy, electricity, and rain forests definitely fall under your jurisdiction.

Right now, Hawai`i imports oil in huge amounts. Hawai`i needs to burn oil in order to make steam so the islands can have electricity. Almost 90 percent of Hawai`i's electricity comes from burning petroleum. Burning oil to generate electricity causes the release of large amounts of carbon dioxide, which contributes to the greenhouse effect. In addition, oil must be transported to the islands in big tankers. Obviously, an oil spill poses a threat to Hawai`i.

As a state employee, you must look out for the needs of the state. Right now, the state needs electricity and it is your job to find some way to meet that need. As Roger Ulverling, the state's director of business and economic development, has said, "We don't find any other alternative source of electricity large enough to put a dent in Hawai`i's consumption." Geothermal energy is a source of energy that could meet nearly all of Hawai`i's electrical needs and end the state's dependence on oil. Geothermal energy has been proven to be safe and reliable. At least twenty countries have made use of it for decades. Figures from the World Resources Institute indicate that replacing oil-generated power with the planned 500 megawatts that geothermal plants could generate will have the same positive effect on global warming as planting 500,000 acres of trees. Geothermal energy seems perfect to you.

Rain forests are in your jurisdiction, too, and as a natural resource, the Wao Kele o Puna rain forest seems fairly valuable. It is, after all, the last lowland rain forest in the United States. It is large — 27,000 acres — and it holds some potential as a source of medicines due to its abundance of unique plants.

On the other hand, True Geothermal Energy is only planning to clear 300 out of 27,000 acres total. And some experts say that Wao Kele is not a very healthy rain forest, anyway. Wild pigs, mongooses, and cats have moved in with various waves of immigration to the islands. Many alien species of plants have also established themselves on the edge of the forest. Besides, you have done a pretty good job with forest conservation. Just look at how Hawai`i compares with other states. Although it is the fourth smallest state, its rank is seventh in the nation for the most state-owned forest land.

In the short term, it seems that you might want to keep the forest as healthy as possible. For the distant future of Hawai`i, though, geothermal energy seems to offer low risk and high gain in terms of natural resources. Since there is a lot of money to be made from investments in the construction of geothermal wells and other technological breakthroughs, as well as all of the money the state would save from cutting back on oil consumption, you might want to think about who you should support — especially since you are state-funded.

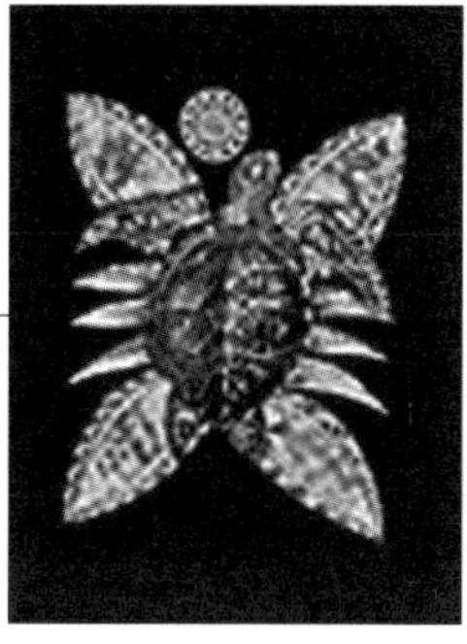

# Pele vs. Progress Role Play

## Role: John Waihee, Governor of Hawai`i

You represent the position of Governor John Waihee. You have a huge problem: Hawai`i must import oil in order to generate 90 percent of the electricity it needs. This is unacceptable to you, and it may be in the best interest of the state for you to pursue the idea of geothermal energy.

Your communications director, Chuck Friedman, has said, "The state is trying to end its slavery on oil for two basic reasons. Economically, we're at the far end of the oil supply line, and environmentally, it's murder on the ozone layer and dangerous to transport." And he's right. You are thousands of miles away from the nearest oil source, so the cost to you and the state is tremendous. In addition, having so many oil tankers in the waters around the islands is a very serious risk for crashes and oil spills. Geothermal energy will solve this problem for you.

As Hawai`i's governor, you don't see many options. With the support of Hawai`i's Senator Daniel Inouye, you can obtain $15 million in financial aid from the federal government for drilling. This added money will be used to create jobs right here in the islands. This would help with unemployment and provide a boost to the economy. In addition, many companies, such as Hawai`i Electric, would benefit from the prospective profits involved. Big business wants you to drill!

Geothermal energy does seem safe, after all. It is used in over twenty countries worldwide and in other U.S. states like California and Nevada. It has proven to be reliable and sustainable. Geothermal energy only produces a tenth of a percent of the carbon monoxide that burning oil does. Besides, the plan calls for only 300 out of a total of 27,000 acres of forest land to be cleared, a pittance by anyone's standards. What a small price to pay for Hawai`i to get the oil monkey off of its back!

But the Wao Kele o Puna rain forest has become a huge pain in the neck for you. You are the first Native Hawaiian governor ever in the history of the state. You reached office with the support of ordinary people, particularly Native Hawaiians. Now the Hawaiians don't want the forest to be touched. You have already angered them by authorizing a land trade, swapping Hawaiian Trust land for a site where another geothermal well had been destroyed by a volcanic eruption. Further, the volcano does represent the goddess Pele in Hawaiian culture, and the forest there holds cultural significance to the Hawaiian people. Can you sell out for money, or do you do what your people want you to do? If you go against the will of the Hawaiians, will you be able to be re-elected? What about if you go against the big business interests — which, by the way, own much of the news media and are in support of geothermal energy? As Hawai`i's governor, what should you do?

# Pele vs. Progress Role Play

## Role: True Geothermal Energy Corporation

You represent the position of True Geothermal Energy Corp. The drilling of geothermal wells in the Wao Kele o Puna rain forest, although not your idea originally, is now your baby.

You have a vision of the future, in which more than twenty geothermal wells at this site alone will produce 500 megawatts of electricity. We're not talking just geothermal wells here; we're talking steam-gathering systems, converter stations, transmission lines, and a deep water cable system to transport all of this juice to the island of O`ahu. The cable system will be placed on majestic towers more than 100 feet high that will stand as a monument to the good things that you are doing in Hawai`i. From these towers, the cables will drop 6,000 feet under water and become the world's deepest undersea cables ever. This project will make history.

Everyone seems to be complaining about the drilling in the Wao Kele o Puna rain forest. You can't understand what the big deal is. From your perspective, the forest is not that special. Wild pigs have been spreading all sorts of alien species of plants and insects for a long time, and in comparison to all of the other states in this country, Hawai`i ranks seventh on the list of who saves the most forest land. Cats and mongooses have invaded the pristine borders of the Wao Kele o Puna rain forest as well.

Safety is of no real concern to you either. Geothermal energy is a known and reliable technology. It is used in California, Utah, and Nevada, as well as in twenty other countries including Italy, Iceland, and New Zealand. This form of energy is not only safe, it has been proven to work.

Besides, the work that you do will hardly do any harm to the forest. As your plan goes, you are only going to clear about 300 acres out of this huge 27,000-acre forest! Most of that will only be roads anyway — we're not talking about a massive clear-cut here. In addition, figures from the World Resources Institute say that replacing oil-generated power with our proposed 500 megawatts of geothermal energy has the same positive effect on global warming as planting 500,000 acres of trees. You're not destroying anything: True Geothermal Energy Corp. is working to make things better.

Bill DeMent, an administrator for True Geothermal Energy Corp. says that all the controversy is just "a lot of emotional hype. They [anti-geothermal drilling groups] don't have their facts. That's typical of them."

# 7. The Philippines

Baltazar Pinguel
Eliza Fabillar
Stephen R. Shalom
Teresita Bautista
Rene Ontal
Oscar Penaranda

THE PHILIPPINES is a tropical archipelago consisting of more than 7,000 islands located at the western edge of the Pacific Ocean. Prior to contact with the Europeans, various social systems existed in the Philippines, ranging from a feudal sultanate in the south; to *barangay* (village) confederacies, mostly semi-slave societies, found in the coastal plains; to semi-communal societies in the interior.

The first Europeans arrived in the Philippines on March 16, 1521, under the command of Ferdinand Magellan, who was sailing for the king of Spain. Magellan and his men immediately intervened in a conflict among local tribal chieftains, favoring one over the others. This was a classic divide-and-rule tactic intended to advance the interests of the Spanish throne. Less than a month after he landed, Magellan was killed in a clash between warring tribes on the island of Mactan. (Lapulapu, who is mentioned in Lesson 1.1, was one of these local chieftains.)

Members of Magellan's expedition who survived the battle continued the voyage back to Spain, completing the first circumnavigation of the globe. Their account of the riches of the Philippines triggered successive expeditions. The permanent Spanish occupation of the Philippines came in the wake of the expedition of Miguel Lopez de Legazpi, who arrived in 1565.

The Spanish instituted the *encomienda* system, under which large tracts of land, together with their inhabitants, were awarded by the Spanish governor general to those who faithfully served the crown. This evolved into the *hacienda* or plantation system, which favored large-scale cultivation of crops like sugar, tobacco, indigo, and *abaca* (Manila hemp) for the world market. Under the Spanish, many Filipinos were deprived of the use of their traditional lands, subjected to forced labor, and burdened with oppressive taxes. The Spanish also imposed Catholicism on much of the population, banning native religious practices.

LIBRARY OF CONGRESS

***Philippine government in exile, 1890s. Standing at the rear (third from right) is Emilio Aguinaldo.***

## Resisting Spanish Rule

Over the next three centuries, there were hundreds of localized uprisings against Spanish rule. One of the most significant revolts took place in 1762 in the Ilocos region. It was led by Diego Silang and, after his death, by his widow, Gabriela Silang. Until the end of the nineteenth century, however, the Spanish were always able to defeat their opposition.

A crucial struggle for national freedom began on July 7, 1892, with the establishment of a revolutionary organization known as the Katipunan. The group's founder, Andres Bonifacio, who came from a working-class background, was influenced by the Philippine "Propaganda Movement," which was led by a small group of wealthy Filipinos whose families had sent them to Europe to be educated. This movement called for political reforms,

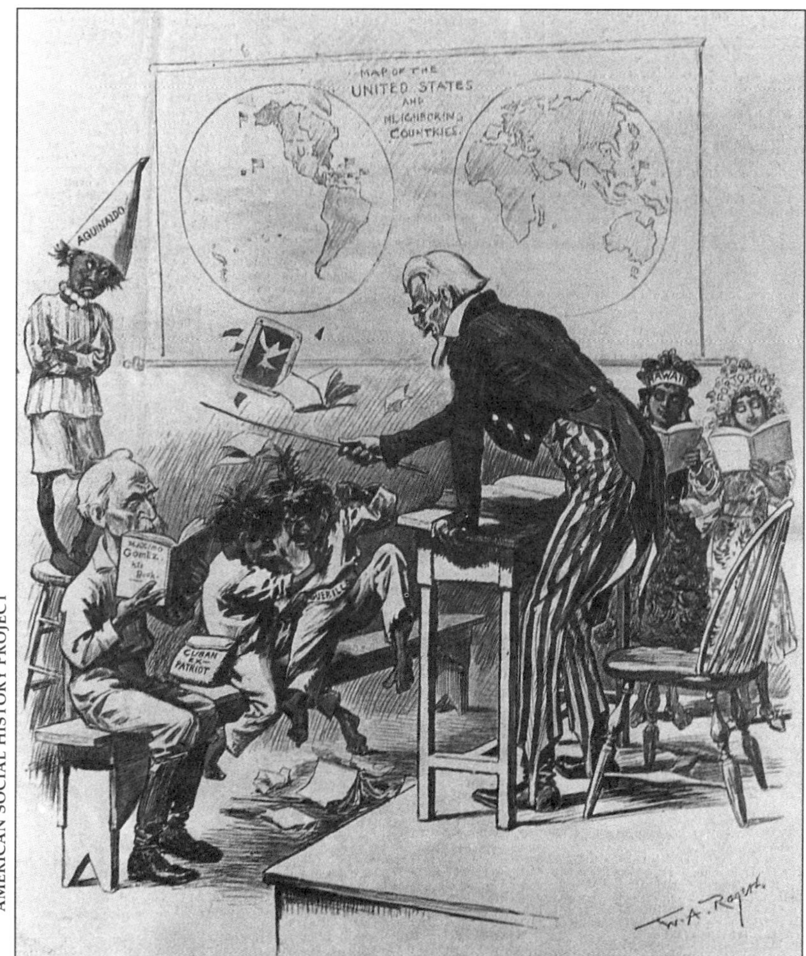


*"Uncle Sam's New Class in the Art of Self-Government." In this 1898 cartoon, Cuba and the Philippines are shown as unruly boys fighting in class, while Hawai`i and Puerto Rico are well-behaved girls learning their lessons. Aguinaldo, shown in a dunce cap at the back, was a leader of the Philippine independence movement.*

AMERICAN SOCIAL HISTORY PROJECT

especially Philippine representation in the Spanish Parliament.

Before the Katipunan could establish itself nationwide, the Spanish authorities uncovered the group's plans, and the revolutionaries had to act without adequate preparation. On August 23, 1896, the Philippine Revolution against Spain commenced. Katipunan members tore up their *cédulas* (residence certificates) in an act of defiance against Spain and declared, "Long Live Philippine Independence!"

Just as the revolution was starting, internal strife began to undermine the unity of the Katipunan. The heart of this internal struggle was the desire by wealthy Filipinos — the *ilustrados* — to wrest leadership from Bonifacio. In March 1897, Emilio Aguinaldo was elected president of the Katipunan. Two months later, Bonifacio was executed for treason. With the leadership in the hands of the *ilustrados*, the revolution took a more conservative course. In August 1897, Aguinaldo and the Spanish governor-general, Primo de Rivera, negotiated the Truce of Biak-na-Bato. Aguinaldo and his companions agreed to lay down their arms and voluntarily go into exile in Hong Kong, in return for 800,000 pesos, to be paid in three installments.

The Biak-na-Bato truce was still in force when hostilities broke out between the United States and Spain. Meanwhile, in Hong Kong Aguinaldo and a member of his group disagreed over the division of the initial payment received from the Spanish government. Aguinaldo was sued before the Hong Kong Supreme Court and left for Singapore in order to avoid appearing in court. In Singapore, he had a talk with the U.S. consul, who convinced him to cast his lot with the United States. According to Aguinaldo, he was promised that the United States would leave the Philippines to the Filipinos.

On May 7, 1898, Aguinaldo, through an arrangement between the U.S. consul in Hong Kong and U.S. admiral George Dewey, returned to the Philippines aboard a U.S. Navy vessel. Dewey, who had just won a decisive battle over the Spanish naval forces in Manila Bay, entertained Aguinaldo aboard his flagship, assuring

CORBIS-BETTMAN

*Cartoon from 1900 celebrating U.S. annexation of the Philippines. The flag reads, "the expansion of good government and commerce."*

him that Washington would recognize Philippine independence in exchange for the Filipinos' help in defeating Spain. With arms given by the United States, Aguinaldo and the forces under his command renewed their fight against Spain. By the end of May, Filipino revolutionary forces had taken some 5,000 prisoners and captured key towns in the provinces near Manila. On June 12, 1898, the Filipinos declared independence from Spain, inaugurating Asia's first republic.

The true intentions of the United States for the Philippines grew clearer to the Filipino revolutionaries day by day. Even once the Filipinos were clearly in control of the suburbs of Manila, U.S. general Thomas Anderson forbade Aguinaldo's forces to enter the city. This order was consistent with a secret agreement between Spanish and U.S. representatives that Spanish forces would surrender after a mock battle with U.S. forces; the Filipinos were to be prevented from participating. The Mock Battle of Manila and the subsequent surrender of the Spanish forces took place on August 13, 1898. The broader Spanish-American War officially ended a few months later with the signing of the Treaty of Paris on December 10, 1898. Representatives of the new Philippine government were excluded from the peace talks.

## From Colony to Neocolony

On February 4, 1899, just as the U.S. Senate was about to vote on the question of annexing the Philippines, four Filipino soldiers crossing the San Juan Bridge near Manila were killed by U.S. forces, sparking the Philippine-American War, which is known in U.S. military annals as the "Philippine Insurrection." The clash sealed the vote for annexation in the Senate.

The capture of Aguinaldo on March 23, 1901, did not end Philippine resistance. Filipino patriots like Macario Sakay and Gen. Vicente Lukban continued the struggle. The United States suffered greater casualties during this second war than it had in the conflict with

AMERICAN SOCIAL HISTORY PROJECT

*African American soldiers in the Philippine-American War.*

Spain. Ultimately, however, the U.S. troops prevailed, committing widespread atrocities in the process. For example, the island of Samar was turned into what one U.S. general called "a howling wilderness," and the Muslims of the southern Philippines, or Moros, suffered massacres at Bud Dajo and Bud Bagsak.

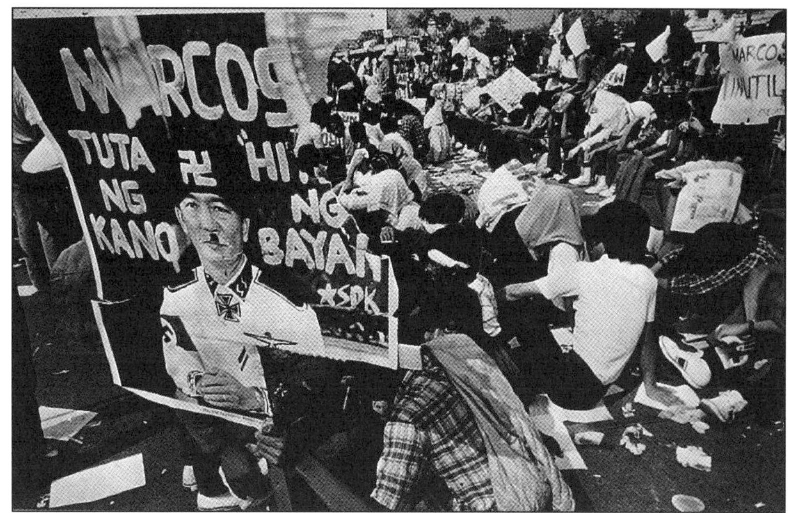


FREE LIBRARY OF PHILADELPHIA

*Marcos is depicted as a Nazi in this 1971 student protest in Manila.*

The Philippines was a direct colony of the United States from 1899 until the inauguration of a Commonwealth Government in 1935. The ten-year commonwealth period was to be a "preparatory stage" for Philippine independence, with Filipinos selecting a president, vice-president, and congress, under a constitution that would have to be approved by the U.S. president. Throughout the commonwealth period, matters of currency, trade, and foreign relations, as well as military affairs, remained in the hands of the United States.

In the U.S. Congress, some of those voting for Philippine independence were motivated by genuine support for the Filipinos. For many members of Congress, however, independence was seen as a way to restrict Philippine immigration to the United States, at a time when race riots against Filipino and other Asian immigrants were frequent on the U.S. West Coast. Likewise, such elements in Congress sought to keep Philippine agricultural goods out of the United States, thereby reducing competition with U.S. farmers. Finally, they wanted to eliminate a distant military base that the U.S. armed forces at the time considered too difficult to defend.

The Philippine Commonwealth was still in force when World War II broke out. In December 1941, the Japanese invaded the Philippines and, defeating Filipino and U.S. forces, conquered the islands. Many Filipinos, however, joined guerrilla organizations to resist the occupation. One of the most significant guerrilla groups was the Hukbalahap, or the Anti-Japanese People's Army, made up of radical peasants from the Central Luzon region. The U.S. military once again invaded the Philippines in October 1944 and, with the help of the guerrillas, defeated the Japanese over the next few months. Filipinos paid a horrendous price in lost lives — among both civilians and soldiers — and war damage (which was caused by U.S. forces as well as the Japanese).

On July 4, 1946, the United States granted the Philippines its independence. The formal granting of independence, however, was in many ways incomplete. Full payment of much-needed financial aid to rehabilitate war damage was made conditional on the Philippines' agreeing to the inclusion of the "Parity Amendment" in its constitution. This amendment said that U.S. citizens must be treated the same as Filipinos, giving U.S. companies an unrestricted opportunity to exploit the country's natural resources. The Philippines also signed a trade agreement, a military bases agreement, and a military assistance pact with Washington.

In subsequent years, the Philippines signed the Mutual Defense Treaty of 1951, the Manila Pact of 1954 (which created the Southeast Asian Treaty Organization), and the Laurel-Langley

Agreement of 1954. This last agreement not only reaffirmed the "Parity Amendment," it extended its coverage to all kinds of businesses. The net effect of these agreements was to make the Philippines a "neocolony" — formally independent, but subject to foreign domination as if it were a colony.

Opposition to neocolonialism, as this type of arrangement is termed, manifested itself in various ways. A guerrilla rebellion was conducted by the Hukbalahap ("Huks" for short), the former anti-Japanese guerrilla organization, now fighting for agrarian reforms. The leadership of the Huks were Philippine communists. A nonviolent approach was pursued by Sen. Claro M. Recto and his colleagues in the Nationalist Citizen's Party, who ardently opposed the Parity Amendment and the U.S. military bases. The Huks were defeated in the early 1950s by intensified Philippine military actions (aided by the U.S. Central Intelligence Agency), combined with grave errors on the part of the guerrillas. Recto and his colleagues, meanwhile, remained an insignificant minority in the Philippine Congress and were no match for the dominant political parties.

Resistance to foreign domination stepped up during the late 1950s and early 1960s among students influenced by both Recto and leftist nationalism. Government repression merely strengthened student opposition. By the late 1960s, when social activism was blossoming around the world (including the civil rights and anti-war movements in the United States), student boycotts and labor strikes were erupting in the Philippines. The political underground sprouted in 1968, with the establishment of a new Communist Party of the Philippines, followed by the formation of the guerrilla New People's Army a few months later. From January to March 1970, protest actions occurred throughout Manila on an almost daily basis, focusing on issues ranging from ousting the U.S. military bases to land reform for Filipino peasants.

Unable to stem the rising tide of popular resistance, Philippine president Ferdinand Marcos declared martial law throughout the Philippines on September 21, 1972. Martial law also enabled Marcos to hold onto power, even though his final term in office would soon be over. Opposition leaders like Sen. Benigno Aquino and Sen. Jose W. Diokno, the latter a member of Marcos's own political party but a committed civil libertarian, together with church leaders, trade unionists, journalists, student leaders, and the like, were the first people arrested under martial law. The martial law regime, which spanned the years from 1972 until early 1986, denied Filipinos all their basic rights. Those perceived by the government as a threat to "national security" were arbitrarily arrested, indefinitely detained, tortured, sexually abused, "involuntarily disappeared," or summarily executed — "salvaged," as military intelligence referred to the dreaded practice.

Opposition to martial law came from many sources. Banned organizations that had been

FREE LIBRARY OF PHILADELPHIA

*Demonstrators call for Marcos to resign, 1983.*

GENE STOLZFUS

*Campaigning for Corazon Aquino, January 1986.*

forced to go underground (including the Communist Party, the New People's Army, and elements within the Catholic and Protestant churches) joined together in 1973 and formed the National Democratic Front (NDF). In Mindanao, Muslim activists from the pre–martial law years formed the Moro National Liberation Front and took up arms against the government.

By the mid-1970s, students, teachers and other professionals, and trade unions began to test the country's political waters. They staged "lightning rallies" and demonstrations against the dictatorship. These large-scale actions were brutally suppressed, but the protesters came back in ever-increasing numbers. In the early 1980s, organizations like the League of Filipino Students, the militant labor confederation Kilusang Mayo Uno (May First Movement), and Gabriela, a coalition of women's organizations, were formed.

In January 1981, Marcos tried to blunt criticism of his regime by announcing the formal lifting of martial law. Nevertheless, all of his martial law decrees — more than 1,000 — remained in effect and Marcos retained dictatorial powers. Human rights groups reported that systematic abuses continued.

## The People's Power Revolution

On August 21, 1983, Sen. Benigno Aquino, who was returning from exile in the United States, where he had been allowed to go for medical treatment, was assassinated by military operatives at Manila International Airport. The assassination opened the floodgates of dissent. Even politically apathetic professionals and affluent people held daily protests, throwing yellow confetti at the country's financial center of Makati. Aquino's funeral, attended by more than a million people, became one of the biggest political mobilizations in Philippine history.

The upsurge of discontent refused to die away and only grew stronger as time passed. Eventually, in early 1986, Marcos called for a "snap" presidential election in an effort to create a safety valve for the people's fury, assuming

GENE STOLZFUS

*People's Power Revolution, 1986*

FREE LIBRARY OF PHILADELPHIA

*Squatters live in this shantytown on Manila Bay, in front of the Manila Cultural Center, in this 1971 photograph.*

that he would be able to manipulate the result. Corazon Aquino, widow of the late senator, was the opposition's presidential candidate. As expected, Marcos was declared the winner by the Commission on Elections, despite the testimony of international observers that he had stolen the election. The Philippine people were angered and became more so when U.S. president Ronald Reagan announced that he was prepared to accept Marcos's victory. Daily demonstrations protested Marcos's electoral fraud. Then, the army's acting chief of staff, General Fidel Ramos, and Defense Secretary Juan Ponce Enrile, who had themselves been architects of the martial law regime, announced their support for Corazon Aquino. Marcos ordered his military to attack the headquarters of the mutiny led by Ramos and Enrile. Aquino and Cardinal Jaime Sin, chief prelate of the Catholic Church in the Philippines, asked the Filipino people to come out into the streets and protect with their bodies the military camp where Ramos and Enrile were staging their mutiny. Tens of thousands heeded the call. The unprecedented combination of a popular uprising combined with a military mutiny — all with the blessing of the Catholic Church — became the People's Power Revolution of 1986. The image of masses of people standing in the path of the military's tanks, which flashed over CNN, soon became a worldwide emblem of nonviolent revolution.

In February 1986, Corazon Aquino was inaugurated as president of the post–martial law Philippines. Marcos, who had long been favored by Washington for his support of U.S. military bases and economic interests, was flown to Hawai`i, where he died in 1989, a few years after the fall of his martial law regime.

Aquino embodied the people's hope for social reform. In many respects, however, her administration failed to deliver on its democratic promise. An early indication of trouble was her decision to distance herself from the movement calling for the ouster of the U.S. military bases, a demand she and most opposition leaders had endorsed in 1984. Further, Aquino, herself a large landowner, refused to institute a genuine land reform program to address rural inequality, the tinderbox of revolutions and uprisings since Spanish times. Finally, although she released political prisoners, she approved the formation of "vigilante" units, which, together with elements in the military, conducted a reign of terror against leaders of organizations pressing for social justice.

In part Aquino was pushed to adopt more conservative policies by her military backers. Units of the Philippine armed forces launched six coup attempts during the Aquino administration. Loyal troops helped her crush these revolts, but the price she paid after each failed coup was to move farther and farther away from her original program of social reform. The major reform won during the Aquino years, which neither Aquino nor the military was able to thwart, was the Philippine Senate's rejection in 1991 of a treaty permitting U.S. military bases to remain in the Philippines.

In 1992 Fidel Ramos, Aquino's defense minister, was elected president of the Philippines. Like Aquino, Ramos has not challenged the power and privilege of the wealthy minority, leaving the majority of peasants and workers in extreme poverty. Ramos has been working with the United States to try to find some way to restore U.S. military access to Philippine territory. Early in 1998, he signed an executive agreement with the United States that grants visiting U.S. military forces the right to stop at twenty-two Philippine ports. Critics fear that in so doing, Ramos has single-handedly transformed the entire country into a U.S. military base.

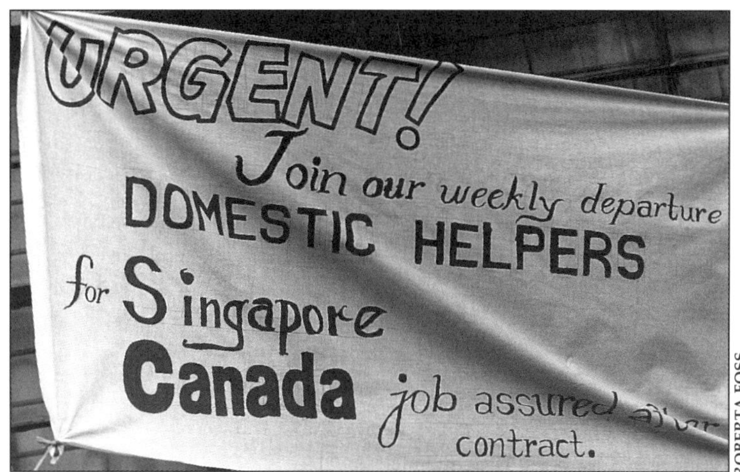


ROBERTA FOSS

*Remittances sent home by overseas Filipino workers — mostly women in domestic service — prop up the Philippine economy.*

At this writing, Ramos has not yet submitted the agreement to the Philippine Senate, the body that is constitutionally empowered to ratify treaties in the Philippines. Meanwhile, while Ramos was unsuccessful in attempts to overturn the Philippine constitution's prohibition on a second presidential term, he nonetheless retains the power to declare martial law or suspend the right of habeas corpus (which prevents governments from holding prisoners without filing formal charges).

Despite the restoration of elected government, the basic conflicts of Philippine society have not been resolved.

## References

Teodoro A. Agoncillo and Milagros C. Guerrero, *History of the Filipino People,* 7th ed. (Quezon City, Philippines: R. P. Garcia Publishing Co., n.d.).

Teodoro Agoncillo, *The Revolt of the Masses: The Story of Bonifacio and the Katipunan* (Quezon City, Philippines: University of the Philippines, 1956).

Stanley Karnow, *In Our Image: America's Empire in the Philippines* (New York: Random House, 1989).

Amado Guerrero, *Philippine Society and Revolution* (Oakland, CA: International Association of Filipino Patriots, 1979).

*American Military History, 1607–1953,* ROTC Manual 145-20 (Washington, DC: Department of the Army, 1956) Readings: Differing Views of Annexation *[Chicago: Rand McNally & Co., 1970], p. 372.)*

---

**Vocabulary:** archipelago, annexation, circumnavigation, feudalism, insurrection, neocolonialism, nonviolence

# LESSON 7.1 The U.S. Annexation of the Philippines

**Objective:** To help students gain an understanding of opposing viewpoints regarding U.S. annexation of the Philippines, through statements from figures on both sides of the debate.

**Themes:** race, gender, justice, rights, liberty

**Vocabulary:** annexation, Providence, suffragist, vassal, dictum

## Suggested Activities

1. Have students read the introduction to this chapter, perhaps as homework the night before. The following day, have them read aloud in class the excerpts given below. The excerpts represent various viewpoints on the U.S. invasion and annexation of the Philippines.
2. Divide the students into small groups and have them restate the meaning of these excerpts in their own words. One student can take the lead in expressing her or his understanding of each excerpt.
3. Ask the students to take the stance of the author of any one of the excerpts. Speaking as this person, each student will write a letter to then-President William McKinley, expressing his or her opinion of U.S. annexation of the Philippines. The letter should state clearly who the author is and how that has shaped his or her views.
4. Each student should share his or her writing with another student.

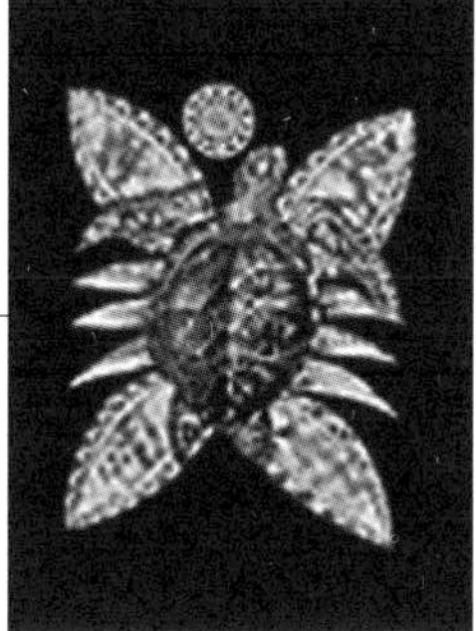

# Readings: Differing Views of Annexation

*When the United States defeated Spain in the Spanish-American War, Spain sold its colony of the Philippines to the United States. But the Filipinos, who had risen up in rebellion against Spain in 1896, were no more interested in being under U.S. control than they had been in Spanish rule. The excerpts below are all statements from the period of the Philippine-American War. The first two reflect contrasting views from U.S. senators. The next two reflect the views of Filipinos who fought against U.S. conquest. Excerpts 5—9 are from organizations and individuals in the United States.*

## Excerpt 1

Lines of navigation from our ports to the Orient and Australia; from the Isthmian Canal* to Asia; from all Oriental ports to Australia, converge at and separate from the Philippines. They are a self-supporting, dividend-paying fleet, permanently anchored at a spot selected by the strategy of Providence, commanding the Pacific. And the Pacific is the ocean of the commerce of the future. Most future wars will be conflicts for commerce. The power that rules the Pacific, therefore, is the power that rules the world. And, with the Philippines, that power is and will forever be the American Republic. . . . The Declaration [of Independence] applies only to people capable of self-government. . . . And you, who say the Declaration applies to all men, how dare you deny it its application to the American Indian? And if you deny it to the Indian at home, how dare you grant it to the Malay** abroad?

— *From a speech by Sen. Alfred Beveridge,* Congressional Record, *Senate, Jan. 9, 1900, pp. 704–711.*

## Excerpt 2

[W]hile there is little else that a democracy cannot accomplish it cannot rule over vassal states or subject peoples without bringing in the elements of death into its own constitution. . . . Is it true . . . that before constitutions and before legislators all men are created equal, or is it only true of some of them?

Is it true that they are endowed by their creator with certain unalienable rights? Or is it only true of some of them?

Is it true that among those rights are life, liberty, and the pursuit of happiness? Or are these for some of them only?

Is it true that governments derive their just power from the consent of the governed? Or is it only from the consent of some of them?

. . . Abraham Lincoln said, "No man was ever created good enough to own another." No nation was ever created good enough to own another.

— *From a speech by Sen. George F. Hoar in the U.S. Senate, Jan. 9, 1899.*

---

* A term for what eventually became the Panama Canal.

** The ethnic group from which most Filipinos are descended.

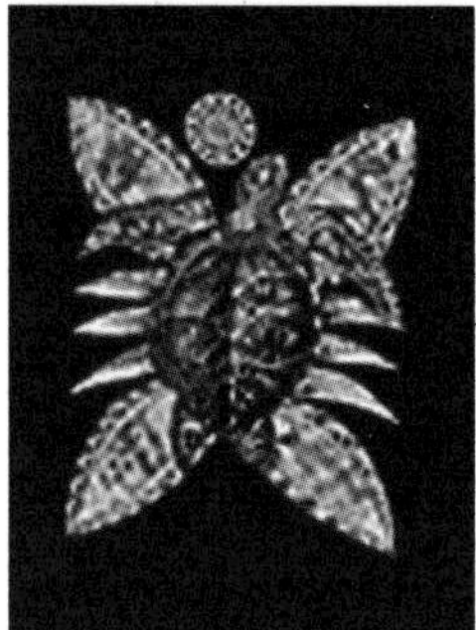

## Excerpt 3

You repeat constantly the dictum that we cannot govern ourselves. With equal reason, you might have said the same thing some fifty or sixty years ago of Japan; and, little over a hundred years ago, it was extremely questionable, when you, also, were rebels against the English Government, if you could govern yourselves. . . . Now, the moral of all this obviously is: Give us the chance; treat us exactly as you demanded to be treated at the hands of England, when you rebelled against her autocratic methods. . . . "[L]ay down your arms," you say. Did you lay down your arms when you, too, were rebels, and the English under good King George demanded your submission? How in the name of all that is serious do you demand that we shall do what you, being rebels, refused to do?

*— From A Filipino, "Aguinaldo's Case Against the United States,"* North American Review, *Vol. 169, 1899, pp. 425–432.*

## Excerpt 4

I believe that we are both striving for much the same object — you for the right to take part in national life; we for the right to have a national life to take part in . . . Mentally, socially, and in almost all the relations of life, our women are regarded as the equals of our men . . . in the name of the Philippine women, I pray the Massachusetts Woman Suffrage Association to do what it can to remedy all this misery and misfortune in my unhappy country. You can do much to bring about the cessation of these horrors and cruelties which are today taking place in the Philippines, and to insist upon a more humane course . . . you ought to understand that we are only contending for the liberty of our country, just as you once fought for the same liberty for yours.

*— From a speech by Clemencia Lopez before the annual meeting of the New England Woman's Suffrage Association, May 29, 1902. Lopez came from a Filipino family that supported Jose Rizal in the 1890s and later was active in the Revolution of 1896, the Philippine-American War, and the continuing opposition to U.S. rule. Her brother Sixto Lopez was secretary to the delegation sent to the United States in 1898 to negotiate recognition of Philippine independence.*

## Excerpt 5

I think one of the results of meeting [Clemencia Lopez] . . . is the deeper sense of sympathy we all feel in a people far off, struggling for liberty. . .We Anglo-Saxons are prone to think that no people is civilized that isn't made after our pattern; and we are peculiarly given to attempts at imposing our civilization upon other peoples. [Our deepest concern] is for our country . . . we long to have it free from the stain of injustice and greed.

*— Remarks by Fanny Baker Ames at a farewell luncheon in honor of Clemencia Lopez, October 5, 1903. Ames was vice-president of the Anti-Imperialist League from 1913 until 1921.*

## Excerpt 6

Resolved, that the colored people of Boston in meeting assembled desire to enter their solemn protest against the present unjustified invasion by American soldiers in the Philippine Islands. Resolved, that, while the rights of colored citizens in the South, sacredly guaranteed them by the amendment of the Constitution, are shamefully disregarded; and, while frequent lynchings of Negroes who are denied a civilized trial are a reproach to Republican government, the duty of the president and

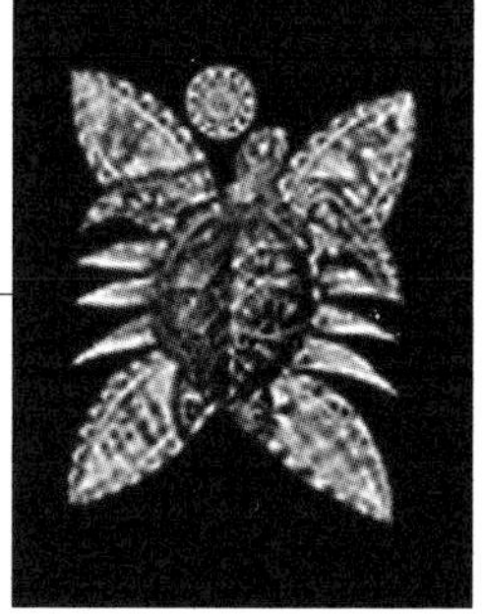

country is to reform these crying domestic wrongs and not to attempt the civilization of alien peoples by powder and shot.

— *Colored Citizens of Boston,* The Boston Post, *July 18, 1899.*

## Excerpt 7

The principle that the higher civilization is justified in supplanting the lower is a dangerous one to admit, because of every nation regarding its own type as the highest, but there are certain broad facts which must force the impartial observer to admit the superiority of our own race, the Anglo Saxon, in the qualities that contribute to human advance. At any rate, we hold to the opinion that we have done more than any other race to conquer the world for civilization in the past few centuries, and we will probably go on holding to this opinion and go on with our conquests.

If we believe that there is a distinct purpose in all that is about us and in our own presence here, we cannot escape the conclusion that man's express duty is the uplifting of man. The duty to improve and elevate himself and his fellows thus becomes an end in itself and a justification of life. . . . Any nation which blocks the way of human progress must expect to be brushed aside by more powerful and vigorous blood.

— *Theodore Marburg, editor, May 1898. (Source: William Appleman Williams, Ed.,* The Shaping of American Diplomacy: Readings and Documents in American Foreign Relations, *Vol. 1, 1750–1914, 2d ed.*

## Excerpt 8

Morally and religiously, we should not shun an opportunity to lift up a barbarous people. . . . Who knows but that this is a plan of Providence to bring the land favored of God and flowing with religious speech into touch with a land in need of the Gospel?

—The Advance, *publication of the Congregationalist Church, May 19, 1898. (Source: Julius Pratt,* Expansionists of 1898: The Acquisition of Hawaii and the Spanish Islands *[Baltimore: Johns Hopkins Press, 1936], reprinted by Quadrangle Books, New York, p. 301.)*

## Excerpt 9

But what have we to gain by taking possession of the Philippines and holding them as a colony or dependent state? . . .

We would have an unsurpassed point in the Far East from which to extend our commerce and trade and gain our share in the immense distribution of material prizes that must follow the opening of China, operating from Manila as a base. . . .

We would have in the Philippines themselves, one of the greatest undeveloped opportunities in all the world — a group of islands with numberless riches and resources awaiting exploitation, and capable of providing a market for a large quantity of our manufactured products.

— *John Barrett, U.S. diplomat. (Source: Richard E. Welch, Jr.,* Imperialists vs. Anti-Imperialists: The Debate Over Expansionism in the 1890's [ *Itasca, IL: F. E. Peacock, 1972], p. 64.)*

---

**Sources:** *Except as noted above, J. Zwick (Ed.),* Anti-Imperialism in the United States, 1898–1935 *(an electronic publication on the World Wide Web at http://www.accinet.net/~fjzwick/ail98-35.html) and D. B. Schirmer and S. R. Shalom (Eds.),* The Philippines Reader *(Boston: South End Press, 1987), p. 32.*

# LESSON 7.2 Letters Home from U.S. Soldiers

**Objective:** To recognize the importance of U.S. soldiers' observations and opinions of the Philippine-American War, illustrating through their eyes the atrocities that took place during the war.

**Themes:** soldiers' viewpoints, Philippine-American War

**Vocabulary:** oppressor, insurrection, regiment, savage, exterminate, deprecate

## Suggested Activities

1. As an introduction to this activity, you may wish to tell students that they will be reading letters home from U.S. soldiers in the Philippine-American War. Ask them whether they believe that it is worthwhile to look at history through the eyes of ordinary people. Why or why not?
2. Pass out the reading provided at the end of this lesson. The final excerpt, reflecting the racist attitudes held by many people in the United States at the time, refers to Filipinos as "little better than a savage." You may want to draw the students' attention to this term and engage them in a discussion of why the author of that letter might use such language. What conception of the Filipinos does it reflect? What do they think may have influenced that particular soldier to see Filipinos in that light? Historically, how did Europeans and European-Americans view the non-European peoples with whom they came in contact as they began to expand throughout the globe?
3. Have students read the introductory paragraph and the excerpts. As they read, ask them to underline key words or phrases. Using those selected words, in no particular order, and adding their own words, the students will create a poem.
4. Have the students share their poems in small groups.
5. The class should reconvene to react to the poems. What similarities or differences do they notice in the words chosen from the letters by different students?

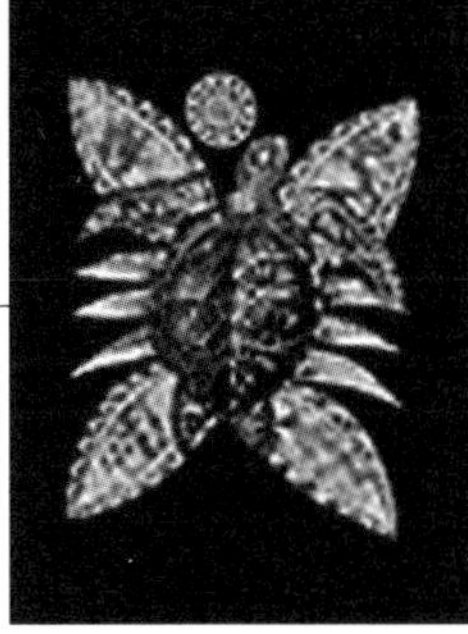

# Reading: Letters from U.S. Soldiers in the Philippine-American War

*Many soldiers who fought in the Philippines had initially volunteered to fight in the Spanish-American War. Some soldiers supported the war against the Filipinos, while others questioned what they and their country were doing. These letters show the range of attitudes held by U.S. soldiers at the time: some held racist attitudes toward Filipinos, while others identified with their quest for independence and admired their courage. The letters caused great controversy when they were published in 1899 by the Anti-Imperialist League, a turn-of-the-century group opposed to U.S. intervention in the Philippines.*

---

We came here to help, not to slaughter, these natives; to fight the oppressor Spain, not the oppressed. It strikes me as not very fair to pursue a policy that leads to this insurrection, and then keep us volunteers out here to fight battles we never enlisted for. I cannot see that we are fighting for any principle now.

*— Soldier in Nebraska regiment*

---

We advanced four miles and we fought every inch of the way; . . . saw twenty-five dead insurgents in one place and twenty-seven in another, besides a whole lot of them scattered along that I did not count . . . It was like hunting rabbits; an insurgent would jump out of a hole or the brush and run; he would not get very far . . . I suppose you are not interested in the way we do the job. We take no prisoners. At least the Twentieth Kansas do not.

*— Arthur Minkler of the Kansas Regiment*

---

I deprecate this war, this slaughter of our own boys and of the Filipinos, because it seems to me that we are doing something that is contrary to our principles in the past. Certainly we are doing something that we should have shrunk from not so very long ago.

*— General Reeve, former colonel of the Thirteenth Minnesota Regiment*

---

They will never surrender until their whole race is exterminated. They are fighting for a good cause, and the Americans should be the last of all nations to transgress upon such rights. Their independence is dearer to them than life, as ours was in years gone by, and is today.

*— Ellis G. Davis, Company A, 20th Kansas*

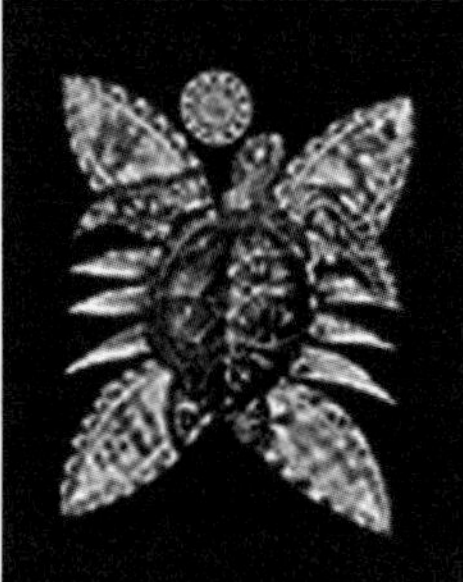

I haven't had any fighting to do since I've been here, and don't care to do any. You would not believe the abuse suffered by the natives . . . The first thing in the morning is "nigger" and the last thing at night is "nigger." The [Filipinos] are a patient, burden-bearing people. I must not say much, as I am a soldier.

— *Sgt. Patrick Mason, 24th Infantry (Colored). (Written two weeks before he was killed in action.)*

Most of the general officers think it will take years, and a large force of soldiers, to thoroughly subjugate the natives. And the unpleasant feature of this is that unless the conditions change radically there will be few soldiers who will care to stay there. There's no use trying to conceal the fact that many of the men over there now, especially the volunteers, are homesick, and tired of fighting way off there, with nothing in particular to gain. There is not one man in the whole army now in the Philippines who would not willingly give up his life for the flag if it was necessary, but it isn't pleasant to think about dying at the hands of a foe little better than a savage, and so far away from home. And the thought of its not ending for several years is not an especially pleasant one, either.

— *Sergeant Elliott, of Company G, Kansas Regiment*

---

**Sources:** *Letter from Patrick Mason is reprinted from Willard B. Gatewood,* Smoked Yankees and the Struggle for Empire: Letters from Negro Soldiers, 1898–1902 *(Fayetteville: University of Arkansas Press, 1987). Other excerpts are from J. Zwick (Ed.),* Anti-Imperialism in the United States, 1898–1935 *(an electronic publication on the World Wide Web at http://www.accinet.net/~fjzwick/ail98-35.html).*

# Lesson 7.3 U.S. Military Bases in the Philippines

**Objective:** To provide insight into the enduring debate over the presence of U.S. military bases in the Philippines.

**Themes:** militarization, national security, toxic hazards, prostitution

**Vocabulary:** dissident, hazardous waste

Up until 1991, the Philippines was a key site for U.S. military bases in Asia. Their presence was hotly debated by Filipinos, with opponents arguing that the bases undermined the country's sovereignty and safety. It was also argued that they had a negative social and environmental impact on the Philippines. At this writing (in early 1998), the United States has just signed an agreement with the government of the Philippines to restore access for its military to Philippine soil. This agreement has not yet been ratified by the Philippine Senate.

## Suggested Activities

1. Have students review the reading provided at the end of this lesson, either in class or as homework the night before.
2. Students will articulate and defend their views through a forced-choice activity. Divide the classroom in half. Label one side of the room "Agree," and the other side "Disagree."
3. Explain to students that they will be asked to take a stand. The teacher will read a statement out loud to the class regarding the U.S. military presence in the Philippines and students must choose which side of the room to stand on. They may not stand in the middle: they must either agree or disagree with the statement.
4. Once students have taken their stand the teacher should call on various students to explain why they have chosen to move to that side of the room. A student may change sides during the course of the exercise if he or she hears a compelling argument from the other side which changes his or her mind.
5. The teacher should read each of these statements one at a time, stopping long enough after each statement for students to choose which side of the room to go to. After students have had a chance to thoroughly discuss the reasons why they have chosen a particular position, move on to the next statement.
6. Following the activity, have students write an editorial explaining and defending the positions they have taken.

### Forced-Choice Statements

- The U.S. military presence in the Philippines has been good for the Philippine economy.
- The girls and women who work in the so-called "hospitality" industry servicing the U.S. bases are free to do as they choose and are working in these jobs of their own free will.
- The United States is the strongest country in the world and its job is to protect the world, so the Philippines should welcome the U.S. military to its country.
- The U.S. government should take responsibility for cleaning up any toxic waste left by the U.S. military in the Philippines, regardless of what it costs.
- The United States should take financial responsibility for the health, education, and general well-being of children fathered by U.S. military personnel in the Philippines.

# Reading: U.S. Military Bases in the Philippines

*In the changed circumstances following World War II, the U.S. government decided that it wanted a string of military bases throughout the Pacific. In 1947 the U.S. and Philippine governments signed a Military Bases Agreement, giving the United States vast tracts of Philippine land over which the U.S. flag would fly. This land was conceded to be used rent-free for military bases for a term of ninety-nine years.*

*Clark Air Force Base and Subic Bay Naval Station were the two main U.S. facilities. Critics of the agreement argued that it was inconsistent with Philippine independence and that it violated Philippine sovereignty (the right of a country to control its own fate). The length of the agreement was later reduced and some specific details were amended, but under the agreement the U.S. military always maintained the right to use the bases as it saw fit.*

*For the next forty-four years a vigorous debate took place in the Philippines about these U.S. bases. Finally, in 1991, after a volcano caused a great deal of damage at Clark Air Base, the Philippine Senate voted against renewing the Military Bases Agreement. Today, re-establishing U.S. bases in the Philippines is once again under discussion. The excerpts that follow illustrate the arguments that were frequently raised during this lengthy debate.*

## Excerpt 1:

*Testimony of U.S. military officials under questioning by U.S. Senator Symington.*

**Sen. Symington:** You said . . . "The Board considers the principal threat to the Philippines to be Communist China with possible assistance from internal dissident groups." What is the capacity from the military standpoint of the Red Chinese today in the Pacific to menace the Philippines[?] . . .

**Admiral Kauffman:** I would say at the moment, sir, very small.

**Sen. Symington:** General, what would you say?

**General Gideon:** Very small, very small.

**Sen. Symington:** But you say it is the principal threat.

**Admiral Kauffman:** Of the threats that exist, I would say it is the principal threat; yes, sir. . . .

**Sen. Symington:** . . . [W]hat you are actually saying is that today there is no threat to the Philippines except an internal threat? . . .

**Admiral Kauffman:** Yes, sir, using the word "today."

— *From U.S. Senate, Foreign Relations Committee, subcommittee on U.S. Security Agreements and Commitments Abroad, United States Security Agreements and Commitments Abroad: The Republic of the Philippines, Hearings, Sept.-Oct. 1969, pp. 60-61.*

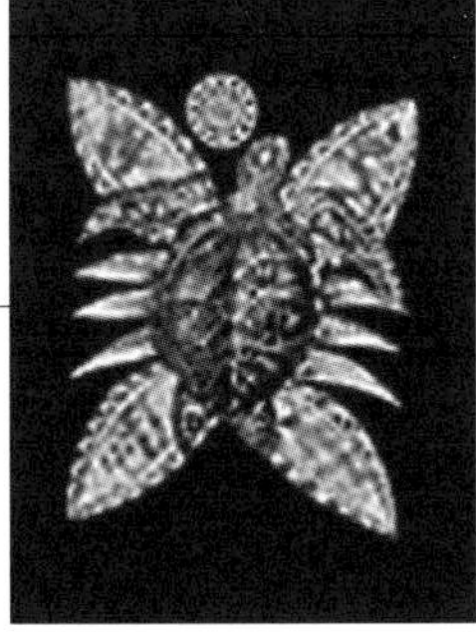

## Excerpt 2.

*U.S. government data on the economic impact of the bases.*

In September 1987 the American facilities in the Philippines employed 23,168 full-time workers, 22,834 contract workers, 22,068 domestic and private hires, and 444 concessionaires, for a total direct employment of 68,514 Filipinos.

Annual salaries for Filipino workers in 1987 totaled $96,075,957. . . the second-largest payroll in the Philippines after the Philippine government itself.

—*United States Information Service, "Background on the Bases: American Military Facilities in the Philippines," 2nd ed., Manila, 1988, p. 16.*

## Excerpt 3.

*Report on the environmental impact of U.S. military bases in the Philippines, by a Filipino-American environmental analyst.*

The U.S. Department of Defense has admitted the presence of 14,401 toxic hot spots in 1,579 [U.S.] bases . . . which possibly endanger public health and the environment. . . .

An internal Defense Department report reveals hazardous waste disposal problems in several overseas bases including the Philippines. The report concludes that the U.S. military ignored effective methods for protecting the environment from hazardous materials in favor of a lax regulatory climate in foreign countries. Given the multitude of activities taking place inside the U.S. bases in the Philippines, many of which have been shown to be environmentally destructive in the U.S., there is no doubt that hazardous waste and toxic contamination will be found in many sites in the base lands.

— *Jorge Emmanuel, "Environmental Destruction caused by U.S. Military Bases and the Serious Implications for the Philippines," presented at Crossroad 1991: Towards a Nuclear-Free, Bases-Free Philippines: An International Conference, Manila, May 1990, p. 1.*

## Excerpt 4.

*Study of the bases by a Filipino professor.*

In Olongapo City alone [near Subic Bay Naval Base], 4,356 women are licensed to work as "hospitality girls." In Angeles [near Clark Air Force Base] where there are around 500 bars, these hospitality girls number 3,430. . . . These numbers are understated, for they do not include the unlicensed streetwalkers, who if combined with the licensed hospitality girls, would number around 9,000 in Olongapo City alone and 7,000 in Angeles City. The figures of Filipino women degraded into prostitution are often not cited by proponents of the bases who claim that U.S. installations provided significant employment for Filipinos.

The increasing growth of the "hospitality industry" around the bases[,] which attracts mostly teen-age girls from the most depressed areas of the Philippines . . . has its attendant social problems. There are the problems of unwed mothers, abandoned children, broken homes, drug abuse, and sexually transmitted diseases.

— *Roland G. Simbulan,* The Bases of Our Insecurity: A Study of the U.S. Military Bases in the Philippines *(Metro Manila: BALAI Fellowship, 1983, p. 253).*

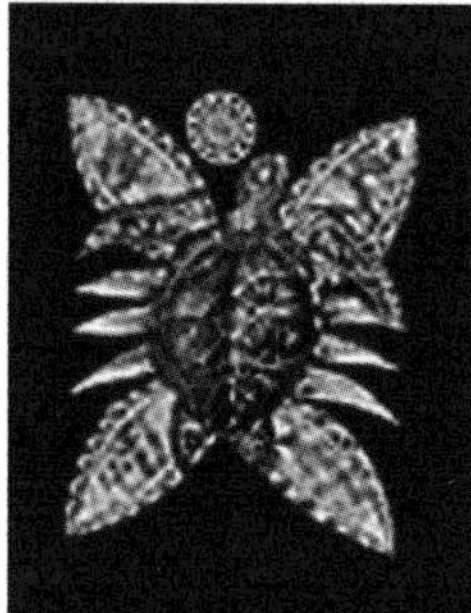

## Excerpt 5.

*Letter by former Philippine Senator Lorenzo Tañada.*

Far from defending us — for until now there is no defense against nuclear missiles and we have no foreign enemies — [the bases] would pull us into the arena of nuclear conflict in the event of war between the United States and Soviet Russia. Because of their nuclear capability and the actual existence of nuclear weapons in the bases, we have become real targets for attack by any power at war with America, whether or not we ourselves are at war with that power.

— *Letter to Constitutional Commissioners, excerpted in Roland G. Simbulan,* A Guide to Nuclear Philippines: A Primer on U.S. Military Bases, Nuclear Weapons and What the Filipino People are Doing About These *(Manila: IBON Databank., 1989), p. 122.*

## Excerpt 6.

*U.S. Senate report explaining U.S. government support for the declaration of martial law in the Philippines.*

. . . U.S. officials appear prepared to accept that . . . military bases and a familiar government in the Philippines are more important than the preservation of democratic institutions. . . .

*—"Korea and the Philippines: November 1972," staff report prepared for the use of the U.S. Senate Committee on Foreign Relations, Feb. 18, 1973, p. 45.*

# Lesson 7.4 Martial Law

**Objective:** To help students imagine the impact martial law would have on themselves and their communities.

**Themes:** human rights, civil liberties, repression

**Vocabulary:** decree, martial law, recourse, subversion, surveillance

## Suggested Activities

1. Read the following fictitious letter, inserting the name of your city or town and its mayor:

> Dear Students,
>
> This message is being sent to every teacher in (town/city), as well as to every newspaper, television, and radio station.
>
> The (town council/ city council) is hereby suspended. From noon today, all laws and rules for (town/city) will be issued by me and me alone. All students must go straight home after school and stay indoors until further notice. In order to protect public safety, the leaders of certain student clubs and organizations are being arrested. Television, radio, and newspapers may not publish or broadcast without the explicit approval of the mayor.
>
> Signed,
>
> ____________, Mayor

2. Ask the students what they think about this directive from the mayor. After they have expressed their opinions, tell them that this directive was fictitious, but that something similar did happen in 1972 in the Philippines. Explain to students that in September 1972 Philippine President Ferdinand Marcos declared martial law, replacing democratic government with military rule and setting up a dictatorship. Martial law in the Philippines included the following measures:
   - The Philippine Congress was suspended and Marcos was able to rule by decree, meaning that whatever he said became law.
   - Although Marcos's term of office was supposed to end the following year, under martial law he could stay in office indefinitely.
   - Tens of thousands of people were arrested — including political opponents of the president, journalists, and student leaders — and the use of torture was widespread. Hundreds were killed without any legal proceedings.
   - Newspapers could only print what the government allowed them to print.
   - Labor unions were no longer allowed to go on strike without the government's permission.
3. Have the students review the readings at the end of this lesson.
4. Divide the class into groups of four or five. Each group should choose a recorder to note down answers to the following questions: What are some examples of human rights violations that are given in the readings? How do you think people in the United States would react if martial law were really declared here? How would they react to abuses of human rights like those experienced by the Filipinos? What do you think life would be like? How would it be different from your life now?
5. Gather the whole class together and have the recorders report their group's conclusions. You may wish to conclude this exercise with a general discussion of democratic freedoms. How do students understand this term? Do they believe they are able to exercise such rights as the right to freedom of speech or freedom of association? Why or why not?
6. Following the activity, you may wish to assign a writing exercise based on the reading. For example, students can write a journal entry, assuming the character of a Filipino living under martial law. Alternatively, they can assume the character of a human rights activist, and write a letter denouncing human rights abuses.

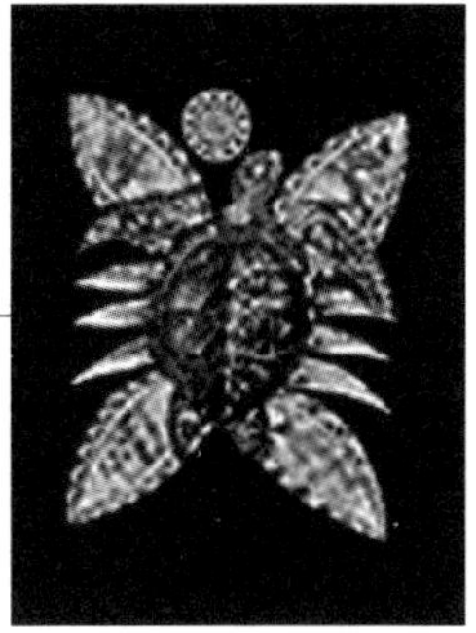

# Reading: Human Rights and Martial Law in the Philippines

*The following accounts illustrate human rights abuses in the Philippines during the martial law period. As the final excerpt indicates, such abuses did not automatically stop once the dictatorship came to an end. The United States remained a strong supporter of Philippine dictator Ferdinand Marcos until the end of his life, and allowed him to settle in Hawai`i after he was forced out of the Philippines.*

**Excerpt 1:** *Testimonies on women's human rights.*

I heard the story of Jennifer Balunggay while viewing a documentary on the "rape of the Marag Valley." Marag Valley is a thickly wooded area, a "virgin forest" in fact, located in the municipality of Luna, in the province of Kalinga-Apayao. It used to be only a simple, clean, and refreshing village, of simple folks and simple children like Jennifer. But in 1980, the logging companies came into Marag and besieged its lush green vegetation, mercilessly cutting down trees. Then two years later, in 1982, the New People's Army [guerrillas] came into the valley and successfully drove the loggers away. On the same year a contingent of the 106th Company of the Philippine Constabulary was sent to keep peace and order in the area. An encounter took place between the Constabulary and the NPA. The soldiers of the government, residents say, were wiped out. Then war began. And Marag was never the same again.

Jennifer was seven years old when the war began. Now, at 13, she looks like a malnourished nine-year-old, frail and thin and pale. Her mother died when the war began. . . . In 1988, her father was suspected of being an NPA and was summarily executed (or "salvaged"). Now orphans, she and her brother and sister go from one relative to another to be fed and clothed. It is no wonder Jennifer's eyes, they say, do not light up even when she smiles . . .

Like Jennifer, Aling Dora is a resident of Marag Valley. She is the woman leader of some 350 families living in a *barrio* [neighborhood] in Kalayukay, where she heads the women's organization. She is a tribal woman, an Isneg. At 48, she is a picture of a woman hardened by fate. Her husband, like many other men of Marag, had been salvaged. . . . Evacuation took its toll on her seven children: three of them died of malaria. She has since been requesting to be allowed to return to Marag, to plow her own field and partake of the valley's bounty once more. But it has become, according to the town mayor, a "no-man's-land," and if she dares enter Marag she is "as good as dead, for the military will shoot, even at her shadow" . . .

Hilda Narciso and Cherry Mendoza are women activists. In 1982, Hilda was arrested on subversion charges by the military in Davao. She was sexually molested and raped. Cherry was on her way to Bataan from Manila with two friends, Eric and Cecile, when they were arrested, brought to camp blindfolded, and later interrogated. Because of fatigue and perhaps a tranquilizer put in her food, Cherry fell asleep during the interrogation. The next day she found herself in pain, having been raped by her interrogators. . . .

*— Lilia Quindoza Santiago, "Reclaiming the Right to Be Human in a Land That Shoots Even at Shadows,"* Laya Feminist Quarterly, *Vol. 1, No. 2, 1992, pp. 24–26 (Quezon City, Philippines).*

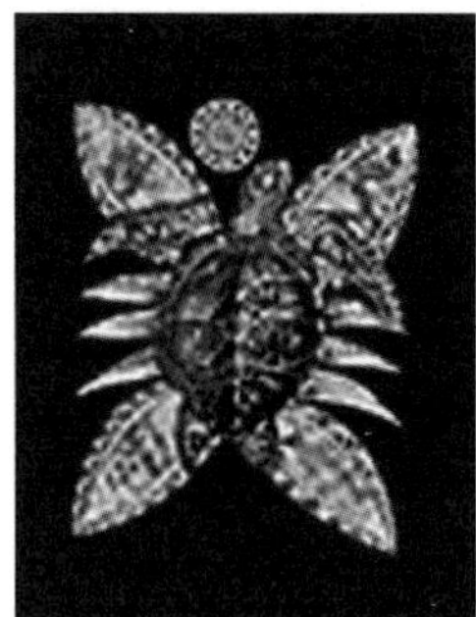

**Excerpt 2:** *Testimony of Romeo Regato, 16 years old, Hilongos, Leyte.*

At about 4:40 in the afternoon of 10 June 1985, while Felicisimo Milano, Leticio Milano, Gregorio Pontino, and I were cleaning the *abaca* plantation . . . a group of eight army soldiers and two CHDF volunteers . . . arrived.*

We did not mind them then for we were busy with our work. But all of a sudden, the CHDF volunteers and two army soldiers opened fire. Three of us, Felicisimo, Leticio, and I, were hit, while Gregorio was able to run away.

The two died on the spot. I was hit in the left shoulder blade and in the left ear when I attempted to flee. With the three of us bloodied on the ground, I heard a soldier giving instructions to finish us off so I pretended to be dead. They left the scene after sensing that none of us was alive.

*— "Philippines: Testimonies on Human Rights Violations," CCIA Background Information, Commission of the Churches on International Affairs, World Council of Churches, Geneva, Jan. 1986, pp. 106-07.*

**Excerpt 3:** *Sworn statement of Anastacia Caputol, 64-year-old widow of Paterno Caputol, in Midsalip, Zamboanga del Sur.*

On 10 March 1985 at about 3:00 in the morning some people woke us up and told Paterno to come out, saying that they would attend a meeting at the Purok Hall. My husband went downstairs and went with them. Reaching Purok I saw from our house that five of our neighbors also went with them. There the armed men ordered Paterno and the others to line up. I saw them bring out [rifles]. . . . they shot Paterno and the rest. I saw my husband and my neighbors fall to the ground. . . . Running away from the area, I saw the things in our house taken by the armed men who later set our house on fire. And then I saw other houses looted and burned. It was a big fire. My estimate is that twenty-seven houses were burned down including the Purok Hall. I believe the armed men were from the ICHDF and 4Ks** based on their uniforms and the red cloth tied around the handles of their long knives. When the morning came, my neighbors and I gathered around the burned Purok Hall. There I saw the completely charred bodies of my husband and our five neighbors.

*— "Philippines: Testimonies on Human Rights Violations," CCIA Background Information, Commission of the Churches on International Affairs, World Council of Churches, Geneva, Jan. 1986, p. 158.*

*CHDF is the Civilian Home Defense Force, a paramilitary group working with the military. *Abaca* is Manila hemp.

**ICHDF is the Integrated Civilian Home Defense Force; same as CHDF. The 4Ks were a fanatical religious paramilitary group that worked with the military.

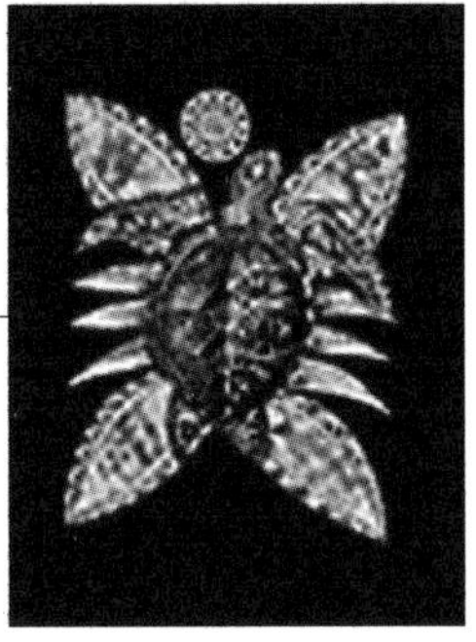

**Excerpt 4:** *Amnesty International on continuing human rights abuses.*

Amnesty International is concerned about a continuing pattern of serious human rights violations in the Philippines. . . . The violations have included extra-judicial executions by members of government and government-backed forces. Trade union members and activists have been among the victims of arbitrary arrest and "disappearance" and many have suffered torture and ill-treatment while in police or military custody. A number of prominent trade unionists have also been sentenced in trials which may not have been fair. . . . Amnesty International believes that all workers should be free to carry out peaceful and lawful trade union activities without fear of being subjected to human rights violations . . .

The forces involved in the government's counterinsurgency campaign have included the Philippine Army, the paramilitary Philippine Constabulary, auxiliary paramilitary units known as Citizen Armed Force Geographical Units (CAFGU), Special CAFGU Active Auxiliaries (SCAAs), and authorized civilian groups known as Civilian Volunteer Self-Defense Organizations (CVOs). In addition, a range of semi-official armed groups, such as anti-communist "vigilante" groups and company security guards, are known to have the support or acquiescence of government forces. Trade unionists have been victim to human rights abuses perpetrated by members of all of the forces named above, but have in particular fallen prey to violations by members of paramilitary and unofficial armed groups. . . .

Evidence of the overlap between "vigilante" groups, company security guards, and officially recognized SCAAs was clearly demonstrated in the testimonies of union leaders and workers from the Atlas Consolidated Mining Development Corporation . . . Workers at the mine alleged that members of their union were victims of a campaign of anti-union violence perpetrated by the "vigilante" group, KADRE, in cooperation with management, the local military command, and local civilian authorities. The workers alleged that from March 1987 to February 1989 alone, nine members of [their union] had been killed, nine had been wounded, five had received death threats, and 13 incidents of harassment of union officials and members had been reported. . . .

— *"Philippines: Human Rights Violations and the Labor Movement," Amnesty International, New York, 1991, pp. 1, 7, 11.*

# Glossary

*Definitions are given below for the vocabulary words signaled in this guide, as well as for other key terms. Most words have more than one meaning; the definitions given here explain the way that words are used in this book. Foreign words are defined in the text when first used; definitions are also included here for foreign terms that appear frequently.*

**Abrogate** — To cancel or do away with, especially by authority.

**Acculturate** — To adopt the customs of a different (usually dominant) culture. Often involves giving up previous values or traditions.

**Adaptation** — In ecology, the process through which a species changes to improve its relationship to its environment.

**Aggression** — The act of initiating hostilities or invasion.

**Agrarian reform** — Policies to achieve a more equal distribution of farmland by granting land to the landless. Such policies have been used in some Third World countries to reduce poverty and injustice caused by centuries of living under a plantation system.

**Agribusiness** — Large companies involved in commercialized agriculture as well as food processing and distribution.

***`Āina*** *(Hawaiian)* — Land.

**Allegiance** — Loyalty, to a nation, government, or cause.

**Americanize** — To make someone or something assimilate into or resemble U.S. culture. *See also* assimilate, acculturate.

**Animosity** — Hostility.

**Annexation** — To take over new territory as part of an existing country.

**Antagonism** — Hostility.

**Apocalyptic** — Involving widespread devastation or ultimate doom.

**Appendage** — Something that is attached to something of greater importance or size.

**Archipelago** — A group of islands.

**Assets** — Property owned by a person, organization, or country.

**Assimilate** — To become a part of the prevailing society or group. Often involves giving up previous values or traditions.

**Atoll** — An island consisting of a ring of coral surrounding a lake.

**Atrocities** — Acts of cruelty and violence inflicted by an enemy armed force on civilians or prisoners.

**Autonomy** — a. Self-government or self-determination. b. Self-government with respect to local or internal affairs.

**Bayonet** — A blade adapted to fit the muzzle end of a rifle and used as a weapon in close combat.

**Bloc** — A group of nations, parties, or persons united for common action.

**Bondage** — A state of subjection to a force or power.

**Boricuas** — People from Borinquen (*see*), that is, Puerto Rico.

**Borinquen** (*also spelled* Boriken) — Name given to the island of Puerto Rico by its original inhabitants, the Tainos. The name means "land of the brave people" in the Taino language.

***Caciques*** (*Spanish*) — Tribal chiefs. In modern Spanish usage, this word is also for political bosses.

**Canvass** — To conduct a poll or survey of public opinion.

**Caribs** — Native inhabitants of the lower Antillean Islands. The Caribbean Sea is named after them.

**Cede** — To yield something to another, especially through a treaty.

**Chamorros** — Indigenous people of the Mariana Islands, including Guam.

*Cimarrones* (*Spanish*) — Fugitive slaves.

**Circumnavigation** —Traveling completely around, for example, by sailing around the world.

**Civil disobedience** —Refusal to obey laws or rules which are contrary to one's values or beliefs. Often nonconfrontational and nonaggressive.

**Clan** — A traditional social unit of a number of families tracing descent from a common ancestor.

**Codify** — To organize something (such as a law) into a code; to give something the force of law.

**Colonial** — To be characteristic of colonialism (*see*).

**Colonialism** — A system in which one nation exercises military, economic, and political control over another. The era of colonialism was begun in the sixteenth century by European nations, later followed by the United States. *See also* decolonization.

**Colonization** —The process by which a nation occupies and settles in territory belonging to another people (or unoccupied territory).

**Colonized** — Subjected to foreign rule (*see* colonialism).

**Colony** — A settlement; also, a region or country over which another country is exercising colonial rule (*see*).

**Commemorate** — To honor the memory of with a ceremony.

**Commodify** — To turn something into an object that can be bought and sold.

**Commonwealth** — A self-governing, autonomous political unit voluntarily associated with the United States.

**Compact** — An agreement.

**Condemned** —Pronounced judgment against; sentenced.

**Conquistador** — Conqueror. Used of Spanish soldiers who traveled to the Americas in order to conquer local inhabitants and create Spanish colonies.

**Conquistadorial** — To act in the manner of conquistadors (*see*).

**Conservation** — The protection of natural resources, such as forests, soil, and water systems.

**Consortium** — A group of organizations or companies that work together for a particular purpose.

**Contemptibly** — Deserving contempt or scorn.

**Conversion** — The adoption of a new religion.

**Covert action** — Attempts to achieve a political or military goal by secret action or action that is not openly acknowledged.

**Decimation** — To kill or destroy nearly all of something (literally, to reduce something to one-tenth of its original size or strength).

**Decolonization** —To free a colony from dependent status.

**Decree** — An order having the force of law.

**Defray** — To cover costs or expenses.

**Degradation** — The state of being degraded; lowering.

**Delusive** — False, misleading.

**Deprecate** — To express disapproval of; belittle.

**Destabilization** — Attempts to weaken the stability of a government, usually through covert action (*see*).

**Detrimental** — Causing damage or harm; injurious.

**Dictatorship** — A government imposed by military force without the consent of the population.

**Dictum** — An authoritative, often formal, pronouncement.

**Dilatory** — Intended to cause delays.

**Diplomacy** — The art or practice of conducting international relations, as in negotiating alliances, treaties, and agreements.

**Displaced** — Moved or shifted from the usual place or position; especially, forced to leave a homeland (*see*).

**Dispossess, Dispossession** — To deprive someone of the possession or use of something, such as land.

**Dissident** — Someone who expresses views that go against a government.

**Economic development** — The development of economic capacity, for example, by creating new industries or building up infrastructure (roads, utilities, etc.).

**Electromagnetic radiation** — Radiation that is emitted by power lines or other devices using electricity.

**Emanates** — Sends forth, as from a source.

**Embargo** — A prohibition by a government on trade with a foreign nation.

**Eminence** — A position of great distinction or superiority.

***Encomienda*** (*Spanish*) — System under which large tracts of land in Spanish colonies, together with their inhabitants, were awarded as property by the Spanish government to individual settlers.

**Evacuation** —To withdraw or depart from an area.

**Export** — Goods or services that come from one country and are sold to another.

**Expropriation** — Governmental action to take possession of land or property.

**Exterminate** — To systematically and utterly destroy.

***Faasamoa*** (*Samoan*) —"The Samoan way," including communal land ownership, collective decision making, and other elements of traditional Samoan culture.

**Feudalism** — A political and economic system based on the rule of landowners or "lords." In such a system, "vassals" are people who owe allegiance to a lord and "serfs" are peasants who live in a condition of near-slavery.

***Fino' Chamorro*** (*Chamorro*) — Language spoken in the Mariana Islands by the indigenous Chamorro people.

**Foments** — Promotes the growth of; incites.

**Forefather** — Used of a person who is from an earlier time and has originated or contributed to a common tradition shared by a particular group.

**Foregone** — A foregone conclusion is one that cannot be avoided.

**Formidable** — Arousing fear, dread, or alarm.

**Genocide** — The planned extermination of an entire national, racial, political, or ethnic group.

**Genealogy** — A family tree or other record of a person's ancestors and family relationships.

**Geothermal energy** — A system that uses the internal heat of the earth to generate electrical power.

**Greenhouse effect** — The phenomenon in which the earth's atmosphere traps the heat of the sun, caused by the presence of gases such as carbon dioxide in the atmosphere. Incoming sunlight passes through but the heat that it creates is retained.

**Guerrilla** — Used of military or paramilitary units that operate in small bands to attack a more powerful enemy.

***Hacienda*** (*Spanish*) — Plantation.

**Half-caste** — Insulting term for a person of mixed racial origin.

***Haole*** (*Hawaiian*) — Foreigners from the United States or Europe; white people.

**Hazardous waste** — A substance, such as nuclear waste or an industrial byproduct, that is damaging to the environment and harmful to human health.

**Homeland** —A region that is closely identified with a particular people or ethnic group.

**Humanitarian** — Person or organization that acts to reduce human suffering and promote human well-being.

**Hygiene** — Conditions and practices that serve to promote or preserve good health.

**Immersion** — To be completely surrounded by something, as if in water.

**Imperative** — Impossible to deter or evade; pressing.

**Imperialism** — The use of military force by one nation to exercise economic and political control over another.

**Imprisoned** —To put in prison; confine.

***Inafa'maolek*** (*Chamorro*) — Peaceful cooperation and interdependence.

**Inalienable** — Something which cannot be denied or taken away.

**Independence** — Freedom from outside control.

***Independentistas*** (*Spanish*) — Independence fighters and supporters of independence, specifically, in Puerto Rico.

**Indigenous** — People or culture that is native to an area.

**Infant mortality** — Death of babies between birth and one year of age. The rate of infant mortality (that is, the number of children who die before their first birthday) is one of the most basic indicators of the well-being of any group of people.

**Infantile** —To be childish or lacking in maturity.

**Influenza** — An acute contagious viral infection characterized by inflammation of the respiratory tract and by fever, chills, muscular pain, and prostration. Also called flu.

**Insurrection** — An open revolt against a government or governmental authority; rebellion.

***Insurrectos*** (*Spanish*) — People involved in an insurrection (*see*), especially in the Cuban fight for independence from Spain in the late nineteenth century.

**Interdependence** —A condition of mutual dependence. Families, groups of relatives, and also different communities and nations may depend on one another for their survival and well-being.

**Legacy** — Something that is inherited from a person, a time period, or a group of people.

**Liberation** — Freedom from oppression or outside control.

***Libertos*** (*Spanish*) — Free Africans and people of African descent in Spain's colonies in the Caribbean.

**Manifesto** — A public declaration of principles or intentions. Usually of a political nature.

**Martial law** — Military rule over a civilian population, which may be imposed by a government during a period of emergency.

**Megawatt** — One million watts; unit used to measure the capacity of electrical generation systems.

***Mestizo*** (*Spanish*) — Person of mixed Indian and European ancestry in Spain's former colonies. Also used of the culture created by such people.

**Militarization** — The dominance of a group or area by military forces and military institutions.

***Mulato*** (*Spanish*) — Mulatto; a person of mixed African and European ancestry.

**Naturalization** — The granting of full citizenship to a foreign-born person.

**Natural resources** — Aspects of the natural environment that are essential or useful for

survival or economic activity, such as soil, water, minerals, etc.

**Neocolonialism** — A system in which countries that were once colonized gain formal political independence but are still subjected to foreign domination in economic affairs.

**Neocolony** — A country which is subjected to neocolonialism (*see*).

**Nonconformity** — Refusal or failure to conform to accepted customs, beliefs, or practices.

**Nonviolence** — The doctrine, policy, or practice of rejecting violence in favor of peaceful tactics as a means of gaining one's objectives.

**Normalization** — Restoring diplomatic and trade relations following a period of war or hostility.

**Oppressed** — *See* oppression.

**Oppression** — To keep down by severe and unjust use of force or authority.

**Oppressor** — One who causes oppression (*see*).

**Outrigger** —A beam that projects from the side of a boat and is used to secure the masts. Also, a boat fitted with such a beam.

***Palagi*** (*Samoan*) — A white person.

**Perpetuate** — To cause to continue indefinitely.

**Pillory** — A wooden structure in which people are confined in order to be punished by public scorn.

**Plantain** — A tropical fruit similar in appearance to the banana.

**Plebiscite** —A direct vote in which the entire electorate is invited to accept or refuse a proposal. Used especially of votes regarding political status.

**Plenipotentiaries** —Diplomatic representatives with the full authority of their government.

**Pompous** — Full of high-sounding phrases; pretentious.

**Progenitors** — Ancestors.

**Propaganda** — Information reflecting the views and interests of those people advocating a doctrine or cause.

**Protectorate** — A relationship of protection and partial control assumed by a superior power over a less powerful country or region.

**Providence** — A way of referring to God or divine power.

**Provisional** — In use only for the time being; temporary.

**Provocation** — Something that causes anger or resentment; also, an action that is intended to create a confrontational situation.

**Rain forest** — Forests that grow in areas of high rainfall, especially in the tropics.

**Ratification** — The process by which approval of a political document or proposal is confirmed.

***Reconcentración*** (*Spanish*) — A policy used by the Spanish to suppress resistance movements by forcing the civilian population into heavily garrisoned zones in order to cut off support to rebels.

**Recourse** — Turning to a person or thing for aid or security.

**Regiment** — A military unit of ground troops consisting of at least two battalions, usually commanded by a colonel.

**Remittances** — Money sent over a distance, for example, to family members in another country.

**Remnants** —Surviving traces; the last remainder of something that barely exists.

**Revenue** — Income, particularly that of a government.

**Reparations** — Compensation for past wrongs, especially wrongs committed during warfare.

**Repulse** — To drive out; for example, to drive out invading forces.

**Rudder** — Mechanism used for steering a boat.

**Sabotage** — Destruction of property or obstruction of normal operations, as by civilians or enemy agents in time of war.

**Sanction** — a. Permission or approval. b. A penalty, imposed either by withholding specific benefits or by applying moral pressure, that acts to ensure compliance.

**Salvaging** — Slang used by the Philippine military for "extrajudicial executions," that is, the killing of individuals outside of any legal process; assassination.

**Sanitation** — a. Measures designed to protect public health. b. Disposal of sewage.

**Satire** — Sarcasm or irony used to attack something the writer or artist sees as wrong.

**Savage** — Term formerly used by Europeans or people of European descent to devalue unfamiliar cultures or customs. Today this term is considered insulting when used in this way.

**Scourge** — Widespread, dreadful affliction and devastation such as that caused by disease.

**Sedition** — Conduct or language inciting rebellion against the authority of a state.

**Self-determination** — Freedom of the people in a given area to determine their own political status; independence.

**Sovereign** — a. The ruler of a country or region. b. Self-governing; independent (*see* sovereignty).

**Sovereignty** — The right of a country or people to control its own fate.

**Strategic** — Important or essential in relation to a plan of action.

**Subsidiary** — A corporation that is wholly owned by another, larger corporation.

**Subversion** — Action to undermine the power and authority, for example of a government.

**Suffrage** — The right to vote.

**Suffragist** — One who supports the right to vote, used especially for movements that favored extending the vote to women. Advocates of women's right to vote were formerly known as "suffragettes," a term that some people think belittles their movement.

**Supplanted** — Took the place of, especially through underhanded tactics.

**Surveillance** — Close observation of a person or group, especially by a government or police agency.

**Theologized** — Interpreted in the light of ideas about religion or God.

**Unalloyed** — Complete; unqualified.

**Uncivilized** — Not civilized; barbarous. As with the word "savage," the use of this word has historically reflected the tendency of European and U.S. explorers to devalue other cultures and customs.

**Vagrancy** — Used to describe the condition of being without employment, land, or other economic resources.

**Vassal** — Subordinate or dependent.

**Viable** — To be capable of sustaining life or existence.

**Wage labor** — Work that is performed for money. Although working for wages is virtually universal in modern society, examples of other systems include slavery, where work is forced by violence, or feudalism (*see*), where work is performed according to traditional social obligations.

**Wake** — Visible track left behind as something moves through water.

**Wards** — A group of people under the protection or care of a person, institution, or government.

---

**Source:** *Definitions are adapted from* The American Heritage Dictionary of the English Language, *3d ed. (New York: Houghton Mifflin, 1992) and* Webster's Deluxe Unabridged Dictionary, *2d ed., (New York: Simon & Schuster, 1983).*

# Historical and Geographical Names

*Numbers in parentheses refer to the chapter or lesson in which the people, events, and organizations in this list are discussed.*

**Aana** (4) Island in the Samoan archipelago.

**Aguinaldo, Emilio** (7) An early leader of the Philippine independence movement who later attempted to form an alliance with the United States.

**Anti-Imperialist League** (1) Political organization formed at the turn of the century by leading citizens such as Mark Twain; its members opposed U.S. annexation of the Philippines and military intervention abroad.

**Apology Bill** (6) 1993 joint resolution (PL 103-150) signed by U.S. President Clinton, acknowledging the U.S. role in the loss of Hawaiian independence. It offers a legal foothold to the Native Hawaiian sovereignty movement.

**Aquino, Benigno** (7) Philippine senator assassinated by military operatives in August 1983. His death sparked a huge outpouring of dissent among the people of the Philippines.

**Aquino, Corazon** (7) Widow of assassinated Philippine senator Benigno Aquino, she ran for president of the Philippines in 1986 and was ostensibly defeated in a fraudulent election. She assumed power as the Philippines' head of state after the nonviolent People's Power Revolution of the same year.

**Arawak** *See* Taino-Arawak

**Atua** (4) Island in the Samoan archipelago.

**Batista, Fulgencio** (2) Strongman of Cuban politics beginning in the 1930s and dictator of Cuba from 1952 to 1959. He was ousted by the revolutionary movement led by Fidel Castro (*see*).

**Battle of Manila Bay** (1) In this battle of the Spanish-American War on May 1, 1898, Spain lost its entire fleet in the Philippines and the United States overturned Spanish rule there while sustaining only light casualties.

**Bay of Pigs** (2) Site of an unsuccessful 1961 invasion of Cuba by exiles seeking to overthrow the government of Fidel Castro. The exiles were armed and trained by the U.S. Central Intelligence Agency.

**Bayonet Constitution** (6) Constitution which replaced the former Hawaiian constitution in the late 1880s. It was written by foreign settlers who coerced the Hawaiian monarchy into accepting it, and it served to undermine Native Hawaiian power.

**Berlin Treaty** (4) 1899 treaty which divided the Samoan Islands into two colonies, German (Western) Samoa and American (Eastern) Samoa.

**Biak-Na-Bato** *See* Truce of Biak-na-Bato.

**Bonifacio, Andres** (7) Founder of a Philippine revolutionary organization known as the Katipunan, which launched the Philippine Revolution on August 23, 1896.

**Borinquen,** *also spelled* "Boriken" (3) Original name of the island of Puerto Rico, which translates as "land of the brave people" in the Taino-Arawak language.

**Borinqueña, la** ("The Song of Borinquen") (3.2) National anthem of Puerto Rico, written in the late 19th century and embraced by Puerto Rican freedom fighters, and revised in 1952.

**Brigandage Act** (1) U.S. tactic in the Philippines through which independence fighters were reclassified as bandits.

**Butcher of Cuba** (1) Valeriano Weyler, Spanish governor of Cuba under whom the policy of *reconcentración* (*see glossary*) was enforced.

**Campos, Pedro Albizu** (3) Leader of the nationalist movement in Puerto Rico in the early to mid-twentieth century.

**Castro, Fidel** (2) A central leader of Cuba's 1959 revolution and Cuban head of state until the present.

**Chamoru Chelus** (Chamorro Brothers / Sisters) (5.2) Indigenous rights activist group, led by Angel Santos, which aims to define and support Chamorro culture. Now known as the Nasion Chamoru (Chamorro Nation).

**Chinese Exclusion Act** (1) Legislation passed in 1882 to exclude Chinese immigrants. The only law in U.S. history to restrict immigration on such a specific national basis.

**Crash of 1893** (1) Crash of the U.S. stock market and resulting financial panic.

**Cry of Pugadlawin** (4) Battle marking the beginning of Philippine revolution against Spain, August 23, 1896.

**Cuba Liberty and Democratic Solidarity Act** (Helms-Burton Act) (2) 1996 law seeking to deter foreign investment in Cuba by imposing sanctions on investment in or trade with Cuba by third countries. Also codifies existing embargo so that any modification would require an act of Congress.

**Cuban Assets Control Regulations** (2.3) Issued in 1963 by the U.S. Treasury Department; these regulations embody the essence of the U.S. economic embargo against Cuba that has been in effect ever since.

**Cuban Democracy Act** (CDA) (2, 2.3) 1992 legislation that outlaws trade with Cuba by foreign subsidiaries of U.S. corporations.

**Cuban Humanitarian Relief Act** (2) Proposed legislation (H.R. 1951) to lift the U.S. embargo on sales of food and medicine to Cuba.

**Cuban Missile Crisis** (2) 1961 confrontation between the United States and the Soviet Union, following the placement of Soviet nuclear missiles in Cuba. Six days after then-President John F. Kennedy ordered a U.S. naval blockade of Cuba, the Soviets agreed to withdraw their missiles. Recently declassified documents revealed that Kennedy had secretly promised not to invade Cuba in order to win this concession.

**Deeds of Cession** (4) Treaties signed in 1900 and 1904, under which the traditional chiefs of Samoa granted governing rights to the United States in return for certain guarantees. Differences between the Samoan and English versions of these treaties have caused continuing differences in interpretation.

**Eastern bloc** (2) A name for the former Soviet Union and its allies in Eastern Europe.

**Fernandez Juncos, Manuel** (3.2) Author of the revised version of "La Borinqueña" (The Song of Borinquen), the Puerto Rican anthem.

**Fuerzas Armadas de Liberación Nacional** (National Liberation Armed Forces) Puerto Rican nationalist organization, fourteen of whose members were convicted of sedition and sentenced to time in U.S. prisons.

**Gallego, Francisco** (3) A *liberto* (free African) who settled in Puerto Rico as an entrepreneur.

**Garrido, Juan** (3) A *liberto* (free African) who accompanied explorer Juan Ponce de Leon to Florida in 1506. He is known for bringing the first wheat seeds to the Americas.

**Grito de Bayre** (Cry of Bayre) (1) Battle marking the beginning of the Cuban war of independence against Spain, on February 24, 1895.

**Grito de Lares** (Cry of Lares) (1) 1868 uprising by Puerto Ricans seeking independence from Spain.

**Hatuey** (2) Taino-Arawak (*see*) chieftain who resisted the Spanish conquest of Cuba.

**Haymarket Affair** (1) Following a labor demonstration in Chicago's Haymarket Square in 1886, a bomb exploded, killing seven police officers. Seven labor leaders were convicted of conspiracy in the bombing and sentenced to death, although their trial spakred an international movement protesting its unfairness.

**Helms-Burton Act** *See* Cuba Liberty and Democratic Solidarity Act.

**Hukbalahap** (*also known as* "Huks") (7) Philippine guerilla organization which fought against the Japanese in World War II, and after the war fought for a Philippine revolution.

**Indian Appropriation Act** (1) 1871 U.S. legislation nullifying all treaties between the U.S. and Indian nations, thereby opening huge amounts of land to white settlers.

**Jones Act** (3) 1917 legislation making Puerto Ricans citizens of the United States.

**Kalākaua, David** (6) King of Hawai`i at the end of the nineteenth century; he was coerced into accepting the Bayonet Constitution (*see*).

**La Borinqueña** *See* Borinqueña.

**Lapitas** (4) Ancestors of the Samoans, they came to the Pacific from the island of Pulotu.

**Lapulapu** (1.1, 7) Filipino chieftain who led the resistance in 1521 against Ferdinand Magellan and other Spanish invaders.

**Lebron, Lolita** (3) Puerto Rican Nationalist who took part in an attack on the U.S. House of Representatives on March 1, 1954.

**Lili`uokalani** (6) Queen of Hawai`i in the late nineteenth century and successor to King Kalākaua, she favored abrogating the Bayonet Constitution and was thus a threat to foreign control of the island. She abdicated in 1893 to avert a potential war; Hawai'i was officially annexed by the United States five years later.

**Lopez, Clemencia** (1, 7.1) Filipina independence activist.

**Lopez de Legazpi, Miguel** (7) Spanish explorer of the Philippines, who arrived in 1565.

**L'Ouverture, Toussaint** (2) A former slave and leader of an 1801 slave rebellion in Haiti, then a French colony. This uprising drove the French from Haiti, which thus became the second independent republic in the Americas.

**Magellan, Ferdinand** (1.1) Portuguese-born Spanish explorer killed in 1521 while invading the Philippine Islands.

**Māhele** (6) Division of lands in Hawai`i between 1848 and 1852, under which *haoles* (foreigners) took over millions of acres of land which had formerly belonged to Native Hawaiians.

***Maine*** *See* U.S.S. *Maine.*

**Manu'a** (4) Island in the Samoan archipelago.

**Marcos, Ferdinand** (7) President of the Philippines; he declared a period of martial law in 1972, which lasted until the People's Power Revolution of 1986. After that nonviolent revolution, he fled to Hawai`i, where he died in exile a few years later.

**Marti, Jose** (2, 2.1) Cuban patriot and writer who wrote the famous essay "Our America" and was killed during Cuba's 1895 battle for independence from Spain.

**Mau** (4) Nonviolent political movement that eventually led to independence for Western Samoa (now called Samoa). Another achievement of the movement was the replacement of the military administration of American Samoa by a civilian (although still foreign) government.

**Middle Passage** (3) The route across the Atlantic Ocean from Africa to the Americas taken by slave ships. Millions of kidnapped Africans met their deaths during this journey.

**Muñoz Marin, Luis** (3) First Puerto Rican governor elected by the people of Puerto Rico. He was elected in 1948 and served until 1965.

**Nafanua** (4) An important Samoan historical figure, she was responsible for the introduction of *faasamoa* (the Samoan way).

**Nasion Chamoru** (Chamorro Nation) *See* Chamoru Chelus.

**Office of Hawaiian Affairs** (6.3) Agency of the U.S. federal government that handles Native Hawaiian issues.

**Operation Bootstrap** (3) Development strategy for Puerto Rico promoted by both the U.S. and Puerto Rican governments which involved promoting industrial development to replace the island's traditional agricultural economy.

**Organization of People for Indigenous Rights** (5.2) Chamorro activist group advocating sovereignty for Guam.

**Pan, Tierra y Libertad** (Bread, Land, and Liberty) (3) Slogan of the Popular Democratic Party of Puerto Rico.

**Paris Treaty** *See* Treaty of Paris.

**Parity Amendment** (7) 1946 amendment to the constitution of the Philippines, giving U.S. citizens the same rights as Filipinos in the Philippine economy. U.S. financial aid for postwar recontruction was contingent on the inclusion of this amendment.

**Pazos, Angel de** (5) Spanish governor of the Mariana Islands who was assassinated on August 2, 1884, by a Chamorro named Jose de Salas.

**People's Power Revolution of 1986** (7) Nonviolent revolution in the Philippines, sparked by the assassination of Sen. Benigno Aquino and fueled by fourteen years of martial law. The revolution helped to overturn a fraudulent 1986 election and install Corazon Aquino as president.

**Philippine-American War** (1, 7) Fighting sparked in February 1899, after Philippine forces had nearly won their independence from Spain only to be betrayed by the U.S., their supposed ally. Recorded in U.S. history as the Philippine Insurrection, it was a deciding factor in the U.S. Senate's vote to annex the Philippines.

**Philippine Insurrection** Name used in U.S. military history to refer to the Philippine-American War (*see*).

**Pili** (4) Great chief of old Samoa, who divided Samoa into its (precolonial) confederations.

**Platt Amendment** (1, 2) Written by U.S. Senator Orville Platt, this document was incorporated into the Cuban constitution of 1902 as a condition for the withdrawal of U.S. military forces from the island. It acknowledged the right of the U.S. to intervene militarily in Cuban affairs and established the U.S. naval station at Guantanamo Bay. Although the amendment was abrogated in 1934, the U.S. naval station is still maintained on Cuban soil.

**Pluto Plan** (2) A secret U.S. plan to destabilize the Cuban government, approved in 1959 by then-President Dwight D. Eisenhower.

**Ponce Massacre** (3) Incident in which eighteen people were killed when Puerto Rican police fired on a peaceful protest march by the Nationalist Party.

**Pulotu** (4) Island believed to be the original homeland of the Samoan people.

**Ramos, Fidel** (7) Philippine politician who supported Corazon Aquino in the People's Power Revolution of 1986, then served as her defense minister. He himself was elected president in 1992.

**Rodriguez de Tió, Lola** (3.2) Nineteenth-century Puerto Rican patriot and advocate of Puerto Rican independence. Author of the original version of "La Borinquena" (The Song of Borinquen) (*see*), the Puerto Rican anthem.

**Sakay, Macario** (6) Philippine independence fighter and national hero reclassified by the U.S. as a "bandit." (*See* Brigandage Act.)

**Salamasina** (4) Descendent of the important Samoan historical figure Nafanua (*see*). She ruled during a peaceful period in Samoan history.

**Salas, Jose de** (5) Chamorro (indigenous person of the Mariana Islands) who assassinated Spanish colonial governor Angel de Pazos on August 2, 1884.

**Sherman Anti-Trust Act** (8) 1890 legislation against the operation of business monopolies; the law was first applied against labor unions, for example during the Pullman Strike of 1894-95.

**Silang, Diego and Gabriela** (7) Husband and wife who led a 1762 revolt against the Spanish in the Philippines.

**Spanish-American War** (1; mentioned throughout) Ten-month war between the United States and Spain in 1898, which begun after the sinking of the battleship U.S.S. *Maine* (*see*) and ended with the Treaty of Paris. As a result of the war, the United States replaced Spain as the ruling power in Cuba, Puerto Rico, Guam, and the Philippines.

**Tagaloa** (4.1) According to the Samoan creation story, the great god who created Samoa and the Samoan people.

**Taino-Arawak** (2, 3) Indigenous inhabitants of the Caribbean before the arrival of the Europeans. They occupied the areas of present-day Cuba, Puerto Rico, Jamaica, Haiti, and the Dominican Republic, and were largely destroyed by Spanish colonization.

**Tamasese, Tupua** (4, 4.5) Leader of the nonviolent Mau movement in Samoa, who was shot by police during a peaceful protest on "Black Saturday."

**Ten Years War** (2) War seeking Cuban independence from Spain begun in 1868 at the same time as the Grito de Lares (*see*). Although neither side was able to gain a decisive victory, concessions made by the Spanish to end the war included home rule for Cuba and, eventually, emancipation of the island's slave population.

**Treaty of Paris** (1; mentioned throughout) December 10, 1898, treaty between the United States and Spain which ended the Spanish-American War (*see*).

**Truce of Biak-Na-Bato** (7) Truce negotiated between Philippine rebels and the Spanish government in August 1897; it involved payment of a sum of money to certain rebel leaders in exchange for their voluntary exile.

**Tuamasaga** (4) Island in the Samoan archipelago.

**Tui Manu'a** (4) Ruler of the island of Manu'a, whose family was called "Moa," possibly indicating the origin of the name "Samoa."

**Tutuila** (4) Island in the Samoan archipelago.

**Upolu** (4) Island in the Samoan archipelago.

**Urayoan** (3) A *cacique* (chief) of the Tainos (*see*), who led indigenous resistance against the Spanish.

**U.S.S. *Maine*** (1, 2) U.S. battleship that exploded on Feb. 15, 1898, while docked in the harbor of Havana, Cuba, then under Spanish rule. The Spanish were blamed for the explosion, although a 1976 exploration of the wreck determined it was caused by a fire in a coal bunker.

**Velazquez, Diego** (2) Spanish conquistador who conquered Cuba in 1510.

**Wao Kele O Puna Rain Forest** (6) The last lowland tropical rain forest in the United States, a sacred site to Native Hawaiians, and a potential source of geothermal power (electricity generated indirectly from volcanoes).

**Women's International League for Peace and Freedom** (1) Progressive social organization founded by Jane Addams; supported suffragist and anti-militarist causes.

**Wounded Knee** (1) Site of the massacre of Sioux Indians by U.S. soldiers on December 28, 1890.

**Young Bill** (3) Legislation introduced in the United States in 1997 (H.R. 856) addressing the issue of Puerto Rico's political status.

**Young Lords** (3) Puerto Rican political organization of the 1960s and 1970s, modeled in part on the Black Panther Party, which organized community protest actions to demand human and civil rights.

# Notes on Contributors

**Bonnetta Adeeb** is a specialist in African American history and multiethnic/racial history from Maryland. She has written and advocated regarding the incorporation of liberation struggles into curricula for English and Social Studies and has developed teaching material in this area.

**Nancy Aleck**, an education activist, holds a master's degree in education from the University of Hawai`i. She is the project director for Rethinking the U.S. in "Paradise," a training course for educators which will be given in Hawai`i during the summer of 1998. She has been a volunteer with AFSC's Hawai`i program for ten years.

**Wayne Wah Kwai Au** is a humanities teacher at Middle College High School, an alternative public school in Seattle, Washington. He writes on the teaching of Hawai'i in the continental United States, the importance of hip hop in education, and radical pedagogy. His articles have appeared recently in *Rethinking Schools* and *Beyond Heroes and Holidays.*

**Teresita Bautista** is a Filipina activist in Oakland, California. She served as the Filipino Liaison for the Oakland School District in the 1970s and has conducted workshops for teachers on the history, culture, and concerns of Filipinos and Filipino Americans, as well as the experience of other ethnic groups and the experience of women. She has also worked in direct services that assist immigrants and refugees.

**Juan Antonio Blanco,** a philosopher and historian, has been a professor at the University of Havana and a diplomat serving in the Cuban mission to the United Nations and other posts. He is the founder and former president of the Centro Felix Varela, an independent Cuban nongovernmental organization.

**Keith Lujan Camacho,** an indigenous Chamorro from Guam, will complete his work in the master's program in Pacific Islands Studies at the University of Hawai`i at Mānoa in the spring of 1998. He intends to continue his studies in a doctoral program.

**Eliza Fabillar** currently works for the American Social History Project/Center for Media and Learning of the City University of New York Graduate Center. She coordinates a professional development program for teachers in secondary education and is involved in developing interdisciplinary curriculum resources for the teaching of U.S. history and culture. Eliza holds a master's degree in cultural anthropology from Columbia University. As an active member of the Gabriela Network, a multiethnic women's solidarity organization, Eliza speaks at university forums and public events on issues surrounding global sex trafficking, particularly of Filipinas.

**Anne Perez Hattori,** an indigenous Chamorro from Guam, is a Ph.D. candidate in Pacific history at the University of Hawai`i at Mānoa. She hopes to soon join the faculty at the University of Guam.

**Liz Hottel** is a writer, activist, and staff member of the Network of Educators on the Americas. She lives in the Washington, DC area.

**Johnny Irizarry** is a Program Specialist for Latino Studies for the School District of Philadelphia's Office of Curriculum Support. From 1986 to 1998, he served as Executive Director of Taller Puertorriqueno (the Puerto Rican Workshop), a community cultural arts center in Philadelphia. He also teaches Puerto Rican arts and cultural history and art appreciation at La Salle University in Philadelphia.

**Eric Joselyn** teaches at a Philadelphia public high school. He is a contributing member of the *Public School Notebook,* a newspaper seeking to document and promote school reform.

**Rachael Kamel** is a Research and Interpretation Specialist for the American Friends Service Committee. She has written and edited many publications for AFSC and other groups, including AFSC's 1990 organizing guide, *The Global Factory: Analysis and Action for a New Economic Era.*

**Erwin Bordallo Manibusan** is a Chamorro, born and raised in the village of Chalan Pago, Guam. After graduating from the College of Education at the University of Hawai`i at Mānoa, Erwin plans to pursue a career in teaching. He will begin teaching social studies at a high school on Guam in the 1998-1999 academic year.

**Dan Taulapapa McMullin** is a Samoan playwright from Los Angeles, currently living in Minneapolis. His work has been performed at Theatre Mu in Minneapolis, Soho Rep in New York, the New Zealand International Arts Festival, and the Pacific Arts Festival in Samoa. He is working on a screenplay, "Bikini Boy," with Hawaiian filmmaker Christine Walker. His new play, *The Demon Anchors,* takes place in American Samoa.

**Deborah Menkart** is an education activist and the director of the Network of Educators on the Americas, based in Washington, DC. She also serves on the board of National Coalition of Education Activists.

**Maria E. Mills-Torres** is the Multicultural Curriculum Specialist for Latino American Studies for the School District of Philadelphia. She is an experienced classroom teacher of world languages (Spanish, French, and English as a Second Language) for K-12 students. She also works as a museum teacher at Taller Puertorriqueno, a community cultural arts center in Philadelphia.

**Marta Moreno Vega** received her Ph.D. from Temple University in May 1995 in African Philosophy. The founding director of the Caribbean Culture Center in New York City, she is presently writing two books and is teaching in the Black and Puerto Rican Studies Department at Baruch College.

**Rene Ontal**, an activist and writer, is currently writing a screenplay about David Fagen, an African American "Buffalo Soldier" who joined the Filipino freedom fighters against U.S. military occupation forces at the end of the nineteenth century.

**Jonathan Kay Kamakawiwo'ole Osorio**, a Native Hawaiian, is assistant professor at the Center for Hawaiian Studies at the University of Hawai`i at Mānoa. He holds a Ph.D. in history from the University of Hawai`i and is a specialist in Hawaiian and Pacific Island history. His dissertation examines the legislatures of the nineteenth century Hawaiian Kingdom. He is also a composer and recording artist in the Hawaiian music industry and a deacon in his church. He is married to Mary Dunn Osorio and has four children.

**Oscar Penaranda** is a writer and an educator. He is a cofounder of the first ethnic studies program in the country, at San Francisco State University, and the founding president of the Filipino American National Historical Society, San Francisco Chapter. He taught for twelve years at San Franciso State and is currently on the faculty of Logan High School in Union City, California.

**Baltazar Pinguel** is the Program Assistant/Office Manager of AFSC's Third World Coalition. He has been a peace and justice activist in the Philippines since the early 1970s. He was a political prisoner for almost five years (1980–1985) under the Marcos dictatorship.

**Anita Rivera** is a Puerto Rican activist living in the Bronx, New York. She is an active member of the National Congress for Puerto Rican Rights and teaches in the New York public school system. She is currently a Library Media Specialist at the Raul Julia MicroSociety Dual Language School.

**Joaquin Cepeda Sablan** is a Chamorro creative writer, currently pursuing his bachelor's degree in literature at the University of Hawai`i.

**Mary Perez Hattori Sasaki**, an indigenous Chamorro from Guam, works as an instructor in educational technology at the University of Hawai`i at Mānoa. She lives in Honolulu with her husband, David, and her son, Timothy.

**Stephen R. Shalom** teaches political science at William Paterson University in Wayne, New Jersey. He is the author of *The United States and the Philippines: A Study of Neocolonialism* (1981) and coeditor of *The Philippines Reader* (1987). He is on the editorial boards of the *Bulletin of Concerned Asian Scholars* and *New Politics* and is a member of the Montclair Civil Rights Coalition.

**Noenoe Silva** is a Ph.D. candidate in political science at the University of Hawai`i at Mānoa. Her research has focused on the resistance movement among Kānaka Maoli (Native Hawaiians) following the 1893 overthrow of the Hawaiian Kingdom.

**Deborah Wei** is the Curriculum Specialist for Asian Pacific American Studies for the School District of Philadelphia. She is a long time teacher and community activist, and has taught in high schools in both Hong Kong and Philadelphia. She is a founder and board member of Asian Americans United and a member of the AFSC's National Community Relations Committee.